*Understanding
Biblical Prophecy*

Books in the series *Preparing for a Bahá'í/Christian Dialogue*

   Volume 1: *Understanding Biblical Evidence*
   Volume 2: *Understanding Christian Beliefs*
   Volume 3: *Understanding Biblical Prophecy*

Other books by the same author:

   Jesus Christ in Sacred Bahá'í Literature
   The Prophecies of Jesus
   A Study of Bahá'u'lláh's Tablet to the Christians

*Preparing for a
Baháʼí/Christian Dialogue*

VOLUME 3

UNDERSTANDING
BIBLICAL PROPHECY

MICHAEL SOURS

ONEWORLD
OXFORD

Preparing for a Bahá'í/Christian dialogue
Volume 3
Understanding Biblical Prophecy

Copyright © Michael Sours 1997

All rights reserved
Copyright under Berne Convention
A CIP record for this title is available
from the British Library

ISBN: 978-185-168-111-2

Cover design by Peter Maguire
Printed and bound by Lightning Source, UK

Oneworld Publications
10 Bloomsbury Street
London WC1B 3SR
England

Stay up to date with the latest books, special offers, and exclusive content from Oneworld with our monthly newsletter

Sign up on our website
www.oneworld-publications.com

contents

PREFACE...xi

PART 1
THE NATURE OF PROPHECY

Chapter 1
THE IMPORTANCE OF BIBLICAL PROPHECY

Biblical prophecy and the Bahá'í Faith......................3
The benefits of studying prophecy..........................5

Chapter 2
UNDERSTANDING PROPHECY AND ITS SYMBOLS

The theological message of prophecy........................9
The symbolic nature of prophecy...........................12

Chapter 3
THE BOOK OF CERTITUDE AND THE MAJOR THEMES OF PROPHECY

The three major themes of Biblical prophecy................22

Different symbols used to signify the same themes. 30

Chapter 4

THE LIMITATIONS OF PROPHECY

The problem of interpreting symbolic language. 33
The circumstantial nature of some prophecies. 36
The limited testability of some prophecies. 40

PART 2

INTERPRETATION AND
THE FULFILMENT OF PROPHECY

Chapter 5

THE BOOK OF CERTITUDE AND
THE INTERPRETATION OF PROPHECY

Studying how prophetic terminology and symbolism are used in other
    parts of the Bible and/or sacred literature. 47
Considering both the literal and symbolic meanings of the text. 48
Studying how the symbol functions and what it points to. 49
Deciding whether a symbol has a limited or broader historical meaning. . 51

Chapter 6

THE FULFILMENT OF PROPHECY

Ways of understanding fulfilment. 53
The progressive fulfilment of prophecy. 57
The literal fulfilment of prophecy. 65
Old Testament prophecy in the Gospel. 68

Chapter 7

RESPONDING TO CHRISTIAN OBJECTIONS

Reasons some Christians believe prophecy must be fulfilled literally. . . . 73
'Abdu'l-Bahá's explanations concerning Christ's fulfilment
    of prophecies. 76
Biblical references for chapter 7. 82

Contents

PART 3
THE RETURN OF CHRIST AND THE 'DAY OF GOD'

Chapter 8
BASIC THEMES IN NEW TESTAMENT PROPHECY

The presence of God. 85
Old Testament symbols in the New Testament. 87

Chapter 9
THE TRIBULATION

Christian beliefs about the tribulation 90
Bahá'í teachings concerning the tribulation. 92

Chapter 10
THE RAPTURE

Christian beliefs about the rapture. 102
Bahá'í beliefs about the rapture. 107

Chapter 11
THE RETURN OF CHRIST IN THE CLOUDS OF HEAVEN

Christian beliefs about the return of Christ in the clouds of heaven. . . 113
Bahá'í beliefs about the return of Christ in the clouds of heaven 114

Chapter 12
THE BATTLE OF ARMAGEDDON

Christian beliefs concerning Armageddon. 123
Bahá'í teachings relating to Armageddon. 126

Chapter 13
THE MILLENNIAL KINGDOM

Christian beliefs concerning the Millennial Kingdom 131

Bahá'í beliefs concerning the Millennial Kingdom. 132
Biblical references for Part 3. 137

PART 4
BAHÁ'U'LLÁH
IN BIBLICAL PROPHECY

Chapter 14

PROPHECIES REFERRING TO BAHÁ'U'LLÁH

Introduction. 141
Identifying Biblical prophecies mentioned in Bahá'í writings. 142

Chapter 15

OLD TESTAMENT PROPHECIES
THAT REFER TO BAHÁ'U'LLÁH

The Glory of the Lord 151
The Glory of the God of Israel 155
The Lord of Hosts and the King of Glory 157
The Everlasting Father and Prince of Peace 161
The Desire of all Nations. 164

Chapter 16

NEW TESTAMENT PROPHECIES
THAT REFER TO BAHÁ'U'LLÁH

The Comforter. 170
The Spirit of Truth. 171
The Prince of this World. 174
The Son of Man. 177
Alpha and Omega. 179
The Glory of God. 182
Biblical references for Chapters 15 and 16. 184

Chapter 17

PROPHECIES CONCERNING
THE 'MOST GREAT NAME'

The 'no other name under heaven' argument. 186

The 'same name' argument.........................187
The meaning of 'name' in the Bible and the meaning of the names
    'Jesus Christ' and 'Bahá'u'lláh'..................187
Jesus had many names............................190
A Biblical example of a prophet who returned with a new name......192
The Bible foretells a new name......................195
The 'Most Great Name'...........................198
Biblical references for Chapter 17....................200

PART 5

BIBLICAL PROPHECY AND THE QUR'ÁN

Chapter 18

THE BOOK OF DANIEL AND THE QUR'ÁN

The Seal of the Prophets..........................203
The Qur'án and the Bible.........................205
The term 'Seal' in the Book of Daniel..................207
Christ as 'Seal of the Prophets'......................209
The Hebrew *hátam* as 'Seal' and 'Last'.................211
The origin of the Qur'ánic usage.....................215

Appendix: The Glory of God in the Biblical tradition............217
Abbreviations.................................221
Bibliography..................................222
Index of Biblical references........................225
Index......................................231

Preface

This book is the third in a series intended to help Bahá'ís study the relationships between Bahá'í Scripture, the Bible, and Christian beliefs. First some general principles of prophecy will be explained, and then a few specific prophecies will be examined in order to show how these principles can be applied. It is hoped that this knowledge will then enable the student of Scripture to understand other prophetic sections of the Bible not presented in this book. Although many prophecies will be examined, this book seeks not only to explain specific prophecies, but to assist study of the overall subject of prophecy.

This book is introductory and, like the first two volumes of *Preparing for a Bahá'í/Christian Dialogue*, is written for those interested in the study of Scripture who are looking for information that will assist them in their efforts to answer Christian questions, to demonstrate the truth of Bahá'í claims and to defend Bahá'í teachings from criticism when necessary. It has been written with the Bahá'í reader who has only a minimal knowledge of the Bible and Christianity in mind, and an effort has been made to keep the book as simple as possible. References to books other than Bahá'í Scripture and the Bible have been kept to a minimum. References to commentaries and scholarly opinions have been deferred to footnotes whenever possible, and every effort has been made to avoid technical religious terminology, or to explain it in simple language.

An attempt has been made to confine much of the information in this book to those prophecies specifically mentioned in authoritative Bahá'í Scriptures and writings. The main guiding light for this volume are several key principles explained by Bahá'u'lláh in His pre-eminent doctrinal work, *The Book of Certitude* (*Kitáb-i-Íqán*). Following the pattern of the previous volumes, both a Christian and a Bahá'í perspective on each issue are presented when appropriate. In most cases, Christian literature of a conservative or traditional nature has been consulted, and special effort has been made to search out those Christian beliefs that Bahá'ís are most likely to encounter, and which may seem the most challenging. In many cases, as will be shown, there are great similarities between Christian and Bahá'í beliefs about prophecy.

The spirit in which things are said and shared can be far more important than what is said. In the previous volumes, emphasis has been placed on the importance of developing a spiritual attitude towards the interaction with Christians, and on finding areas of agreement between Christian and Bahá'í beliefs as a basis of building friendships. There are numerous passages in Bahá'í Scripture concerning the appropriate spirit in which Bahá'ís engaging in inter-faith dialogues should seek to discover truths of which they are unaware and share the truths they know. From these passages, it is possible to discern an etiquette for dialogue. This etiquette is governed by the desire to seek ways of conversing that will foster friendship and avoid the needless contention that inevitably undermines both friendship and the search for truth.

Not every answer finds a receptive listener, and in some instances, those beliefs valued the strongest and loved the most may be met with the most severe criticism. At such moments, it is especially important to avoid arguments. Tactfully and sincerely reiterating the praises of Christ and the Bible in Bahá'í Scripture can do much to dispel the apprehensions of Christians about the Bahá'í Faith. Overcoming such apprehensions can sometimes take a long time but, once this has been achieved, it may then become possible to share 'a reason for the hope that is in you' (1 Pet. 3:15). This approach is useful for interactions with people of all religions and can be a strong foundation for building friendship. More has been said about practical steps for positive dialogue with Christians in the previous two volumes, and it is hoped that the reader will consult them.

part one

THE
NATURE OF PROPHECY

chapter 1

THE IMPORTANCE OF BIBLICAL PROPHECY

BIBLICAL PROPHECY AND THE BAHÁ'Í FAITH
Throughout His most important Tablets, Bahá'u'lláh calls attention to the fulfilment of prophecy. He writes, 'The promises of God, as recorded in the holy Scriptures, have all been fulfilled' and, in the same connection, He adds, 'Happy is the man that pondereth in his heart that which hath been revealed in the Books of God, the Help in Peril, the Self-Subsisting' (*Gleanings* 13). In another passage, Bahá'u'lláh writes that today is the day to arise and cry out,

> I testify that, through Thy Revelation, the things hidden in the Books of God have been revealed, and that whatsoever hath been recorded by Thy Messengers in the sacred Scriptures hath been fulfilled. (*Gleanings* 163)

In His Tablet to Queen Victoria, Bahá'u'lláh writes, 'He, in truth, hath come unto the world in His most great glory, and all that hath been mentioned in the Gospel hath been fulfilled' (*Proclamation* 33). To Pope Pius IX, Bahá'u'lláh writes, 'Lo! The Father is come, and that which ye were promised in the Kingdom is fulfilled!' (*Proclamation* 84–5). And, in another passage written to the bishops of the Christian churches, He writes, 'This is what the Spirit (Jesus) prophesied when He came with the truth...' (*Proclamation* 94).

In *God Passes By*, Shoghi Effendi's historical account of the first hundred years (1844–1944) of the Bahá'í Faith, each major phase and aspect of the Bahá'í Revelation is linked in some way to the Bible, either by reference to a Biblical parallel or, as in most cases, by a reference to the direct fulfilment of Biblical prophecy.

These links include, for example, the appearance of the Báb (*God Passes By* 56-7, 58, 276); the gathering of the Báb's disciples (ibid. 8); the death of the Báb's leading disciple, Quddús (ibid. 49); the prophesied earthquake that marked the Báb's martyrdom (ibid. 53); the appearance and first emanations of Bahá'u'lláh's Revelation (ibid. 92, 110); the declaration of Bahá'u'lláh's mission to His companions (ibid. 151); the revelation of *The Book of Certitude* (ibid. 139), the Tablets to the Kings (ibid. 213), *The Book of the Covenant* (ibid. 239, 249), and His Most Holy Book, the *Kitáb-i-Aqdas* (213); the rebellion of Mírzá Yahyá (ibid. 163-4); and Bahá'u'lláh's exiles, arrival in Palestine, imprisonment in 'Akká, and visits to Mount Carmel (ibid. 107, 183, 194).

When Shoghi Effendi sets out to explain 'the relationship between the religious Systems' established before Bahá'u'lláh, and Bahá'u'lláh's 'own Revelation' (*God Passes By* 93), he turns to the prophecies found in past Scriptures. His references to these prophecies demonstrate the importance of Biblical prophecy to the Bahá'í Faith. While he refers to Buddhist, Hindu, and Zoroastrian prophecies, most references are from the Bible and the Qur'án, the holy Books of 'two of the most widely diffused and outstanding among the world's recognized religions' (*World Order* 145). More than half a page is devoted to listing Qur'ánic prophecies, but nearly two full pages are given to Biblical ones. This does not necessarily mean that Biblical prophecy is more important to the Bahá'í Faith, but owing to the fact that Christianity is the most widespread religion in the world, Biblical prophecy may well be of special importance to the propagation of Bahá'u'lláh's message. Biblical prophecy is also important for understanding much of the terminology and symbolism in Bahá'í Scripture.

The prophecies Shoghi Effendi selected from the Bible and the Qur'án on pages 94–6 of *God Passes By* are introduced under what could be regarded as three categories:

1. those that refer directly to Bahá'u'lláh,
2. those that refer to His advent, and
3. those that refer to His Day.

Among the Qur'ánic prophecies cited, most refer to His 'Day', and one refers to Bahá'u'lláh as the 'Great Announcement' (ibid. 96); whereas among the Biblical references, many of the most familiar titles of Bahá'u'lláh are found, the 'Everlasting Father', the 'Prince of Peace', the 'Lord of Hosts', the 'King of Glory', the 'Desire of All Nations', the 'Comforter', the 'Glory of God' and so on (ibid. 94–5). Moreover, the student of Biblical prophecy will recognize that even the Qur'ánic prophecies build on themes and terminology rooted in Biblical terminology and tradition. Even though the Bahá'í Faith was born out of Islam in the same way that Christianity was born out of Judaism, many elements have combined – such as the power and influence of Christianity, especially in the nineteenth century, Bahá'u'lláh's Tablets to rulers of Christian nations, 'Abdu'l-Bahá's missionary journeys to the Christian nations of the West, and the Jewish and Christian presence in Palestine – to imbue Bahá'í Scripture with Biblical terminology and symbolism, and to heighten the awareness that the Bahá'í Faith fulfills the hopes expressed in Biblical literature. All these factors suggest the importance and benefits of studying Biblical prophecy, its symbolism and message.

THE BENEFITS OF STUDYING PROPHECY
Prophecy is not merely about prediction – it is not merely a divine or magical knowledge of things that should and/or would come about in the future. Prophecy is about God's promises, and these promises teach us important things about the nature of God and the purpose of life. Biblical prophecy teaches that

God is a personal God, a God Who cares about humankind, Who makes promises and keeps them. Prophecy calls attention to God's presence, and awareness of this can provide an important confirmation of faith. From what the prophecies say about the future, humanity is reminded of where it is headed and what it can attain through faith and obedience – its spiritual potential and destiny.

The prophecies, as recorded in the great Biblical tradition, also give meaning to the history of humankind. This history is one of 'redemption'. That is, there is a divine plan running through human history. Redemptive history is a theme common to the Bible, the Qur'án, and other Scriptures; it is also one of the main themes of *The Book of Certitude* (see *God Passes By* 139). Some events may be cyclical or recurring, like a wheel, such as the rise and fall of civilizations and the successive appearances of divine Messengers; but this wheel is also moving in a particular direction – towards the redemption of humankind.

In each age a greater degree of redemption is obtained as the salvation and peace resulting from the teachings of each new Prophet reach larger numbers of people. Prophecy provides a vision of the day when not only a few, but all humankind is united in its recognition of God.

Through prophecy, not only can the will of God for this age be discerned, it is possible to discern God's activity in the past as well. Many people have ceased to believe that the ancient Scriptures have any divine authority. Bahá'u'lláh, however, gives the assurance that God, through His grace and love, has protected His testimony recorded in the Scriptures (*Certitude* 89–90). When we understand the nature of prophecy and see its fulfilment, we more easily see the spirit of God in the ancient Scriptures and accept that His spirit is working in history and in our lives today.[1]

---

[1]. Bahá'u'lláh writes, 'Every discerning observer will recognize that in the Dispensation of the Qur'án both the Book and Cause of Jesus were confirmed'

It is important to appreciate this link between ancient Scriptures and their subsequent fulfilment, not just with regard to the Bible, but also with regard to the sacred Scriptures of other world religions. The fulfilment of prophecy provides compelling evidence of the validity and worth of this sacred heritage that belongs to the entire human race. It is evidence that can help many people appreciate and accept the truth of other religions and sweep away the barriers separating the great religions of the world (*God Passes By* 139). Bahá'u'lláh did not view the Biblical record of prophecies as hopelessly corrupted by human hands or the passage of time, nor as the mere wishful thinking of ancient peoples. Following references to several prophecies from the Book of Isaiah, Bahá'u'lláh writes, 'This is the Day which *the Pen of the Most High* hath glorified in all the holy Scriptures' (*Gleanings* 13, emphasis added).

In addition to enriching personal faith, strengthening certitude, and broadening individual knowledge of Scripture, the study of prophecy also provides information useful in discussions about the Bahá'í Faith with Christians. Christian expectations about the return of Christ and the future are, for example, shaped by their beliefs about prophecy. For this reason some Christians will want to test the truth of the Baháí Faith by examining how the events of Bahá'u'lláh's life and this age correspond with Biblical prophecy.

(*Certitude* 20) and again, He says, 'He [Muḥammad] recognized the truth of the signs, prophecies, and words of Jesus, and testified that they were all of God' (*Certitude* 21). From these passages we can observe God's divine will linking events together into a great redemptive history that spans the ages. If the true Gospel had been lost, what guidance could Christians have turned to when Muḥammad appeared? When Muḥammad affirmed the Torah and the Gospel, this was not solely because these sacred Scriptures testified to Him and to the truth of the Qur'án, but because this affirmation testified to God's active presence throughout history. And although the merits of the Gospel are self-evident and stand in no need of additional proof, the fulfilment of its prophecies is a great affirmation of the Gospel's divine inspiration. Today, any visitor to the exhibition room of the Library of the British Museum can view copies of the Gospel pre-dating Muḥammad which, although containing minor scribal errors and some variants, record the same prophecies that can be read in any current edition of the Bible.

Christians may feel that the proofs demonstrating that Bahá'u'lláh is a Manifestation of God are convincing yet still have difficulty accepting the essential oneness of Bahá'u'lláh and Christ, the relationship between Christianity and the Bahá'í Faith, and the fact that humanity has entered a new age with new requirements. Showing that the prophecies concerning the return of Christ have been fulfilled by Bahá'u'lláh can help Christians to see more clearly why Bahá'u'lláh is Christ in Spirit and to understand that there are special and great spiritual victories that they as individuals can win in this age – today, they can become the heirs of His Kingdom (*Tablets of Bahá'u'lláh* 14).

There are also some specific characteristics of the Bahá'í Faith to which Christians frequently object, such as its new name. Referring to prophecies can demonstrate that such characteristics were anticipated and revealed as part of God's plan and, therefore, cannot be validly rejected. The Bahá'í administrative order is another such example. All of these things that prophecy can teach – about God, about history, about ourselves as individuals – as well as the way it can substantiate many aspects of the Bahá'í Faith's claims and teachings, point to the benefits to be gained by studying prophecy.

Chapter 2

UNDERSTANDING PROPHECY AND ITS SYMBOLS

Prophecy has two main characteristics or aspects: (1) its *theological message* and (2) the *symbolic nature* of prophetic language. These constitute the major characteristics of the prophecies explained in Bahá'u'lláh's *Book of Certitude*. This book, according to Shoghi Effendi, 'broke the "seals" of the "Book" referred to by Daniel, and disclosed the meaning of the "words" destined to remain "closed up" till the time of the end' (*God Passes By* 139; cf. Dan. 12:4, 9). The full significance and scope of these features cannot be considered here, but some of the essential principles for understanding them will be outlined in the following sections.

THE THEOLOGICAL MESSAGE OF PROPHECY

All the prophets were deeply concerned with communicating knowledge about the nature of God, His activity and plan. This underlying message about God – His relationship to humankind and humankind's relationship to Him – runs through all the prophecies and can be referred to as the 'theological' message of prophecy. The term *theology* simply refers to that field of study concerned with the understanding of God. By concentrating on *what* and *how* prophetic language is communicating about God, it is possible to gain an understanding that will help unlock the meaning of prophetic Scripture.

The central feature of the Bible is its concept of God and His presence in the world. Much of the Bible is a record of historical events. Some stories are symbolic (such as the account of Adam and Eve), but most are actual historical events *interwoven with symbolism*. The symbolism is used to communicate the significance of the events, which might otherwise have gone unnoticed and unappreciated.

The most important historical event in Israelite history is the 'exodus', which refers to the freeing of the Israelites from slavery in Egypt and their migration back to their original homeland (*Secret of Divine Civilization* 76). This event is not presented in the Bible as simply the history of an oppressed people escaping from tyranny, but as evidence that God had actively liberated them. This distinctive perspective concerning the activity of God is one of the characteristics that distinguishes the Bible from modern historical books. The prophets interpreted history in a way that revealed God for people who otherwise did not perceive God's presence. The exodus demonstrated God's love and care for oppressed people and showed that He was just and compassionate. It also provided the standard and model by which people should live in relation to one another. Symbolism is interwoven in this account to show that this event occurred because of God's presence in the world. It reveals not just the fact of God's existence and presence, but the nature of God that we as human beings can know.

These accounts and this understanding of God enabled the people to realize God's *presence* in their own human experience. God's presence was most clearly seen in the consequences of individuals' and nations' responses to God's laws. Turning to God led to prosperity and turning away led to ruin; one brought strength, the other enslavement to self and passion. The Biblical account, therefore, offers an important way of understanding God's presence in human history and experience. This vision is reflected in the prophecies of those prophets who came to Israel after the exodus, such as Isaiah, Jeremiah and Daniel. The prophets knew how God had acted in the past and foresaw how He would act in the future; they knew how the Law of God operated and could foresee what would and should take place.

This way of interpreting history as a response to the will of God can be seen in Shoghi Effendi's writings about our own age in his book *God Passes By* and in collections of his letters, such as *The Promised Day Is Come*. He sees history unfolding according to the world's response to Bahá'u'lláh's message (*Promised Day* 111). God's presence and activity in history did not cease with the events described in the Bible – it continues in the events occurring even now. The fall of monarchs, the decline of nations, and wars such as World War II, for example, cannot be separated from this divine and pervasive process (see *Promised Day*, especially 3–4)

The central theological message of prophecy therefore concerns the awareness of the presence of God – and true salvation, or eternal well-being, is obtained through the recognition and attainment of this presence. This is the main concern of the holy Books. Bahá'u'lláh writes, 'no theme hath been more emphatically asserted in the holy scriptures' (*Certitude* 139). God's presence is wrath for those who turn away and blessing for those who turn towards Him. The latter involves recognition of the revelation of the divine Law – those principles that reveal the will of God – and then abiding by them. These laws are most discernible through the Prophets and Manifestations of God, either by their actions or the direct ordinances they reveal. The 'Law' of God need not be expressed in a written code of legislation – Jesus, for example, revealed a few specific laws, but through His example and His many teachings, spiritual principles and parables, people understood how they should live and govern their lives. As 'Abdu'l-Bahá states, 'Jesus, then, founded the sacred Law on a basis of moral character and complete spirituality' (*Secret of Divine Civilization* 82). Moses, Muḥammad, the Báb and Bahá'u'lláh, however, also revealed many specific laws pertaining to individual and community life – and Bahá'u'lláh, in particular, has laid down laws and teachings relating to the conduct and responsibilities of nations, and the governing of a world-wide community of nations.

Because God is a transcendent Reality, a Reality the nature of which no language can adequately communicate, the 'presence' of God is not the same as the presence of a physical being; rather it signifies the signs and evidences of divinity that can be apprehended. Referring to the prophetic theme of attaining the presence of God in the last Day, the Báb explains:

> On that Day all men will be brought before God and will attain His Presence; which meaneth appearance before Him Who is the Tree of divine Reality [i.e. the Manifestation of God] and attainment unto His presence; inasmuch as it is not possible to appear before the Most Holy Essence of God, nor is it conceivable to seek reunion with Him. That which is feasible in the matter of appearance before Him and of meeting Him is attainment unto the Primal Tree. (*Selections from the Writings of the Báb* 108)

In other words, because God is not a physical or limited being, the attainment of His presence means the attainment of the presence of the Manifestations of God (that is, recognition of the Manifestation of God and following His teachings; see *Certitude* 170). This spiritual fact points to the importance for every true seeker after the presence of God to recognize and follow the teachings of these Manifestations.

The theological message of prophecy and the theme of the 'presence of God' will be further discussed in Chapter 3. Here, some attention is given to how this message is communicated in Biblical symbolism.

THE SYMBOLIC NATURE OF PROPHECY
Most of the prophetic Scriptures use symbolic terminology in order to reveal their message. In Biblical prophecy, much of the central symbolism is based on a few specific events described in the early portions of the Old Testament. Almost all of these events communicate similar or related messages about God's

relationship with humankind. Therefore, by studying these events and their significance, it is possible to understand most of the symbolism used in later Biblical prophecy. In other words, the 'symbolic method' of prophecy uses certain events or persons in religious history to communicate important themes. As will be shown later, these themes find their highest realization in the appearance of Bahá'u'lláh.

As most of the important symbolism originates in the Old Testament, it will be easier to understand if we divide the Old Testament into two historic periods:

1. the period before the divided kingdoms, the 'pre-divided kingdom' period,[2] and

2. the period after the division of the kingdom, the 'divided kingdom' period.

In Israelite history, a period covering roughly three thousand years of scriptural history led up to the unified kingdom established by King David (c. 1000–961 BC) and maintained by his son and successor King Solomon (c. 961–922 BC). After Solomon, the kingdom became divided (922 BC), and consequently the Israelites were later defeated and subjugated by other empires (a period of roughly 900 years up to the time of Jesus Christ).

Most of the prophecies from the Old Testament period, as well as most of the prophecies that are applicable to the Bahá'í Revelation, originate with prophets who spoke during the 'divided kingdom' period. When these prophets prophesied about the future they used symbolism based on Israelite sacred history during the 'pre-divided kingdom' period to express their central message.

To understand these prophecies it is therefore helpful to study those main aspects of the pre-divided kingdom period from which they derived their symbolism – to discover the

---

2. It is not called simply the 'united kingdom' period because it covers a long period of sacred history before the united kingdom was created.

theological significance of these symbols and how they functioned in a predictive way. Some aspects of Israelite history are more central than others and they are used more often to form the basis of prophetic symbolism. Many secondary symbols are derived from each of the main ones. For the purpose of this study, five symbols will be explained. These are:

1. The first seven days of Genesis
2. The original garden of Eden (or garden of God)
3. The Tabernacle (and the Temple)
4. The promised land
5. The reign of King David

In Part 3 (see Chapter 8) Old Testament symbolism will be examined in relation to similar New Testament symbolism. By understanding these examples, it will be possible for the student of Scripture to understand other examples not explained here.

1. The first seven days of Genesis
The opening chapter of the Book of Genesis describes God actively creating the cosmos in the first seven days. This is done in a specific order, leading to the creation of human beings. The account is of course symbolic. This symbolism expresses many spiritual truths, some of which can be simplified as follows:

- there is a divine order to creation,
- each new day is initiated by God, and
- each day represents a further stage in the development of God's plan.

This symbolism is incorporated into prophecy in many ways, such as in pervasive references to the 'Day of God'. When a Manifestation of God appears, according to prophetic symbolism He ushers in a new Day. In the Genesis account, the cosmos is created through God's Word, and in the same way, the Manifestations of God, acting as His representatives, bring into being a new age created through their Word, the Word of God. Also, according to the Genesis account, on the seventh day (the day of completion) God rested. This symbolism is used in Scripture to indicate that the final day is a day of rest, signifying peacefulness (or simply peace). Peace among all human beings is the goal and culmination of God's plan. If people turn away from God, this peace is not possible and God's day becomes in effect a 'day of wrath' (Zeph. 1:15, *God Passes By* 95).

2. The original garden of Eden (or garden of God)
The garden of Eden or of God (which later came to be called the Garden of Paradise) was made by God for Adam and Eve (humankind) to live in (Gen. 2:8-9). Although this is not literal history, but a symbolic story, it forms a part of the Old Testament's historical narrative. It is 'sacred' history – a narrative that explains many truths applicable to real history and the real experience of humankind's relationship with God.

One of the main messages of this story is that God establishes an order, and that by living according to this arrangement, human beings can live in happiness and prosperity. Resisting this order leads to unhappiness and suffering. The experience of living in harmony with God, in the world of His original divine order, is symbolized by life in the garden, where Adam and Eve lived in the 'presence' of God. The story says that God came and walked in the garden (Gen. 3:8), suggesting the close fellowship and communion between humankind and God. When Adam and Eve violated God's order (that is, broke His commandment or law not to eat the forbidden fruit), it is said that they then hid themselves from the 'presence of the LORD[3] God' (Gen. 3:8).

---

3. Throughout many translations of the Old Testament, the term 'Lord' appears in small capital letters, 'LORD'. This is because the sacred Hebrew name of God is

Later prophetic writings, such as those of Ezekiel, would refer to this Garden as a symbol for the future renewal of Israel (Ezek. 36:35). Similarly, in the New Testament the Book of Revelation describes the Kingdom of God using symbolism also based on the story of the original garden (Rev. 22). Because this Genesis story captures so well the idea of close communion with God and ideal life, the symbols it uses appear many times in prophecy to suggest these ideal spiritual relationships and themes. Aspects of the garden, such as the tree of life, for example, appear many times in prophecies that are applicable to Bahá'u'lláh and they are used in Bahá'u'lláh's writings to indicate the fulfilment of these prophecies (see, for example, Persian *Hidden Words*, nos. 19, 34; also note Arabic *Hidden Words*, nos. 21, 68).

3. The Tabernacle (and the Temple)

After Moses led the Israelites out of captivity in Egypt, they travelled to Mount Sinai, where God revealed the 'Law' to Moses. This Law was written on Tablets of stone and God instructed Moses to build a *container* for these Tablets and a special *tent* for the container. God made a *promise* to be with the Israelites if they obeyed the Law.

This promise is called a 'covenant'. The container that held the Law was called the 'Ark of the Covenant' and the tent for the container was called the 'tent of meeting' or 'Tabernacle'. The expression 'tent of meeting' emphasized that the Law represented the point of meeting between the people and God.

---

indicated in the original language, the Hebrew letters of which can be transliterated in Roman letters as YHVH (the original text of the Old Testament had no vowels). Attempts by scholars to arrive at the original pronunciation with vowels have led to the constructions *Jehovah* and more recently *Jahweh* (or *Yahweh*). Since the name refers to the 'Lord', translators have simplified these difficulties by translating it as Lord and using small capitals to indicate the name YHVH in the text. For more information see, Richardson, ed. *A Theological Word Book of the Bible* 97, or most any other Bible dictionary or Bible word book.

After the Ark of the Covenant was placed in the Tabernacle, according to Scripture, God indicated that He was present among the people by putting a 'cloud' over the Tabernacle. If the people made sacrifices according to the Law (obeying the Law entails personal sacrifice, the giving up of one's own desires for the well-being of others) then they would be able to see the glory of God (Lev. 9:6). The 'glory of God' means the 'light and splendour' of God. Even as the presence of the sun is known by the presence of light, this 'glory' signifies the light of God (*God Passes By* 94). When the Scriptures say the people were able to see the glory of God, it means that through following the Law of God as revealed by Moses, they were able to become aware of God and attain His presence.[4] The portion of the Tabernacle that contained the Ark of the Covenant was called the 'Holy of Holies'. According to 'Abdu'l-Bahá, the Holy of Holies symbolizes the unchanging 'spiritual virtues and divine qualities', 'the essence of the Law of Adam, Noah, Abraham, Moses, Christ, Muḥammad, the Báb, and Bahá'u'lláh' (*Some Answered Questions* 47).

After Moses died, the Israelites entered the promised land (that is, the land promised to the descendants of Abraham) of Canaan. For a long time they lived alongside each other as a group of separate tribes. Then David, from the tribe of Judah, united the Israelites and moved the Ark of the Covenant to Jerusalem. In Jerusalem, his successor, King Solomon built a permanent *Temple* for the Ark of the Covenant. This Temple replaced the Tabernacle, the movable tent the Israelites had taken with them wherever they went. The presence of the Ark of the Covenant made the city of Jerusalem (also called the 'City of David' and 'Zion') especially holy for the Israelites.

All of these terms – the Ark of the Covenant,[5] the Tabernacle, the cloud, the glory of God, the Temple, the Holy

---

4. For more on the Biblical significance of the term 'glory', see Appendix.

5. Another form of symbolism related to the Ark of the Covenant is Noah's ark. This Ark signified God's law of reward and punishment. Those who entered were

City of Jerusalem, and Mount Zion, where Jerusalem is situated – have special significance relating to the revelation of the Law by Moses and the presence of God among those who recognized Moses and God's revealed Law. When the Israelites had neglected God's Law and became disunified, they were defeated by other empires (first the Assyrians and later the Babylonians) and made captives, the Temple at Jerusalem was destroyed and the Ark of the Covenant was lost. When later prophets spoke of the future revelation of a new Law, they looked back to these former times and spoke using these symbols.

The prophet Ezekiel, for example, lived during the period of the divided kingdom. He was taken in captivity to Babylon with the Israelites and during this time was called upon by God to prophesy many things to come. Because the people were living in another country they had become familiar with the religion and symbolism of that country, and consequently Ezekiel sometimes used their symbols when he spoke of the future. Nevertheless, these were generally secondary to the main symbolism he used to express his central themes. He spoke of the re-establishment of an ideal Temple, the return of the presence ('glory') of God to that Temple, the re-establishment of the reign of King David, and the reunification of the divided kingdoms of Judah and Israel. He used these symbols to convey the plan of God for the future, a plan that can be seen in the Bahá'í Revelation today. Each of these symbols represents in different ways the presence of God that is revealed by, and can be attained through recognition of, God's Manifestation.

In the time of Christ, the prophecy of the re-establishment of the Temple was fulfilled through Him (John 2:19–21, Heb. 9). Later it was fulfilled through Muḥammad, and today it is

---

saved and those who did not perished. The thematic significance of this ark can be seen in many phrases used by Bahá'u'lláh (*Certitude* 62, 187). Bahá'u'lláh often alludes to this symbolism in relation to His laws and the Bahá'í administrative order (*Tablets of Bahá'u'lláh* 5, 71, 97).

fulfilled through Bahá'u'lláh (*Gleanings* 315, *God Passes By* 213). They are all the fulfilment of the prophesied Temple because they are all the revealers of God's Law, all signify the presence of God, all are 'the Temples of the Cause of God' and all are 'abiding in the same tabernacle' (*Certitude* 153).

4. The promised land

Long before Moses, God promised to Abraham that He would raise up great nations from his offspring (Gen. 17, also 22:18) and that He would give his descendants the land of Palestine (Israel today).[6] Because this land was promised to them by God, it came to be called the 'promised land'. During a period of drought the descendants of Abraham migrated to Egypt in search of food and settled there. In time, the Israelites became oppressed by the Egyptians. Moses freed them from this bondage and captivity and led them back to their original homeland of Palestine (*Secret of Divine Civilization* 76). The land had, however, become occupied by other tribes, many of which were hostile to the Israelites. Over a period of time and through the course of many battles, defeats and trials, the Israelites regained the land and established a great culture and nation. These events were later recorded in the Bible and the historians and prophets who looked back on those times understood and taught that God was present in them. It was He Who had led them in their battles, and Who had caused them to be defeated or victorious according to whether or not they were living in right relation to His laws, teachings and spirit.

Much of the later prophetic symbolism expresses this belief that God is the ruler and leader of human destiny. He is, for example, the 'Lord of Hosts' (that is, Lord of the army) Who will lead the people to (spiritual) victory. Centuries after the Israelites conquered Canaan they were defeated by the Babylonians and carried away into exile. After this event,

---

6. Gen. 12:7, 24:7, 15:7–21; Exod. 3:8; Deut. 26:9. See also *God Passes By* 305. What constitutes the exact borders of this promised land is disputed.

prophets arose who looked forward to the day when God's promise to Abraham concerning the land would be realized. In one sense, and especially in the literal sense so far as the Jews are concerned, the promised land is the land of Israel today. In another sense, the promised land may be regarded as any land in which the Manifestations of God appear.

5. The reign of King David

When the Israelites returned to Canaan from their captivity in Egypt, they lived as a loose confederation of tribes. David united these tribes and conquered the rest of the land, expanding and creating a nation and kingdom. During this period, the Israelites were prosperous and independent from the rule of other empires. Learning and civilization developed and their wealth increased. After David's rule, Solomon became king, and there are many traditions and legends about his great wisdom. However, after Solomon's death the kingdom became divided and went into decline.

In many ways the kingdom established by David was the high point in Israelite national history, a sort of golden age. In ancient times, when a king was inaugurated the priests anointed the king, signifying that his reign was consecrated and established with the blessing of God (Jud. 9:15; 1 Kgs. 1:39; 2 Kgs. 11:12; 1 Sam. 24:6, 10). The king was then viewed as a representative of God on earth. To say that he is 'the anointed one', in this sense, is to say that he has the right to be king and to rule the people. After the kingdom established by David had declined and been destroyed, the prophets began to prophesy that God would send a new king like David, the Anointed One (see, for example, Isa. 9:11, 61:1, 2; Ezek. 37:24; Dan. 9:24).

In Hebrew the word for *anointed* is 'Messiah', and in Greek the same word is 'Christos' (in English 'Christ'). Many prophecies were concerned with the coming of this future Messiah who would establish His kingdom and rule the people with justice. Many people rejected the claims of Jesus because they expected a warrior king like David; they did not understand that Jesus would raise up His kingdom without leading a literal army against the Romans. As history shows, Jesus raised up an even greater kingdom than any witnessed in the time of David. Because the rule of David was the greatest period in Israelite national history, it came to symbolize the rule of God on earth. Like many things in past ages that came to be used as symbols for the future, they are mere shadows of the greatness to come. Nevertheless, the prophets used what people were familiar with and that inspired the greatest hope. The 'anointed', 'David', and the 'throne of David' all became symbols of God's future rule on earth. This expectation was first fulfilled by Jesus, then Muḥammad and today by the Báb and Bahá'u'lláh.

These subjects form what can be called the primary symbolic terminology of prophecy – in other words, they are used to communicate the main message. Other symbols, such as the ones that occur in the process of elaboration on these themes, can be regarded as secondary, and it is important not to let secondary symbols obscure the message of the primary ones.

Most of these primary symbols are fulfilled by all the supreme Manifestations of God (Jesus Christ, Muḥammad, the Báb and Bahá'u'lláh – those Who came after the prophecies were made). Each of the prophetic themes and symbols (the Day of God, the ideal paradise, the Temple, the conquests, the Davidic rule) concern one subject – the presence of God and its attainment. All the Manifestations represent this central Reality (*Certitude* 142). The student of Scripture who meditates on this theme and understands this basic Biblical symbolism will be able to understand much of the prophetic language of the Bible with little difficulty. From this starting point, it is possible to learn many other important scriptural truths about God, about how to live, why things happen in life as they do and how to view life.

Chapter 3

THE BOOK OF CERTITUDE
AND THE MAJOR THEMES OF PROPHECY

THE THREE MAJOR THEMES OF BIBLICAL PROPHECY
Christian scholars sometimes divide Biblical prophecy into three major themes or categories. There is much in Bahá'í Scripture to support the existence of these categories, and if the student of prophecy is aware of them, it is much easier to put prophecy into perspective. These categories, in fact, are among the main features or themes of 'redemptive history' explained in *The Book of Certitude*.

The most explicit theme of prophecy is the theological message of the 'presence of God', the central theme examined in this chapter. The two other themes concern the human response to God's presence.

The three prophetic themes can be categorized as:

1. *Prophecies of punishment*: These refer to the judgement of God against the people for unbelief, idolatry, immorality and injustice. Frequently in the Old Testament, the people of Israel are the focus of these prophecies. In the New Testament, a broader world view tends to dominate. These prophecies use symbolism involving wars, famines, hell, death, the destruction of the world and so on, and concern the consequences of turning away from God and rejecting His Manifestations.

2. *Messianic prophecies*: Prophecies in this central category refer to a future redeemer and ruler, and/or

the restoration of the *presence* of God among God's people. Such prophecies include those referring to the reign of God (that is, the Kingdom of God) and the Day of God, and refer to such things as the re-establishment of the Temple, the establishment of the Kingdom of God, and the coming of a new Jerusalem and a new earth.

3. *Prophecies of rewards*: These prophecies are closely tied to messianic prophecies and involve the blessings of living in communion with God and in God's Kingdom where war has ceased and all abide under the protection of God. The message of prosperity and eternal salvation is prominent in these prophecies which use as symbolism the entering of the promised land, the restoration of the garden of Eden, and the end to wars, death, suffering, and so on. These prophecies concern the turning to God and the benefits of recognizing God's Manifestations and following their teachings.

There are some prophecies that do not, strictly speaking, fall within these categories, but these are nevertheless the dominant themes of Biblical prophecy. Of these three main themes, the messianic prophecies – those concerning the presence of God – are obviously central. All the prophetic books of the Bible tend to point to the messianic hope as the ultimate goal of humankind, but with regard to the *time* of the fulfilment of messianic prophecy, it is how each person responds to them (consciously or unconsciously) that determines where he or she stands in relation to the prophecies of rewards and punishments.

Prophecies of Punishments and Rewards

To step back from the particulars of prophecy and to look at these themes broadly is perhaps the simplest way to understand the ancient prophetic vision and its fulfilment. Consider the three themes above: note that apart from the central theme of messianic prophecies, the remaining two themes are opposites. There are the themes of reward and punishment, despair and prosperity, suffering and happiness, evil and good. These opposites – and the ability to distinguish between them – are at the core of religious consciousness and mystical experience. To be near to God is heaven and to be distant is hell (*Epistle* 132). To obey God leads to prosperity and to turn away from God leads to suffering. The prophetic vision is about these contrasting states of being. It is, in its most basic form, a contrast between the spiritual life and life without God. The Christian scholar Charles Briggs described these themes of 'future judgement and redemption' as the 'two poles of predictive prophecy' (*Messianic Prophecy* 45). In explaining certain words of Jesus, Bahá'u'lláh addresses this point in *The Book of Certitude*:

> Whosoever in every dispensation is born of the Spirit and is quickened by the breath of the Manifestation of Holiness, he verily is of those that have attained unto 'life' and 'resurrection' and have entered into the 'paradise' of the love of God. And whosoever is not of them, is condemned to 'death' and 'deprivation', to the 'fire' of unbelief, and to the 'wrath' of God. (*Certitude* 118)

In this passage, Bahá'u'lláh has listed many of the key scriptural terms that appear in the prophecies and which constitute the 'two poles' of predictive prophecy. The truth of these words, especially with regard to the 'death', 'deprivation', and 'fire' of unbelief can be appreciated by reflection on the events commonly reported in any contemporary newspaper. If the people had entered into the life of faith, most of the destruction and horrors afflicting the world today would not be occurring. People often blame political parties, the immigration of 'foreigners', and the influences of other nations, races or religions for the problems in their respective countries; but the real cause is their rejection of Bahá'u'lláh's teachings for this age.

If we reflect on what it is to be 'human',[7] both the purpose of religion and the role of prophecy become more clear. To be truly human is to realize and develop one's spiritual potential through knowing and worshipping God. The purpose of religion, and the reason we can benefit from it, is that it makes us aware of our spiritual potential, and it safeguards the interests and promotes the unity of the human race (*Proclamation* 112). It is not always necessary for people to be openly 'religious' in order for them to acquire spiritual qualities, but, obviously, to be religious is ideally to be conscious of one's spiritual needs and potential as a human being. Such consciousness helps foster our development, and it helps us both to avoid what is harmful and to seek out what is beneficial to our spiritual lives and to the well-being of others.

The study of prophecy reveals that the prophets were keenly aware of God's redemptive activity in the world and in human nature. They spoke with great conviction about God's promises and what should and would occur to those who turned to God and those who turned aside. When humankind turns away from God, when there is a loss of spiritual understanding, destruction and unhappiness spread throughout the community. Recognition of God's new Messenger enables people who have fallen away from the religious life to realize once again their potential and the purpose of their lives, whereas those who reject and oppose God's Messenger cut themselves off from these benefits and blessings. Moreover, those who accept God's new teachings are able to work together for the benefit of all, whereas those who reject them fail to contribute effectively to the needs and prosperity of the community.

---

7. Humankind's unique spiritual reality and potential is implicit in Gen. 1:26, which 'Abdu'l-Bahá often cited (*Promulgation* 28, 69, 76, 259, 403). Concerning human spiritual development and purpose, see also *Certitude* 3, 101; *Gleanings* 149; *Prayers and Meditations* 314; *Secret of Divine Civilization* 1–2.

This simple recurrent pattern of people's rejection and acceptance, and the consequences of each, is told throughout the Scripture, and in our own age it has occurred once again with the appearance of Bahá'u'lláh. Referring, for example, to these two poles of predictive prophecy as they relate to those who accepted the Faith of the Báb and those who opposed it, Bahá'u'lláh writes:

> Reflect: Who in this world is able to manifest such transcendent power, such pervading influence?[8] All these stainless hearts and sanctified souls have, with absolute resignation, responded to the summons of His decree. Instead of complaining, they rendered thanks unto God, and amidst the darkness of their anguish they revealed naught but radiant acquiescence to His will . . .
>
> Do thou ponder these momentous happenings in thy heart, so that thou mayest apprehend the greatness of this Revelation, and perceive its stupendous glory. Then shall the spirit of faith, through the grace of the Merciful, be breathed into thy being, and thou shalt be established and abide upon the seat of certitude. The one God is My witness! Wert thou to ponder a while, thou wilt recognize that, apart from all these established truths and above-mentioned evidences, the repudiation, cursing, and execration, pronounced by the people of the earth, are in themselves the mightiest proof and the surest testimony of the truth of these heroes of the field of resignation and detachment. Whenever thou dost meditate upon the cavils uttered by all the people, be they divines, learned or ignorant, the firmer and the more steadfast wilt thou grow in the Faith. For whatsoever hath come to pass, hath been prophesied by them

---

8. Here, Bahá'u'lláh is referring to the early believers and martyrs of the Bábí era.

who are the Mines of divine knowledge, the Recipients of God's eternal law. (*Certitude* 235–7)

In this passage, Bahá'u'lláh sums up a theme that forms a powerful part of His overall arguments and proofs establishing the truth of the Báb. Here He draws attention to the spiritual achievements of the early believers, the 'Dawn-Breakers', and contrasts these achievements with the low spiritual condition and horrific deeds of those who rejected the Báb and persecuted His followers. In these dramatic historical happenings, the underlying messages of the two poles of predictive prophecy – the themes 'prophesied by them who are the Mines of divine knowledge' – are starkly contrasted. This example helps to create awareness of how these themes are acted out and fulfilled in less dramatic circumstances every day.

Before the heroic age of the Bahá'í era mentioned above by Bahá'u'lláh, this pattern of redemptive history recurred many times and in different ways, and was recorded in the Bible and the Qur'án (the Qur'án recounts many Biblical stories). As we read the great prophetic books of the Bible that record this pattern of redemptive history, certain themes emerge and become more and more clear. Most of the prophecies are about a spiritual struggle: the decline of nations, the destruction that follows irreligion, the acts of God that reveal His will and save humankind, the appearance of divine Messengers, the persecution of their followers, and the rewards of those who are steadfast in their adherence to the spiritual life.

Messianic Prophecies
The high point or goal of prophecy is always the act of God's Revelation through a chosen Messenger, here designated the *messianic prophecies*. All the prophets looked forward to the fulfilment of God's promise to guide humankind. The appearance of divine Messengers is the greatest evidence of a personal God Who seeks communion with His creation. Each Manifestation of God therefore represents God's presence in

the world, and through recognition of Him and obedience to His laws and teachings God's presence is attained – the greatest of all blessings. Most of the prophecies lead to this promise and are fulfilled when a Manifestation of God appears. Even the prophecies about rewards and punishments are most often centred around this coming appearance of God. Bahá'u'lláh writes:

> The highest and most excelling grace bestowed upon men is the grace of 'attaining unto the Presence of God' and of His recognition, which has been promised unto all people. (*Certitude* 138)

Following Bahá'u'lláh's assertion that 'no theme hath been more emphatically asserted in the holy scriptures' (*Certitude* 139) than the attainment of the presence of God, He points out that by this is meant the recognition of God's Manifestation:

> The knowledge of Him, Who is the Origin of all things, and attainment unto Him, are impossible save through knowledge of, and attainment unto, these luminous Beings who proceed from the Sun of Truth. By attaining, therefore, to the presence of these holy Luminaries, the 'Presence of God' Himself is attained. From their knowledge, the knowledge of God is revealed, and from the light of their countenance, the splendour of the Face of God is made manifest. (*Certitude* 142)

Bahá'u'lláh then goes on to give a vital key for unlocking the mysteries of Biblical prophecy:

> Therefore, whosoever, and in *whatever* Dispensation, hath recognized and attained unto the presence of these glorious, these resplendent and most excellent

Luminaries, hath verily attained unto the 'Presence of God' Himself, and entered the city of eternal and immortal life. (*Certitude* 143, emphasis added)

From this passage, it is clear that in every age it has been possible to attain the presence of God and to enter the City of God – the great prophetic theme. This does not mean, however, that attaining the presence of God is limited to those who attain the literal, physical presence of the Manifestation. Bahá'u'lláh clarifies this issue by pointing out that it refers to the Manifestation's 'all-embracing Revelation' (*Certitude* 143). It therefore includes those who in the new 'Day' of God recognize the Revelation, that is, those truths revealed by the Manifestation, His example, laws and teachings (*Certitude* 200–1).

Once the meaning of this theme of 'attaining the Presence of God' – symbolized in many different ways in prophecy – is understood, it becomes much easier to interpret Biblical prophecy. First, it becomes clear that references to the appearance of God (for example, Rev. 21:3; Qur'án 2:46, 249, 18:111) and to future Manifestations such as the return of Christ (for example, Rev. 22:12–13, 20) both relate to the same thing. The appearance of the Manifestation signifies and represents the appearance of God, God's presence, reign and judgement. Second, it becomes possible to understand that the fulfilment of these prophecies can be recognized by human beings in every age. Every time a Manifestation of God appears, these great prophetic themes are fulfilled. Prophecies are rarely so specific that they have a limited and single meaning (*Certitude* 33, 68, 72). They do not so much refer to specific events, as to specific types of events related to the central one of the Revelation of God's presence. The prophecies are fulfilled through specific events whenever these themes occur in history. This understanding of prophecies is one of the divine mysteries that Bahá'u'lláh disclosed in His pre-eminent doctrinal work, *The Book of Certitude*.

DIFFERENT SYMBOLS USED TO SIGNIFY THE SAME THEMES

Throughout the ages different prophets spoke and prophesied on these themes. Each prophet used terminology that reflected the circumstances of his time and his religious heritage. The choice of symbols may differ, but the main theme remained the same. For example, at the time when the prophet Ezekiel had his vision, the people were suffering because they lived in such a way as to make themselves remote from the presence of God. Ezekiel envisioned a time when the people would again attain the presence of God. In his vision this divine promise was represented by the re-establishment of Israel's holy Temple, which had been destroyed literally because of the people's iniquities. The Temple had once contained the Tablets of the sacred Law. As long as the people possessed and obeyed the Law, it was promised that God's presence would be among them (Exod. 40:38). Thus, in the vision of Ezekiel, the *re-establishment of the Temple* is a symbol of the time when people will once again attain the presence of God through recognition of God's law and obedience to it. According to the vision, God would intervene in history to reawaken the people and to call them back to the divine law. As Bahá'u'lláh points out, each Manifestation of God represents the presence of God, and so these same prophecies of Ezekiel were fulfilled by Christ, Muḥammad, the Báb, and Bahá'u'lláh. Each one of these Manifestations represented the re-establishment of the Temple foretold and promised in Ezekiel's vision.

Similarly, when St John had the vision recorded in the Book of Revelation, he foresaw that people would fall away from God and that there would be great struggles between those who had rejected God and those who believed. At the end of his account he too spoke about a time when God would act in history and people would once again attain to the presence of God. Many of the symbols used by Ezekiel reappear, but whereas Ezekiel tends to emphasize the imagery of the Temple, the last part of St John's vision looks to a time when God will dwell among the people as

He did in the Garden of Eden. Each vision carries essentially the same theological message – *the presence of God*.

These particular points and prophecies will be examined in greater detail in the following chapters. Symbols change, but the central themes remain the same. If such prophecies are interpreted in their literal sense, then it is impossible to see how they have been fulfilled by Christ, by Muḥammad, and in our day, by Bahá'u'lláh. But when prophecies are interpreted according to their spiritual significance, their fulfilment in each age becomes apparent. Bahá'u'lláh writes:

> Those things which to them were inconceivable have been made manifest. The signs and tokens of the Truth shine even as the midday sun, and yet the people are wandering, aimlessly and perplexedly, in the wilderness of ignorance and folly. (*Certitude* 239)

Some people argue that prophecies must be fulfilled exactly in every detail, but examples of prophetic fulfilment in the Bible show that this is not the case. In the Old Testament, for example, it was prophesied that the prophet Elijah would return (Mal. 4:5).[9] Jesus indicated that this prophecy was fulfilled by John the Baptist (Matt. 17:11–13). In many ways, Elijah and John the Baptist were very different – they were born to different families in different ages, had different names, and so on – yet in essential details they were the same. Both Elijah and John the Baptist appeared at a time when the nation had fallen away from God, and both preached a powerful message of repentance.

This is not to say that the details of prophecy are not important. Sometimes these details raise issues that help clarify

---

9. Note that the name 'Elijah' is an English transliteration from Hebrew. The name is different in Greek, so in some translations of the New Testament, such as the King James Version, the transliteration is 'Elias' rather than Elijah. 'Elijah' and 'Elias' are different forms of the same name.

the nature of fulfilment, but in many instances the details are intended to make the message relevant to the time when the prophecy was first revealed. Ezekiel's vision illustrates this point. Although it was of the future, it also called the people of Ezekiel's day back to the Mosaic laws from which they had turned away. When Ezekiel's vision unfolds the future, it outlines the re-establishment of the sacred Law by elaborating on aspects of past Mosaic law which had then become neglected. For example, Ezekiel speaks of the re-instatement of animal sacrifices in the restored Temple. Jesus, like Bahá'u'lláh, indicated that He was the 'Temple' of God (John 2:19–21, *Gleanings* 315), and as such, it can be understood that He fulfilled the prophecies of Ezekiel. Nevertheless, the Mosaic laws of animal sacrifices were abolished, *not* re-instated with the appearance of Jesus. It can be understood, however, that Ezekiel's vision of the re-establishment of the Law was expressed in terms that were understandable to the people of his time. Such details made Ezekiel's prophecies especially relevant up to the time when they were first fulfilled in Christ.

Whatever the prophets communicated, they spoke in a way that revealed God. Knowledge of God was never realized by mere abstract philosophical thinking, but through seeking and doing God's will as made known through the prophets, and understanding right and wrong in real social relationships and historical events.[10] The knowledge of right and wrong is woven into the prophecies, communicating the knowledge of God and informing the seeker no matter where he or she may stand in relation to historical events.

---

10. See, for example, Jer. 22:15–16; John 7:17; 1 John 4:7–16.

Chapter 4

THE LIMITATIONS OF PROPHECY

Even though prophecy can help us demonstrate to Christians the truth of Bahá'u'lláh's claims, it is important to know the limitations of prophecy. There are three main difficulties involved in relying on prophecy as a source of evidence:

1. Many prophecies are written in symbolic language and their interpretation is therefore controversial.

2. The fulfilment of prophecies constitutes proof, but not conclusive proof.

3. Some prophecies are difficult to use as evidence because they span a time period longer than our own lives. Determining fulfilment can, therefore, be impossible where it might not occur in our lifetime – such as the outward establishment of the Kingdom of God on earth.

THE PROBLEM OF INTERPRETING SYMBOLIC LANGUAGE

In *The Book of Certitude*, Bahá'u'lláh teaches that Scripture is written in two kinds of language, one 'unconcealed and unveiled' so 'that it may be a guiding lamp and a beaconing light' and another that is 'veiled and concealed, so that whatever lieth hidden in the heart of the malevolent may be made manifest and their innermost being be disclosed' (*Certitude* 255). Bahá'u'lláh explains that the ambiguity caused by the concealed and veiled nature of Scripture makes the interpretation of prophecy one of the principal tools used by the clergy to justify rejection of the Manifestations of God (*Certitude* 18, 26, 80). Most of the prophecies in the Bible are written in this 'veiled' language. Such language is especially characteristic of certain portions of the Bible, such as the Books of Daniel and Ezekiel in the Old Testament and the Book of Revelation in the New Testament.

To perceive the concealed meaning of prophecy one must acknowledge the symbolic nature and spiritual significance of the words used. If prophecy is interpreted literally, and it is imagined that such events will literally happen, then one may expect a truly extraordinary sign and proof that requires little or no spiritual discernment to recognize and acknowledge it.

For example, Christ prophesied 'the stars will fall from heaven' (Matt. 24:29). If, for the moment, what is scientifically known of stars – for example, their relative sizes and heat – is discounted, and this verse is interpreted in its literal sense, then its fulfilment would be clear and evident to everyone; both believer and non-believer would be made unavoidably aware of such an event (*Certitude* 80–1).

Because of such literal expectations, much emphasis has been placed by some Christians on prophecy. If prophecy pertains to clear historical events of such a phenomenal nature, what could be a more definite criterion for discerning where humanity stands in relation to the last days foretold in the Bible? But if the words of such verses are understood symbolically and recognized to have spiritual significance, then they are signs to the spiritually illumined – and only they would be aware of their fulfilment. Only those people who truly seek spiritual things could appreciate the fulfilment of such prophecy. To others, such fulfilment would be meaningless and empty.

The same verse, 'the stars will fall from heaven', can be used to illustrate this point. In *The Book of Certitude* Bahá'u'lláh explains the symbolic meanings of the terms *stars* and *heaven*. The 'stars', He indicates, represent the divines, or clergy, who guided the believers after the ascension of Christ. In allegorical terms, after the setting of the Sun of Righteousness (Christ) the stars (the clergy) rise in the heavens (religion) to guide the believers. In one instance, Bahá'u'lláh explains that 'heaven' symbolizes 'the heaven of divine Revelation' (*Certitude* 44). By applying these explanations given by Bahá'u'lláh to the terms *stars* and *heaven*, the verse 'the stars will fall from heaven' can be interpreted as meaning that the Christian clergy will fall as stars from the heaven of religion, and consequently, the Christian believers will not know where to turn for guidance. The Church will no longer inspire confidence in the people.

This interpretation is consistent with scriptural symbolism. In the same sermon where Jesus prophesied that the 'stars will fall from heaven' (Matt. 24:29), He also urged His followers to read the Book of Daniel (Matt. 24:15), and in that Book religious leaders are likened to stars:

Those who are wise shall shine
Like the brightness of the firmament,
And those who turn many to righteousness
Like the stars forever and ever. (Dan. 12:3)

For those who are troubled by the divisions in the Church and disagreements over the meanings of Scripture, it is possible to see that the 'stars' that once guided Christianity have indeed fallen from the 'heaven' of religion. But for those who interpret the verses literally, the condition of the Church, its divisions and disagreements, are not recognized as having any relationship to the fulfilment of this prophecy. For the literalists, the prophecy is not fulfilled, and it presents none of the evidence perceived by Bahá'ís.

Alluding to this prophecy of Jesus, Bahá'u'lláh wrote to the Christian clergy:

O concourse of bishops! Ye are the stars of the heaven of My knowledge. My mercy desireth not that ye should fall upon the earth. My justice, however, declareth: 'This is that which the Son hath decreed'. And whatsoever hath proceeded out of His blameless, His truth-speaking, trustworthy mouth, can never be altered. (*Tablets of Bahá'u'lláh* 14)

Many Christians find it difficult to accept such interpretations of Scripture, and consequently the Bahá'í explanation of prophecy will not appear conclusive or convincing to them. However, some Christians do interpret many prophecies in their symbolic sense and some do so in essentially the manner that Bahá'u'lláh has explained in The Book of Certitude.

THE CIRCUMSTANTIAL NATURE OF SOME PROPHECIES

Some prophecies constitute only circumstantial evidence, that is, they speak more of the events and circumstances at the time of the appearance of the Manifestation than of His actual life and teachings. It is important to understand this, so that false conclusions are not drawn from the fulfilment of prophecy. This *circumstantial* nature of some prophecies means that they do not offer *conclusive* proof. This is one reason why Volume 1 of *Preparing for a Bahá'í/Christian Dialogue* emphasized other sources of evidence for deciding the most important questions of faith.

Many prophecies, rather than offering direct and explicit evidence that Bahá'u'lláh is a Manifestation of God, provide clues relating to the circumstances of His life and the age in which He was destined to appear. In many instances, it is only by first recognizing the station of a Manifestation that one realizes that He has fulfilled prophecies. For example, once it is recognized that Jesus is the 'Christ' (that is, the Messiah) then it follows that He is the one foretold in the prophecies. In the same way, once it is recognized that Mírzá Husayn 'Alí is 'Bahá'u'lláh' (literally, the *glory of God*), then it follows that He is the glory of God so often foretold in the prophecies.

Many prophecies are therefore limited in terms of evidence. As pointed out in Volume 1, Bahá'u'lláh emphasizes in *The Book of Certitude* that the greatest evidences of a Manifestation of God are His life and teachings. Bahá'u'lláh often refers to prophecy, but it is perhaps significant that in *The Book of Certitude*, He chooses to de-emphasize reliance on it as a form of evidence:

> Although We did not intend to make mention of the traditions of a bygone age, yet, because of Our love for thee, We will cite a few which are applicable to Our argument. We do not feel their necessity, however, inasmuch as the things We have already mentioned suffice the world and all that is therein . . . As the people differ in their understanding and station, We will accordingly make mention of a few traditions, that these may impart constancy to the wavering soul, and tranquillity to the troubled mind. Thereby, will the testimony of God unto the people, both high and low, be complete and perfect. (*Certitude* 237–8)

Of prophecies, Bahá'u'lláh writes, 'We do not feel their necessity'. Rather, He feels that other criteria He has already mentioned are sufficient to 'the world and all that is therein'. Bahá'u'lláh will cite some prophecies, but it appears that He wants the reader to be aware that this type of evidence is not on the same level as the other evidence He has already cited.

This may seem confusing to some readers. Is Bahá'u'lláh really de-emphasizing prophecy, since He uses the word 'traditions' instead of prophecies? A careful examination of the traditions mentioned in *The Book of Certitude* may help answer this question. Two characteristics are apparent: first, the traditions are not in 'veiled' language, a point that Bahá'u'lláh Himself mentions (*Certitude* 238–55); and second, the traditions prophesy certain *circumstances* or *characteristics* concerning the expected Messiah (in this case, the Báb). That is, these 'traditions' are prophecies because each one of them describes things to come. Since the meanings of these traditions are not concealed in symbolic language, they should be easier to use as evidence. Nevertheless, they are still not conclusive.

These traditions can be grouped under nine headings, which prophesy the following:

1. People will oppose the new Revelation.
2. He (the Promised One: in the case of these prophecies, the Báb is intended) will change the laws of the former Revelation and bring new laws.
3. His primary enemies will be the clergy.
4. He will be a descendent of Muḥammad's family.
5. The greatness of His Revelation will exceed that of former religions.
6. He will have the characteristics of Moses, Jesus, Joseph and Job.
7. His followers will be persecuted.
8. The clergy of His day will be very wicked.
9. He will appear in the year '60' (that is, the year AH 1260)

By examining these prophecies, it is possible to see how far they constitute evidence. For example, Bahá'u'lláh cites the following tradition: 'And when the Standard of Truth is made manifest, the people of both the East and the West curse it' (*Certitude* 238). This tradition prophesies that people will oppose the new Revelation. Any impartial survey of the persecution and violence associated with the advent of the Báb and Bahá'u'lláh shows that history testifies to the fulfilment of this prophecy. Nevertheless, it must be admitted that before it can be shown conclusively that the Báb and Bahá'u'lláh have fulfilled this prophecy, we must first demonstrate that they are Manifestations of God – a realization that can come only through an awareness of their lives and teachings. Otherwise, how can it be known that the Bahá'í Faith is *the* Cause that the tradition says will be persecuted? Not every cause that is opposed by the people is the Cause of God. Therefore, this prophecy only offers proof that pertains to *circumstances* relating to the Faith, circumstances which alone do not constitute an irrefutable evidence that the Báb and/or Bahá'u'lláh are Manifestations of God.

One of the traditions Bahá'u'lláh mentions indicates that the Báb's primary enemies will be the clergy, yet it is evident that not every enemy of the clergy will be a bearer of a new Revelation from God. Another tradition indicates that the Báb will be a descendant of Muḥammad's family, yet it must also be acknowledged that not every descendant of Muḥammad's family is a Prophet of God. Another foretells that His Revelation will exceed the greatness of former Revelations, but again, to prove this we must first examine the Revelation itself. And if we ascertain that it is a Revelation from God, what need is there for prophecy or any other type of evidence? Obviously one cannot argue that the Bahá'í Revelation is the true Faith of God and at the same time say that it can only be accepted as such when it fulfils the prophecies of former times.

The following analogy will illustrate this point. Bahá'u'lláh writes, 'The proof of the sun is the light thereof, which shineth and envelopeth all things' (*Certitude* 209). By this, Bahá'u'lláh suggests that everything is known by the qualities that pertain directly to it. It is known that the sun gives light and heat to the earth, and it is possible to predict that it will rise each succeeding day. But with each day the sun is recognized by its characteristic light and heat, not because it fulfilled a prediction by appearing to rise over the horizon. The moon will also fulfil the prediction by rising over the horizon, but it will not have the light and heat by which the sun is recognized. This shows that fulfilment of the prediction is not conclusive. Furthermore, if it is possible to experience the heat and light of the sun, what need is there for the fulfilment of a prediction as evidence?

While considering the above prophecies, it is worth reflecting on the three main themes of prophecy. Notice how almost all the nine different headings given above can be placed into the two categories of judgement (which concerns those who have turned away from God, numbers 1, 3, 7 and 8) and redemption (which occurs through the new Revelation of God, numbers 2, 5 and 6). Only numbers 4 and 9 are so specific as to have a meaning likely to be fulfilled once only.

THE LIMITED TESTABILITY OF SOME PROPHECIES
Added to the difficulties of interpretation and inconclusiveness is the problem of verifying certain prophecies. Some prophecies are fulfilled over a long span of time. Moses, for example, prophesied many things, including the appearance of Christ, yet Christ did not appear until centuries later. Moreover, when Christ did appear, many Christians believed that some Old Testament prophecies still referred to events in the future. The sceptic can argue that until all prophecies are fulfilled the evidence is incomplete, that is, some may never be fulfilled, proving that the prophecies were not inspired, or that it is not possible to know whether they have all been fulfilled.

The eminent and learned Bahá'í scholar Mírzá Abu'l-Faḍl addressed this problem.

> If faith depended on the fulfilment of what is prophesied in the verses, the people would be justified in continuing their unbelief and denial until such time as the prophecies are fulfilled. This is clearly a fallacy, and religions could not soundly proceed on this basis. (*Miracles and Metaphors* 132)

These points have been discussed to show that generally prophecy is neither conclusive evidence nor a necessary proof of a Manifestation's reality. A Manifestation's greatest proofs are His life, teachings and influence on the world. As *evidence*, prophecy does, however, help identify some of the circumstances pertaining to the one foretold in the sacred Scriptures. Prophecy can give indications of what should and should not be expected. The quest for evidence and proofs is only one reason to study prophecy. As shown in the previous chapters, there is another reason for such a study of prophecy – it can assist the pursuit of the spiritual life.

part two

INTERPRETATION
AND THE
FULFILMENT OF PROPHECY

chapter
5

THE BOOK OF CERTITUDE
AND THE INTERPRETATION OF PROPHECY

Once a list of references to specific prophecies or prophetic themes has been compiled from the Bible and Bahá'í writings, it becomes necessary to reflect on their significance and meaning. It is essential to understand the meanings of the prophecies in order to explain them with clarity when discussing prophecy with Christians. The process of studying the prophecies has two stages:

1. Learn what the Bahá'í writings say about each prophecy. When no specific explanations exist, use the explanations given for other prophecies as a guide.

2. Learn some of the common Christian beliefs about each prophecy under consideration and give special attention when necessary to how the Bahá'í view can best be explained. It is also worth noting that both conservative and liberal Christian commentaries can have valuable insights and are often in agreement with Bahá'í teachings on specific points and topics. It can be very persuasive if one is able to show a Christian seeker that a Christian Bible scholar agrees with the Bahá'í interpretation.

Since many of the prophecies that refer to Bahá'u'lláh have already been explained in the Bahá'í writings, it follows that in such cases these references and explanations are naturally the most reliable and representative of 'Bahá'í' belief. In *The Book of Certitude*, for example, Bahá'u'lláh provides a very detailed analysis (24–89) of Jesus' prophecies in Matthew, Chapter 24 (specifically verses 29–31). In the case of Isaiah 2:1–10, 'Abdu'l-Bahá provides an explanation in *Some Answered Questions* (Chapter 12). *Some Answered Questions* also contains explanations of many other prophecies, especially from the Book of Daniel and the Book of Revelation.

In addition to learning specific explanations to specific prophecies, it is important for the student of Scripture to gain a knowledge of how the symbolism of prophecy works. In the preceding chapters some major Biblical symbolism has been explained. There are, however, many other symbols in the Scriptures and it is useful to develop the skill of interpreting them. Bahá'u'lláh never intended the seeker to limit his or her understanding to the specific explanations given in *The Book of Certitude* (237, see also 181, 210–11). Passages, such as Bahá'u'lláh's explanation of Matthew 24, give many details offering insights into numerous other prophecies. These insights are especially important where specific explanations do not exist and it is necessary to understand and interpret prophecy for oneself. Bahá'u'lláh does not just give specific interpretations, He instructs us in the method of interpretation – as He says, 'Thus We *instruct* thee in the interpretation of the traditions' (*Certitude* 32, emphasis added). Similarly, when 'Abdu'l-Bahá explains the symbolism of the Genesis narrative about Adam and Eve, He states, 'This is one of the meanings of the Biblical story of Adam. Reflect until you discover the others' (*Some Answered Questions* 126).

A number of basic interpretive principles implied or stated in *The Book of Certitude* can be applied to understanding prophecy. Some of these can be outlined:

1. Consider whether passages in one part of the Bible can be clarified by referring to other passages.

2. Consider both the literal and symbolic meanings of the text.

3. Study how the symbol functions and what it points to.

4. Based on the symbol's function and conceptual meaning, decide whether it has a limited meaning or a meaning that could be fulfilled in different ages.

In the following pages, each of these steps will be examined more closely.

STUDYING HOW PROPHETIC TERMINOLOGY AND SYMBOLISM ARE USED IN OTHER PARTS OF THE BIBLE AND/OR SACRED LITERATURE

When Bahá'u'lláh explains Jesus' prophecy concerning a 'sign' that will appear 'in heaven' (Matt. 24:30/*Certitude* 61–6), He recounts past Scriptures *and* traditions that mention stars in heaven heralding the Messengers of God, such as the famous Biblical story of the star of Bethlehem (Matt. 2:2) and well-known traditions about stars heralding Abraham and Moses (but which are not recorded in the Bible). This example shows how other aspects of Scripture and traditions can help clarify the meaning of certain terms and/or expressions. Similarly, when 'Abdu'l-Bahá explains the prophecy in Daniel concerning the 'seventy weeks' (490 days), He calls attention to the fact that in another verse the 'day of the Lord is one year', meaning that 490 days is equal to 490 years in prophecy (*Some Answered Questions* 48; see also 46). As 'Abdu'l-Bahá explains, 'the Holy Books have their special terminologies which must be known and understood' (*Promulgation* 246). To understand, for example, the term 'army' in a verse such as Revelation 19:19, it is worth considering whether the word *army* means a literal army with material weapons, or a spiritual army such as St Paul describes (2 Cor. 10:3–5). In Chapter 18, this approach will be applied using the Book of Daniel to help clarify questions arising from the Qur'ánic statement that Muḥammad is the 'Seal of the Prophets'.

One easy way to apply this approach and get a better idea of what a particular term means – for example, 'the New Jerusalem', 'famines' and 'water' – is to consult a concordance and/or Bible dictionary, which are among the study tools described in Volume 1 of the *Preparing for a Bahá'í/Christian Dialogue* series. This reference tool helps make it possible to find out quickly how a term is used throughout the Bible.

CONSIDERING BOTH THE LITERAL AND SYMBOLIC MEANINGS OF THE TEXT

When Bahá'u'lláh explains the meaning of a 'sign' that will appear 'in heaven', He states that 'heaven' has both an inner and an outer meaning. One meaning is literal, indicating a star in the sky, and the other is symbolic, a great herald in the 'heaven of divine Revelation' (*Certitude* 44). This demonstrates that some prophecies may be both literal and symbolic. In most cases, however, prophecy is symbolic, as will be shown by other examples later in this book.

Many verses in Scripture can have several meanings. In connection with the interpretation of Scripture and sacred traditions, Bahá'u'lláh cites a saying of Imám Ṣádiq, a successor of Muḥammad: 'We speak one word, and by it we intend one and seventy meanings' (*Certitude* 255). Nevertheless, although there may be many meanings in a verse of Scripture, it is important not to confuse *significant* meanings with *any* meaning. Not every interpretation, whether it be symbolic or literal, is valid. Bahá'u'lláh points out in *The Book of Certitude* the error of some interpretations (see 40, 47, 113, 115).

Interpretation need not require years of study, but the more knowledge one acquires about the context and language of a particular passage, the more one is able to rule out speculative and unfounded interpretations. Some interpretations, as history has shown, were simply based on a misunderstanding of the text, confusion over the meaning of certain words, grammar, identities of persons and so on. The English in the King James version of the Bible sometimes gives a very different impression when interpreted according to modern English. One way to avoid such errors is to consult different translations and opinions before drawing conclusions.

STUDYING HOW THE SYMBOL FUNCTIONS AND WHAT IT POINTS TO

When Bahá'u'lláh explains the meaning of the prophecy 'they will see the Son of man coming in the clouds of heaven' (Matt. 24:30), He draws attention to the functioning of each term as a symbol. 'Heaven' He says, 'denoteth loftiness and exaltation, inasmuch as it is the seat of the revelation of those Manifestations of Holiness' (*Certitude* 67) and 'clouds prevent the eyes of men from beholding the sun' (*Certitude* 72). From these statements it is clear that the 'heavens' above us, because of their height, their seeming inaccessibility, signify that which is exalted and holy (that is, the Revelation of God). Because it is hard to see through 'clouds' they are used as symbols to signify those things that prevent us from seeing the truth or are difficult to understand.[11] In this context, the 'clouds' of 'Heaven' are, therefore, those things that come from 'heaven' (the realm of God, so to speak, or the Revelation), and which cause some people to reject or fail to see the truth. A new religious teaching annulling past laws is one example Bahá'u'lláh gives of 'clouds of heaven'.

When Bahá'u'lláh explains the meaning of Jesus' prophecy that the 'sun shall be darkened' (*Certitude* 33), He explains that

---

11. Concerning the symbolism of the cloud in the Old Testament, L. H. Brockington, Oxford lecturer in Aramaic and Syriac, writes that God 'came down in the pillar of cloud and went inside the tent of meeting [i.e. the Tabernacle] to talk with Moses face to face while the cloud remained at the door. The people recognized the cloud as the visible sign of God's presence (Exod. 33:7–11). The cloud thus came to be both a symbol of God's presence and a veil to hide the brilliance and strength of it.' See Alan Richardson, ed., *A Theological Word Book of the Bible* 175.

this refers to the obscuring of the light or teachings of the Manifestation (Christ) before the coming of the next Manifestation. In this case, the term 'sun' is a symbol of the Manifestation of God. The symbolism can be understood by considering the similarities between the sun and the Manifestations. Bahá'u'lláh writes:

> These Suns of Truth are the universal Manifestations of God in the worlds of His attributes and names, even as the visible sun that assisteth, as decreed by God, the true One, the Adored, in the development of all earthly things, such as the trees, the fruits, and colours thereof, the minerals of the earth, and all that may be witnessed in the world of creation, so do the divine Luminaries, by their loving care and educative influence, cause the trees of divine unity, the fruits of His oneness, the leaves of detachment, the blossoms of knowledge and certitude, and the myrtles of wisdom and utterance, to exist and be made manifest. (*Certitude* 33–4)

This symbolic equation between the 'sun' and the Manifestation of God can also be observed in Biblical symbolism (Mal. 4:2, *God Passes By* 95). Similarly, much can be understood about the prophecies by considering the conflict between present-day materialism and the spiritual reality of Bahá'u'lláh's teachings. For example, we can understand the meaning of the prophecy that He will come with 'power and great glory' (Matt. 24:30) by considering the spiritual meanings of 'power' and 'glory'. Instead of physical power over His adversaries and the revelation of His glory through the destruction of His enemies in a military battle, His power and glory are related to His spiritual triumph and presence. His power is evident in the invincibility of His truth and the enduring reality of His Word. His glory was not achieved by preventing His oppressors from imprisoning Him, but rather in the splendour and victory of His Cause despite His suffering.

DECIDING WHETHER A SYMBOL HAS A LIMITED OR BROADER HISTORICAL MEANING

Once a symbol has been studied and its function and conceptual meaning are understood, it is possible to decide whether the prophecy refers to only one historical event or to a type of event that occurs in different ages. When Bahá'u'lláh explains the meaning of 'oppression' (or 'tribulation') He says that this refers to the time when people seeking after the truth do not know where to turn for guidance because the religious leaders have become confused, corrupted or are simply ignorant. This event, He says, 'is the essential feature of every Revelation' (see *Certitude* 31). It characterizes the time before a new Messenger of God appears. This view can be supported by passages from the Bible. For example, a prophecy similar to the one in which Christ refers to His second advent, in Matthew 24:29, can be found in the Old Testament (Joel 2:28-32) and is associated with the first advent of Jesus by Peter in Acts 2:14-21. Such examples demonstrate that these signs occur in every dispensation and that some prophecies, such as Matthew 24:30, can be interpreted as references to more than one Manifestation of God. Bahá'u'lláh, for example, points out the universality of other prophetic terms used by Jesus, such as 'sun', 'moon' and 'star' (*Certitude* 37-8), and also the terms mentioned in Qur'ánic prophecies, such as 'heaven' (*Certitude* 68) and 'clouds' (*Certitude* 73-4).

Each of these examples also shows how the language of prophecy is above all concerned with the condition of the soul and the quest to attain the presence of God. When this spiritual content is considered it becomes easier to see that many prophecies are fulfilled in every age and in the experience of every seeker and believer. Where a prophecy may be applicable to many different ages, it is especially important to reflect on how it applies to the age in which we are now living.

Once the Bahá'í writings have been consulted and the spiritual meaning of the prophecies has been considered, it is useful to study what Christians have written and said about the prophecies. Christians have written numerous books about prophecy as well as verse-by-verse commentaries on the Bible, but not all agree with each other. Some books, however, agree with the Bahá'í view and reject the more literal interpretations; these books can provide valuable insights that can be very useful when conversing with Christians. Calling attention to such views can, for example, help persuade some Christians to be more flexible in their own interpretations. If a Christian sees that several well-respected evangelical commentators agree with a particular Bahá'í interpretation, it becomes much easier for them to accept the Bahá'í position.

Studying Christian authors who disagree with Bahá'í interpretations provides the opportunity to consider arguments and responses before discussing the issue with Christians. Some Christians believe Christ will not return as a historical person, others look for a historical person, but await certain specific conditions to herald His advent. It is good to know about such differences in advance. When encountering unexpected beliefs, the best response is to encourage the Christian to explain his or her beliefs as fully as possible, noting relevant verses, etc. In the process, it is likely that much will be learned about Scripture, to the benefit of everyone.

chapter 6

THE FULFILMENT OF PROPHECY

WAYS OF UNDERSTANDING FULFILMENT

The fulfilment of many prophetic themes can be understood in two main ways: fulfilment in the broader sense of history, and fulfilment in the narrower sense of each individual's own spiritual experience.

The theme of 'judgement' can be used to illustrate these different perspectives. When a person is taken before a court to be 'judged' this simply means that the merits of this person (or it could be a nation) are being evaluated. Theoretically, if the person judged has done well then he or she is rewarded; if it is a court of law, for example, and the person has done evil, he or she is punished.

Shoghi Effendi argued that tragic world events of the nineteenth and twentieth centuries were the consequence of the rejection of Bahá'u'lláh's teachings, principally by the world's religious and civil leaders (see *Promised Day Is Come* 18). In this instance, Shoghi Effendi is viewing Biblical and Bahá'í prophecy in a broad historical sense. That is, Bahá'u'lláh appeared, the world turned away, and the prophesied 'Day of Judgement' occurred (see also *Advent of Divine Justice* 68–9). Evidence of this judgement is to be found in all the wars and suffering that have been going on ever since, and which are directly related to the fact that the world has ignored Bahá'u'lláh's teachings concerning the oneness of humankind, the containment of nationalism, the elimination of the extremes of wealth and poverty, the need to overcome racism and so on.

Nevertheless, this judgement also occurs within the experience of every believer. The prophetic verses can refer to theological truths and spiritual experiences that are potentially ever-present in human life. Everyone must face the truth, decide what is right and accept the consequences if they turn away from it. Other aspects of prophecy, such as the prophecy of Armageddon, the tribulation, paradise and so on, can be understood in the same way. We all have our own Armageddon to fight, our own promised land to return to, our own chance to attain to the presence of God.

It is, of course, possible to experience both forms of fulfilment in many different types of experiences throughout one's life and spiritual development. Most people are caught in the cross-currents of the broader historical fulfilment of prophecy, as well as having an individual experience of reward and punishment.

Many Bible interpreters and scholars argue over which events in history fall within the real meaning of the prophecies. Some believe that prophetic literature (such as the Book of Daniel or the Book of Revelation) was written with events contemporary to the author in mind. Some argue that the prophetic verses are purely symbolic of theological truths and spiritual experiences. Finally, some believe that the prophecies are mostly about future events. With the symbolic and thematic nature of prophecy in mind, it is possible to see that all of these views can be correct in certain respects. It is possible that many of the prophecies of Daniel, for example, refer to events in the second century BC, as some scholars today believe, but that, as Christ indicated, they were also applicable to future events (Matt. 24:15).

In some ways the prophecies can, therefore, be understood in three ways: in the light of past social and political events, as present individual experience, and as referring to future events. It can be argued that John's vision of paradise restored (Rev. 21), for example, was realized by many Christians in the golden age of Christianity, or that it is being realized by many Bahá'ís today,[12] or that its true culmination awaits the future golden age of the Bahá'í era. It all depends on how one chooses to understand its meaning, and how much one wants to stress the outward literal aspects of these prophecies. It is important, however, to keep in mind that prophecies are ultimately concerned with the spiritual well-being of humankind. Bahá'u'lláh writes:

> In every age and century, the purpose of the Prophets of God and their chosen ones hath been no other but to affirm the *spiritual* significance of the terms 'life', 'resurrection', and 'judgment'. (*Certitude* 120, emphasis added)

In *The Book of Certitude* there are many passages suggesting how prophetic fulfilment can be realized in individual and personal experience. A number of the key Biblical prophecies, for example, concern the trumpet-blast heralding the new Revelation, the appearance of a new creation as a result of this Revelation, and the believers living eternally in the City of God in the presence of God. Each of these symbols can be understood in relation to the awakening of consciousness and the change in one's inner life. In *The Book of Certitude*, Bahá'u'lláh writes about the importance of striving to enter God's presence. He sets forth the main stages of the seeker's path – sanctification (meaning not just detachment, but dedicating oneself to God), illumination and then union, signified by entering spiritually the City of God (*Certitude* 195–200). He also outlines the essential ethical and spiritual ideals, qualities and practices required: trust in God, humility, avoidance of idle talk and backbiting, contentment with little, companionship with the spiritually minded, prayerfulness, purity of thought, forgiveness of others and so on (*Certitude* 192–200). Bahá'u'lláh uses familiar prophetic symbols to describe the station the seeker will achieve, when he or she has arisen to fulfil these requirements:

---

12. See *Selections from the Writings of the Báb* 79, 82, 110.

Only when the lamp of search, of earnest striving, of longing desire, of passionate devotion, of fervid love, of rapture, and ecstasy, is kindled within the seeker's heart, and the breeze of His loving-kindness is wafted upon his soul, will the darkness of error be dispelled, the mists of doubts and misgivings be dissipated, and the lights of knowledge and certitude envelop his being. At that hour will the mystic Herald, bearing the joyful tidings of the Spirit, shine forth from the City of God resplendent as the morn, and, through the trumpet-blast of knowledge, will awaken the heart, the soul, and the spirit from the slumber of negligence. Then will the manifold favours and outpouring grace of the holy and everlasting Spirit confer such new life upon the seeker that he will find himself endowed with a new eye, a new ear, a new heart, and a new mind. He will contemplate the manifest signs of the universe, and will penetrate the hidden mysteries of the soul. Gazing with the eye of God, he will perceive within every atom a door that leadeth him to the stations of absolute certitude. He will discover in all things the mysteries of divine Revelation and the evidences of an everlasting manifestation. (*Certitude* 195–6)[13]

The experience described in each sentence in this paragraph can be viewed in relation to numerous Biblical prophecies: the tribulation and its end, the appearance of the New Jerusalem and City of God, and so on. After reading Part 3 of this book, study this passage in its context in *The Book of Certitude*. This will help clarify how prophecy relates to personal spiritual experience.

---

13. Notice that the seeker is not at the stage of trying to decide whether or not there is a God or whether or not to become a member of a religion. This is already assumed. The question is not belief or how one identifies oneself, but rather how to become truly close to God.

For the committed seeker, even a moment on this spiritual path may be sufficient to enable him or her to see the new City of God revealed by Bahá'u'lláh and appreciate the deeper significance of prophecy. However, as Bahá'u'lláh states, 'people differ in their understanding and station', and for this reason it is good to be able to explain and share with others some examples of prophecies that have been fulfilled in a literal way that has an outward appearance – 'Thereby, will the testimony of God unto the people, both high and low, be complete and perfect' (*Certitude* 237–8). Examples of literal fulfilment can be very persuasive, causing many to take up the spiritual path which they might otherwise neglect or avoid.

THE PROGRESSIVE FULFILMENT OF PROPHECY

It has been demonstrated that many prophecies are fulfilled in every age. What then is the distinction between this age and past ages? 'Abdu'l-Bahá states that the difference is in the maturity of humankind.

> The Cause of Bahá'u'lláh is the same as the Cause of Christ. It is the same Temple and the same Foundation. Both of these are spiritual springtimes and seasons of the soul-refreshing awakening and the cause of the renovation of the life of mankind. The spring of this year is the same as the spring of last year. The origins and ends are the same. The sun of today is the sun of yesterday. In the coming of Christ, the divine teachings were given in accordance with the infancy of the human race. The teachings of Bahá'u'lláh have the same basic principles, but are according to the stage of the maturity of the world and the requirements of this illumined age. (*Bahá'í World Faith* 400)

From this passage, it is clear that this age is unique and marks a new stage in human evolution. Shoghi Effendi also refers to this distinction when he writes that the Báb stood historically at the 'confluence' or meeting point of 'two universal prophetic cycles' (*God Passes By* 54–5). These two cycles he identified as:

1. the 'Adamic Cycle', which he explained as 'stretching back as far as the first dawnings of the world's recorded religious history', and
2. the 'Bahá'í Cycle', which he said was 'destined to propel itself across the unborn reaches of time for a period of no less than five thousand centuries' (*God Passes By* 54–5).

In another passage, Shoghi Effendi spoke of the Bahá'í Revelation as the 'promise and crowning glory of past ages and centuries' and as the

> Consummation of all the Dispensations within the Adamic Cycle, inaugurating an era of at least a thousand years' duration, and a cycle destined to last no less than five thousand centuries, signalizing the end of the Prophetic Era and the beginning of the Era of Fulfilment. (*God Passes By* 100)

From these passages, it becomes apparent that the prophecies of the 'Adamic Cycle' which would include Biblical prophecies, were pointing toward a consummation, an Era of Fulfilment. Whereas certain prophecies were fulfilled in past ages, such fulfilment never embraced the whole of humankind. Whereas some people were able to enter the inner and outer Kingdom of God in the age, for example, of Christ, there was never a time when all the nations were gathered in this Kingdom. For this reason, and because of people's failures in past ages, there were always wars and conflicts between the nations, religions and races. In this age, all the world will be gathered together into one community, and provisions will be made to end war (*Some*

Answered Questions 63–4). In this way, the peace spoken of in past prophecies will embrace all people and, therefore, reach a 'consummation'.

The unity of humankind has never been achieved in any period of the Adamic Cycle, and once the prophecies concerning this unity have been fulfilled, no future age can hope to achieve a higher level of unification of this world. The unity of humankind represents in many ways the culmination of the highest hopes and prophecies of past ages (see *Promised Day* 108). Bahá'u'lláh writes, 'That which hath been made manifest in this pre-eminent, this most exalted Revelation, stands unparalleled in the annals of the past, nor will future ages witness its like' (see Shoghi Effendi, *Advent of Divine Justice* 65).

Referring to the evolution of human civilization in connection with the prophetic 'time of the end', Shoghi Effendi writes:

> The ages of its infancy and childhood are past, never again to return, while the Great Age, the consummation of all ages, which must signalize the coming of age of the entire human race, is yet to come. The convulsions of this transitional and most turbulent period in the annals of humanity are the essential prerequisites, and herald the inevitable approach, of that Age of Ages, 'the time of the end', in which the folly and tumult of strife that has, since the dawn of history, blackened the annals of mankind, will have been finally transmuted into the wisdom and the tranquility of an undisturbed, a universal, a lasting peace, in which the discord and separation of the children of men will have given way to the worldwide reconciliation, and the complete unification of the divers elements that constitute human society. (*Promised Day* 117)

The centrality of world unity becomes even more apparent in the following passage:

> The Revelation of Bahá'u'lláh, whose supreme mission is none other but the achievement of this organic and spiritual unity of the whole body of nations, should, if we be faithful to its implications, be regarded as signalizing through its advent the coming of age of the entire human race. It should be viewed not merely as yet another spiritual revival in the ever-changing fortunes of mankind, not only as a further stage in a chain of progressive Revelations, nor even as the culmination of one of a series of recurrent prophetic cycles, but rather as marking the last and highest stage in the stupendous evolution of man's collective life on this planet. The emergence of a world community, the consciousness of world citizenship, the founding of a world civilization and culture – all of which must synchronize with the initial stages in the unfoldment of the Golden Age of the Bahá'í Era – should, by their very nature, be regarded, as far as this planetary life is concerned, as the furthermost limits in the organization of human society, though man, as an individual, will, nay must indeed as a result of such a consummation, continue indefinitely to progress and develop. (*World Order* 163)

And finally, in this passage, Shoghi Effendi shows the significance of world unity in relation to the fulfilment of those prophecies referring to the 'Day of God':

> Only those who are willing to associate the Revelation proclaimed by Bahá'u'lláh with the consummation of so stupendous an evolution in the collective life of the whole human race can grasp the significance of the words He [Bahá'u'lláh], while alluding to the glories of this promised Day and to the duration of the Bahá'í Era, has deemed fit to utter. 'This is the King of Days' . . . 'It is evident', He in another passage explains, 'that every age in which a Manifestation of God hath lived is

divinely-ordained, and may, in a sense, be characterized as God's appointed Day. This Day, however, is unique, and is to be distinguished from those that have preceded it. The designation 'Seal of the Prophets' fully revealeth its high station. The Prophetic Cycle hath verily ended'. (*World Order* 166–7)

In this passage, it is clear that the prophecies concerning the 'appointed Day' have also been fulfilled in past ages, as explained above, but it is also evident that this fulfilment was never achieved to the degree that it is destined to reach in this age. Although the central thrust of these passages concerns the unity of humankind, other features are also apparent, such as the establishment of peace, the degree to which civilization will advance in this age, consciousness of world citizenship and so on.

Moreover, what was achieved symbolically or in part in past ages will be achieved, in some ways literally and fully in this age. This distinction between the present age and past ages can be seen in 'Abdu'l-Bahá's comments both on the prophecies concerning peace in this age (Isa. 11:1–10) and on those concerning the Jews' return to Palestine.

> These verses [Isa. 11:1–10] apply word for word to Bahá'u'lláh. Likewise in this marvelous cycle the earth will be transformed, and the world of humanity arrayed in tranquillity and beauty . . . Cooperation and union will be established, and finally war will be entirely suppressed. When the laws of the Most Holy Book are enforced, contentions and disputes will find a final sentence of absolute justice before a general tribunal of the nations and kingdoms, and the difficulties that appear will be solved. (*Some Answered Questions* 63–4)

Here, 'Abdu'l-Bahá interprets the promise of the day when the 'wolf also shall dwell with the lamb' symbolically, as signifying peace among the nations. This peace, He explains, will be a literal peace involving a means of international co-operation, a form of collective security. No former age ever attained such a system of international security. Even when Christian nations were at peace among themselves there were other non-Christian nations that posed a threat.

This literal or outward significance of peace is reinforced by 'Abdu'l-Bahá's later comments about the Jews returning to Palestine. The initial context is that of the above explanation of Isaiah 11:1–10. 'Abdu'l-Bahá states:

> Universal peace and concord will be realized between all the nations, and that Incomparable Branch [Bahá'u'lláh] will gather together all Israel, signifying that in this cycle Israel will be gathered in the Holy Land, and that the Jewish people who are scattered to the East and West, South and North, will be assembled together. (*Some Answered Questions* 65; cf. *God Passes By* 305)

A few passages later He returns to the theme, saying:

> Now see: these events did not take place in the Christian cycle, for the nations did not come under the One Standard which is the Divine Branch. But in this cycle of the Lord of Hosts all the nations and peoples will enter under the shadow of this Flag. *In the same way*, Israel, scattered all over the world, was not reassembled in the Holy Land in the Christian cycle; but in the beginning of the cycle of Bahá'u'lláh this divine promise, as is clearly stated in all the Books of the Prophets, has begun to be manifest. You can see that from all parts of the world tribes of Jews are coming to the Holy Land; they live in villages and lands which they make their own, and day by day they are increasing to such an extent that all Palestine will become their home. (*Some Answered Questions* 65–6, emphasis added)

'Abdu'l-Bahá's commentary focuses on the present successes of the Bahá'í Faith (64–5) and relates these to the fact that it is now possible to witness the beginning of events that will lead to the future realization of Isaiah's prophecies. The return of the Jews to Palestine is not, however, connected here to a *specific* prophecy. 'Abdu'l-Bahá simply mentions it as, presumably, a feature of 'the great events' unfolding in this Day. This event He refers to as a 'divine promise . . . clearly stated in all the Books of the Prophets'.[14]

At the time of 'Abdu'l-Bahá's discourse, the progressive return of the Israelites to Palestine was a well-known phenomenon and a popular topic of discussion. His reference to the return of the Jews may have been incorporated into his discussion in order to illustrate, by an example of literal fulfilment, that the unity of humankind in this age should also be understood as a literal and outward fact. This is suggested by His words, 'in the same way . . .', when He refers to the return of the Jews following explanations about the unity of humankind. This comparison suggests that the promise of the unity of humankind is to be fulfilled literally and also that, like the return of the Jews to Israel, the prophesied process of unification may occur without the direct involvement of the Bahá'í community.

Seven years before 'Abdu'l-Bahá made the above statements, He commented directly on the return of the Jews to Palestine:

> You have asked Me a question with regard to the gathering of the children of Israel in Jerusalem in accordance with the prophecy.
>
> Jerusalem, the Holy of Holies, is a revered Temple, a sublime name, for it is the City of God . . . The gathering of Israel at Jerusalem means, therefore, and

---

14. See, for example, Ps. 147:2; Isa. 11:11, 12; Ezek. 34:13–5, 37:22; Shoghi Effendi, *God Passes By* 305.

prophesies, that Israel as a whole is gathering beneath the banner of God and will enter the Kingdom of the Ancient of Days. For the celestial Jerusalem, which has as its center the Holies of Holies, is a City of the Kingdom, a Divine City. The East and West are but a small corner of that City.

Moreover, materially as well (as spiritually), the Israelites will gather in the Holy Land. This is irrefutable prophecy, for the ignominy which Israel has suffered for well-nigh twenty-five hundred years will now be changed into eternal glory, and in the eyes of all, the Jewish people will become glorified to such an extent as to draw the jealousy of its enemies and the envy of its friends. (According to information received by the National Spiritual Assembly of the United States several years ago, this Tablet was revealed by the Master in the year 1897 to a Jewish community in the Orient: *Bahá'í News*, No. 250, December 1951, p. 5; *Lights of Guidance*, no. 1677, p. 499.)

In this passage, 'Abdu'l-Bahá speaks of the fulfilment of prophecy in its two senses – symbolic and literal. In one sense, the return to the promised land means becoming a Bahá'í, and in another, it means the Jews literally returning to Palestine. 'Abdu'l-Bahá acknowledges that these prophecies contain both aspects, but there is a suggestion that in this age the fulfilment will also be outward.

'Abdu'l-Bahá's interpretation of Isaiah (11:1–11) and other unspecified prophecies concerning the return of the Jews to Palestine provides one way of understanding many other prophecies as well, such as those referring to the establishment of the Kingdom of God on earth. The outward, visible evidences of fulfilment will be greater in this age than in any past age, so much so that it can be said that such prophecies *culminate* in this age.

Other examples of the progressive nature of prophetic fulfilment are the prophecies concerning King David. As mentioned in Chapter 2, many prophets spoke of the future re-establishment of the rule of King David (for example, Isa. 9:7, Ezek. 37:24–5; see also Hos. 3:5, Amos 9:11, Zech. 12:8). When Jesus appeared He established first His spiritual sovereignty and later, through the Christians, this sovereignty also became evident materially (*Secret of Divine Civilization* 80–5). Thus Jesus was the fulfilment of these prophecies about David – Jesus was the new King on the throne of David. The prophets used 'David' as a symbol of the King to come because he was the greatest of the Hebrew kings, yet no one in the days of David witnessed a kingdom as great as the Kingdom established by Christ. For this reason, the fulfilment is much greater in reality than is signified by the symbol. This was anticipated in the prophecies themselves (see Ps. 110:1, Matt. 22:41–6).

Before the appearance of Islam, Christianity had established a great Kingdom, but this Kingdom slipped into a dark age after the time of Muhammad. Then Islam raised up a new Kingdom, once again fulfilling the messianic prophecies, but to an even greater extent than Christianity – so much so that the Islamic nation caused a renaissance in Europe.[15] The same will again prove true with regard to Bahá'u'lláh, for His Kingdom will embrace the entire world. Even though Bahá'u'lláh sits on the throne of David in fulfilment of prophecy, it will be a greater Kingdom than David's; in fact, no past kingdom can compare with the glories of the civilization that will be raised up in the Bahá'í era. For more about the archetypal and progressive fulfilment of prophecy, see Chapter 18.

THE LITERAL FULFILMENT OF PROPHECY
It is not possible to exhaust the meaning of Scripture. Bahá'u'lláh gives the keys in *The Book of Certitude* for understanding the

---

15. See Shoghi Effendi, quoted in Hornby, ed., *Lights of Guidance*, no. 1664, p. 495.

Scriptures, but this is not to say that the full import of Scripture can ever be wholly comprehended (*Certitude* 204). Even a literal fulfilment is not limited to only one age. Examples of the literal fulfilment of prophecies do not preclude the possibility that the same prophecies have deeper spiritual significance, or that the same prophecy may be fulfilled literally and symbolically by more than one Manifestation of God in different ages.

To illustrate that many prophecies are fulfilled literally, and how literal fulfilment varies in degree, the following five prophecies have been selected. It is worth keeping in mind that the term *literal* can have varying degrees of applicability. A prophecy may refer to future wars, for example, and war may then occur, but not in exactly the manner described.

1. The King of Zion (Jerusalem) Riding upon a Donkey
2. The Two Witnesses
3. The Twelve Princes
4. The Strong City
5. The Thief in the Night

1. The King of Zion (Jerusalem) Riding upon a Donkey: The Old Testament prophet Zechariah prophesied that the 'King' of the Jews would come 'having salvation' and being 'lowly . . . riding on a donkey' (Zech. 9:9). In the Gospel according to Matthew, Jesus asked the Apostles to bring Him a donkey from nearby, and He then rode upon it into Jerusalem 'that it might be fulfilled which was spoken by the prophet [Zechariah]' (Matt. 21:1–6). In this instance, it can be said that the prophecy was literally fulfilled. However, in a strict sense, it could be argued that Jesus was not really a king, that is, He had no army or kingdom in this world, literally speaking. So, since He was a king in the true spiritual sense of His sovereignty and Lordship, and because the riding of the donkey was a literal event, the prophecy was fulfilled partly in a spiritual and partly in a literal sense.

2. *The Two Witnesses*: The Book of Revelation speaks of two Witnesses who will prophesy 1260 days (Rev. 11:3). According to 'Abdu'l-Bahá, these two Witnesses are Muhammad and His righthand companion and true successor, 'Alí. In this instance, the 'two witnesses' refer literally to two persons or Messengers, Who did witness (that is, testify) in the literal sense to the truth of God. Nevertheless, the 1260 days signifies, according to the symbolic terminology of Scripture, 1260 years (Num. 14:34, Ezek 4:6). The era of the prophecy of these two Witnesses was literally 1260 years (that is, from AD 622 to AD 1844, according to the lunar calendar of Islam), but this understanding necessitates the awareness that 1260 days means 1260 years. In this instance, real persons, events and times are conveyed in literal *and* symbolic language.

3. *The Twelve Princes*: In the Book of Genesis, God tells Abraham with regard to Abraham's son Ishmael that He has blessed him and 'will make him fruitful, and will multiply him exceedingly. He shall beget twelve princes, and I will make him a great nation' (Gen. 17:20). The people of Arabia trace their ancestry to Ishmael, and with the rise of Islam, this prophecy was fulfilled through the appearance of the Twelve Imáms (the spiritual leaders and successors of Muḥammad), and the great nation was the nation of Islám. This prophecy was first fulfilled in Genesis 25:16 (the twelve sons of Ishmael) and could also be applied in a more symbolic sense to the twelve apostles of Jesus. In either case, this prophecy was fulfilled.

4. *The Strong City*: In the Book of Psalms, King David sang this verse, which can be understood prophetically: 'Who will bring me into the Strong City' (Psalm 60:9). In a symbolic sense, 'me' (meaning King David) signifies Bahá'u'lláh as the ideal Davidic King and Ruler. In a literal sense it can be observed that the Strong City is 'Akká, the prison city where Bahá'u'lláh was confined (*Epistle* 144, *God Passes By* 184). It was well known as a

fortress with strong walls. Like Zechariah's prophecy concerning the King of Zion riding the donkey, this prophecy has a spiritual message as well as details that can be understood literally. It could be applied to Jesus and Jerusalem in the same way.

5. *The Thief in the Night:* In the second epistle of Peter, it is stated that the 'day of the Lord will come as a thief in the night' (2 Pet. 3:10). The description 'as a thief in the night' is a simile, used to convey symbolically how this coming will seem, that is, unexpected, when people do not anticipate it, like a thief entering a house while people are sleeping. Although the language is symbolic, the *message* is literal. The day of the Lord came in fulfilment of prophecy in a way that was unexpected. People expected prophecies to occur literally, and when the most dramatic ones did not occur in that manner, they failed to realize that there had been any fulfilment at all. The second part of the prophecy states that then 'the heavens will pass away with a great noise, and the elements will melt with fervent heat; both the earth and the works that are in it will be burned up' (2 Pet. 3:10; see *God Passes By* 96). This passage is symbolic, for the literal heaven (the sky above) did not pass away, nor was the earth burned up. Yet, since the coming of the Day of the Lord as a thief in the night, the 'heavens' have passed away with a great noise – meaning the world's religions, their laws and influence. People have discarded the religious laws and have been abandoning the religions, and all of this has taken place with a great noise, so to speak. Similarly, the earth – people's understanding, and the whole way of life on the planet – has been transformed and changed.

OLD TESTAMENT PROPHECY IN THE GOSPEL
It is useful to examine the overall use of Old Testament prophecies in the New Testament. By so doing, it is possible to see what kinds of Old Testament passages were considered prophetic, how they were interpreted, and whether the New

The Fulfilment of Prophecy

Testament offers any different or more persuasive prophetic evidence than that cited in Bahá'í Scripture.

In the Gospels, very few Old Testament prophecies are quoted directly. The Gospel according to Matthew refers eleven times to Old Testament prophecy to prove that Jesus was the One foretold by the prophets. These quotations are commonly called 'proof-text' and scholars believe that this version of the Gospel was written especially to persuade Jews. In most cases Matthew introduces these texts by saying this was done so 'that it might be fulfilled which was spoken by the prophets', or some similar phrase. Matthew also quotes Old Testament prophecy to prove other things, such as the ministry of John the Baptist (Matt. 3:3, cf. Isa. 40:3; Matt. 17:11, cf. Mal. 4:5; see also Matt. 21:13, cf. Jer. 7:11; Matt. 21:16, cf. Ps. 8:2; Matt. 26:31, cf. Zech. 13:7), but with regard to Jesus, there are only eleven instances that relate specifically to His life and ministry:

1. Jesus' name will be 'Immanuel', (Matt. 1:22–3, cf. Isa. 7:14);

2. a 'ruler' – meaning Jesus – will come from 'Bethlehem' (Matt. 2:6, cf. Mic. 5:2);

3. 'Out of Egypt I called My Son', is cited in connection with the story that Jesus' parents went to Egypt to save Him from Herod's attempt to massacre all the male children (Matt. 2:15, cf. Hos. 11:1);

4. the massacre of the innocents (Matt. 2:18, Jer. 31:15);

5. a prophecy saying that beyond the Jordan, the people who sat in darkness saw a great light, meaning Jesus (Matt. 4:15–16, cf. Isa. 9:1, 2);

6. 'He Himself took our infirmities/And bore our sicknesses', is cited in connection with Jesus' healing the sick and possessed (Matt. 8:17, cf. Isa. 53:4);

7. a passage from Isaiah cited as prophetic praise of Jesus, His character and ministry to the Gentiles (Matt. 12:18–21, cf. Isa. 42:1–4);

8. He will speak in parables (Matt. 13:35, cf. Ps. 78:2);

9. the Messiah will enter Jerusalem on a donkey (Matt. 21:4–5, cf. Zech. 9:9);

10. a broad statement that 'all this was done that the Scripture of the prophets might be fulfilled' (Matt. 26:56); and

11. a reference to the money awarded to Judas for betraying Christ and what the money was used for (Matt. 27:9–10; cf. Zech 11:12–13/Jer. 32:6–9).

It is Matthew, not Jesus, who quotes the Scriptures to point out when fulfilment has occurred. Jesus is presented as initiating the literal fulfilment of Zechariah 9:9 (Matt. 21:4–5), and only Matthew 26:56 quotes the words of Jesus; but here, it is simply the context that suggests that all that has happened was prophesied. Matthew 27:9–10 is not a direct quotation and consequently it is a passage that has perplexed many readers because Matthew seems to combine two prophecies, emphasizing the greater prophet (Jeremiah), though his words form the smaller part of the prophecy.

Another reference that is worth noting is from the Gospel of Mark referring to Jesus' death among thieves (Mark 15:28, cf. Isa. 53:12). The Gospel according to Luke also contains an affirmation from the risen Jesus that 'these are the words which I spoke to you while I was still with you, that all things must be fulfilled which were written in the Law of Moses and the Prophets and the Psalms concerning Me' (Luke 24:44) – but no direct quotations are given showing which prophecies these might be. Perhaps Luke's most important reference to Old Testament prophecy is to Isaiah 61:1, 2, concerning the 'anointed' (that is, the Messiah) preaching the Gospel (Luke 4:17–19).

In the Gospel according to John, the prophecy concerning the ruler coming on a donkey is corroborated (John 12:14, cf. Zech. 9:9; cf. Matt. 21:4–5). John also refers to several prophecies in relation to the people's disbelief (John 12:38, cf. Isa. 53:1; John 12:39–40, cf. Isa. 6:10); and tells of Jesus quoting certain prophecies, one of which concerns Judas' betrayal of Him (John 13:18; Ps. 41:9) and the other the world hating Him without good reason (John 15:25, cf. Ps. 69:4). In another case, Jesus refers to prophecy without quoting one (John 17:12). John refers to the Roman soldiers dividing Jesus' garments among themselves to fulfil prophecy (John 19:24, cf. Ps. 22:18) and concludes with the broader statement that 'all things were now accomplished, that the Scripture might be fulfilled' (John 19:28). John also sees the fulfilment of prophecy in the fact that the soldiers did not break the bones of Jesus' legs – as was sometimes done with crucifixion victims (John 19:36, cf. Exod. 12:46, Num. 9:12, Ps. 34:20). Finally, John cites Zechariah (12:10): 'They shall look on Him whom they pierced' as a fulfilled prophecy (John 19:37).

A close examination of these passages shows that some of the prophecies were fulfilled literally, many others contain features that were not fulfilled in a strictly literal way, and some are of a very general and circumstantial nature. Moreover, Jesus rarely referred to prophecy, and when He did, He was usually not specific. The most important aspect of Jesus' fulfilment of messianic prophecy was established simply by the fact of His spiritual sovereignty – a fact of Lordship that meant He has fulfilled all the prophecies concerning the promised Messiah, the Davidic Ruler and King. Perhaps one of the most important references in this connection is Jesus' reading of Isaiah 61:1, 2 in the synagogue (Luke 4:17–19). There was no need to provide more Old Testament quotations, since people either recognized or did not recognize the station of Christ. Of the verses cited above, most offer some scriptural and prophetic evidence relating to isolated instances in Jesus' ministry, and very few refer to the station of

Jesus. This is established by way of knowing Who He is, not by reference to prophecy. Once it is known that He is Lord, then it is clear that He is Christ and all the messianic prophecies are fulfilled in Him.

Similarly, it may be asked, is it not clear from the very fact of Bahá'u'lláh's sovereignty and divinity that He is the fulfilment of the prophecies concerning the 'glory of the Lord' – those prophecies that refer to the presence of God among humankind? There are many prophecies cited in Bahá'í Scripture that could be interpreted as having an outward literal meaning, such as the Glory of the Lord coming to the promised land, setting up His Tabernacle on the Mountain of God, Mount Carmel seeing the glory of the Lord, His new name, the Law going forth from the Mountain, His imprisonment in 'Akká, and so on. But the literal sense of these prophecies can never equal the spiritual sense that gives real life to the same verses. As with Christ, it is the recognition of Who He is that seals the prophecies.

The spiritual fulfilment of prophecy will be considered further in the next chapter.

Chapter 7

RESPONDING TO CHRISTIAN OBJECTIONS

One way to demonstrate the spiritual significance of the prophecies concerning Bahá'u'lláh is to make comparisons with prophecies about the appearance of Jesus. There are Bahá'í Scriptures stating that Christ and Bahá'u'lláh fulfilled prophecies in both a spiritual and a literal manner. The real difficulty lies not in finding prophecies that appear to have been fulfilled literally, but rather with Christians asserting that highly symbolic prophecies must be fulfilled in a manner consistent with their literal interpretations and expectations. This chapter looks at some major *symbolic* prophecies fulfilled by Christ.

REASONS SOME CHRISTIANS BELIEVE PROPHECY MUST BE FULFILLED LITERALLY

Christians who are inclined to interpret prophecy literally will challenge the Bahá'í approach. They will want to know if Christ fulfilled prophecies two thousand years ago in a literal way, what basis there is for Bahá'ís to claim that prophecies about Christ's return are intended to have spiritual and symbolic meanings.

This objection is based on the assumption that Jesus fulfilled literally the prophecies referring to Him. But if Christ fulfilled the prophecies of the Old Testament literally, why did most of the Jewish leaders at that time reject Him? Did they interpret prophecy literally or symbolically? Did those who opposed Christ use the correct method of interpreting the prophecies concerning the appearance of the Messiah? How can anyone be sure that they are using a correct method?

Christians who maintain that Jesus fulfilled prophecy literally usually assert that the Old Testament prophecies which were *not* fulfilled literally would be so fulfilled with Christ's second appearance. They argue that the Jews who failed to recognize Jesus did so not because they failed to perceive the spiritual significance of Old Testament prophecy, but because they expected Him to fulfil the wrong prophecies – prophecies that actually referred to Jesus' second appearance. This line of argument can be classified as the 'Smitten Shepherd' and 'Second Coming' arguments.

The 'Smitten Shepherd' and 'Second Coming' Arguments
The Jewish leaders expected a king who would liberate them from Roman domination. According to Christians, these expectations were based on the mistaken idea that the prophecies saying the Messiah would be a ruler were to be fulfilled with the first appearance of Christ. Christians assert that the Jews failed to realize that Jesus' first appearance was to be as the 'smitten Shepherd' described in the Book of Zechariah:

> 'Awake, O sword, against My Shepherd,
> Against the Man who is My Companion',
> Says the Lord of hosts.
> 'Strike the Shepherd,
> And the sheep will be scattered'. (Zech. 13:7)

To support this argument, Christians correctly point out three things:

1. Jesus affirmed that this prophecy referred to Him (Matt. 26:31);

2. the prophecy referred to Him as a shepherd, and Jesus likened Himself to a Shepherd (cf. John 10); and

3. Jesus suffered as the prophecy states.

Some Christians argue that Jesus was not a ruler at the time of His first appearance. Hence, they maintain, only when Christ returns for a second time will He come in glory as ruler of all.

Based on these assumptions, Christians reject the Bahá'í view that the Jewish leaders failed to understand both the spiritual message of the Scriptures and the spiritual significance of Jesus, and therefore could not see how Jesus had fulfilled prophecies of the Old Testament.

However, even though Christ referred to Zechariah 13:7, the Gospel according to Matthew states that when Jesus rode into Jerusalem, He fulfilled another prophecy from the same book, as mentioned above. This prophecy states that:

Your King is coming to you;
He is just and having salvation,
Lowly and riding on a donkey. (Zech. 9:9)

This verse is recorded as being fulfilled in Matthew 21:2–7. It was fulfilled literally except for the part 'Behold, your King is coming to you'. But since this verse refers to Jesus, it follows that the message of Scripture is that He is also a king. Even though there is no reason to doubt that the verses concerning the 'smitten Shepherd' refer to Jesus, it must be accepted that Zechariah also indicates that although 'lowly' (Zech. 9:9), He nevertheless is King. This Kingship can be appreciated from the point of view of Jesus' Lordship, His eternal sovereignty and spiritual power.

The Christian argument asserts that prophecies not fulfilled literally in the first advent of Christ were intended for His second advent. But there is no clear distinction in the Bible between prophecies referring to the first appearance of the Messiah and those referring to the second. Such distinctions have been determined by Christians after the seeming fact of unfulfilment – that is, in the absence of literal fulfilment. The distinctions rest on the assumption that if a prophecy was not fulfilled in a literal way, it must be fulfilled literally in a future age. To respond to this argument, it is necessary to explain how Jesus fulfilled prophecy in a spiritual way and to support this view with Biblical evidence.

'ABDU'L-BAHÁ'S EXPLANATIONS CONCERNING CHRIST'S FULFILMENT OF PROPHECIES

There is evidence in the Bible to support the belief that many prophecies should be interpreted symbolically. On several occasions, 'Abdu'l-Bahá discussed the ways in which Jesus fulfilled prophecy, and these discussions – which can be found in *Paris Talks* (54–7) and *Selections from the Writings of 'Abdu'l-Bahá* (44–6) – are the basis of the following arguments.

According to 'Abdu'l-Bahá, the Jewish leaders did not believe Jesus was the promised Messiah because He did not fulfil prophecies in the literal manner they expected. 'Abdu'l-Bahá argues that Jesus did fulfil the prophecies of the Old Testament, but in a spiritual manner. In this way 'Abdu'l-Bahá seeks to demonstrate the error of insisting upon literal fulfilment of prophecies. There are three essential steps in this argument:

1. Jewish expectations concerning the Messiah at the time of Jesus
2. The Jews' literal interpretations of Old Testament prophecies
3. Jesus' spiritual fulfilment of these same prophecies

Jewish Expectations about the Messiah, as Recorded in the New Testament

In the New Testament, it is recorded that the Jews believed the Messiah would be a ruler.

> When Herod the King heard these things [about the birth of the Messiah], he was troubled, and all Jerusalem with him. And when he had gathered all the chief priests and scribes of the people together, he inquired of them where the Christ was to be born. So

they said to him, 'In Bethlehem of Judea, for thus it is written by the prophet:
"But you, Bethlehem, in the land of Judah,
Are not the least among the rulers of Judah;
For out of you shall come a Ruler
Who will shepherd My people Israel." ' (Matt. 2:3–6)

These verses indicate that the 'chief priests and scribes of the people' believed the Messiah would come as a 'Ruler' to lead the people of Israel. This expectation rested upon the prophecy of Micah in the Old Testament (see Mic. 5:2).

The expectation and belief that the Messiah would be a Ruler had spread among the people, for those who greeted Jesus' entrance to Jerusalem sang from the Book of Psalms (118:26), calling Him 'King of Israel':

The next day a great multitude that had come to the feast, when they heard that Jesus was coming to Jerusalem, took branches of palm trees and went out to meet Him, and cried out:
'Hosanna!
Blessed is He who comes in the name of the Lord!
The King of Israel!' (John 12:12–13)

The exuberant enthusiasm of the people, however, was to change. The priest opposed Jesus and sought to kill Him (Matt. 26, Mark 14, Luke 22, John 12) and the people also rejected Jesus (Matt. 27:25, Mark 15:11–14, Luke 23:18–23, John 19:15). The Romans mockingly referred to Jesus as the 'King of the Jews' (Matt. 27, Mark 15, Luke 23, John 19) and the chief priest shouted 'We have no king but Caesar!' (John 19:15).

Now Pilate wrote a title and put it on the cross. And the writing was:
JESUS OF NAZARETH,
THE KING OF THE JEWS.
Then many of the Jews read this title, for the place

where Jesus was crucified was near the city; and it was written in Hebrew, Greek, and Latin. Then the chief priests of the Jews said to Pilate, 'Do not write, "The King of the Jews", but, "He said, 'I am the King of the Jews.'"' (John 19:19–21)

From these verses it is apparent that many Jews expected the Messiah (which means the Christ) to come as a 'Ruler' (Matt. 2:3–6); that they had hoped Jesus was indeed the expected Ruler or King (John 12:12–13); and that, in the end, they rejected Jesus as the awaited King (John 19).

Jewish Literal Interpretations of the Hebrew Scriptures
Why did the Jews deny that Jesus was the King foretold in Scripture? This question can be answered by examining some of the other prophecies that describe the expected King. According to Old Testament prophecy, the promised Ruler would rule over the people of Israel; He would carry a sword and defeat the enemies of God's chosen people; and He would sit upon the throne of David. Some sources of these prophecies are:

1. He will rule over Israel:
    'But you, Bethlehem Ephrathah,[16]
    Though you are little among the thousands of Judah,
    Yet out of you shall come forth to Me
    The One to be ruler of Israel,
    Whose goings forth have been from of old,
    From everlasting'. (Mic. 5:2)

2. He will carry a sword and defeat the enemies of God's chosen people:
    For by fire and by His sword
    The Lord will judge all flesh;

---

16. 'Ephrathah' is the ancient name of Bethlehem Judah. See Genesis 48:7.

And the slain of the Lord shall be many.
(Isa. 66:16)

3. He will re-establish King David's throne;
   For unto us a Child is born,
   Unto us a Son is given . . .
   Of the increase of His government and peace
   There will be no end,
   Upon the throne of David. (Isa. 9:6–7)

These verses only indicate briefly what is in fact a major theme of many Old Testament Scriptures, such as the Psalms or the Book of Isaiah.

From the Jewish point of view, Jesus could not be the Christ because He did not appear as the expected Ruler. The Romans still ruled over and oppressed the people of Israel, and Jesus had no sword or throne. As 'Abdu'l-Bahá points out, Jesus did not even carry a staff, much less a sword. Nor did He defeat His enemies; instead, He was crucified. 'Abdu'l-Bahá writes:

> In this wise did they object to that Sun of Truth, although that Spirit of God was indeed the One promised in the Torah. But as they did not understand the meaning of these signs, they crucified the Word of God. Now the Bahá'ís hold that the recorded signs did come to pass in the Manifestation of Christ, although not in the sense which the Jews understood, the description in the Torah being allegorical. (*Selections from the Writings of 'Abdu'l-Bahá* 45)

The Biblical verses cited above establish the foundation of the Bahá'í argument. The first and second steps have been demonstrated: some Jews anticipated that the Messiah or Christ would be a sovereign Ruler, a King who would liberate them from Roman domination and return the Jews to the glory of Israel in the days of David; and, in as much as their literal expectations were not fulfilled, the Jews rejected Jesus and persecuted Him and His followers.[17]

Jesus and the Spiritual Fulfilment of Prophecy

Demonstrating from the Bible that Christ fulfilled these prophecies in a spiritual way greatly strengthens the Bahá'í argument. For some Christians such evidence may constitute a compelling reason for searching out the spiritual significance of prophecies about the second advent.

The views held by Christ and those who followed Him during His lifetime (the Apostles) can be cited to illustrate the Bahá'í point of view.

> 1. Jesus claimed to be King/Ruler:
> Pilate therefore said to Him, 'Are You a king then?' Jesus answered, 'You say rightly that I am a king. For this cause I was born, and for this cause I have come into the world, that I should bear witness to the truth. Everyone who is of the truth hears My voice'. (John 18:37; see also Matt. 27:11, Mark 15:2, Luke 23:1–3).

Jesus also points out that King David spoke of the Christ to come as 'my Lord' (see Matt. 22:42–5; Ps. 110:1). This shows that David regarded the future Messiah to be sovereign. The entire Psalm refers to the Messiah as a Ruler, executing kings and judging nations. It is obvious from the context of Matthew 22:41–5 that Jesus thought David was referring to Him. This, of course, does not mean that Jesus thought that this Kingship was to be understood literally.

---

17. It is recognized by Christians that the primary method of interpretation used by Jews at the time of Christ was the literal method. The conservative Christian scholar of prophecy J. Dwight Pentecost, for example, writes, 'The prevailing method of interpretation among the Jews at the time of Christ was certainly the literal method of interpretation' (*Things to Come: A Study in Biblical Eschatology* 17).

2. Jesus said He brought a sword: 'Do not think that I came to bring peace on earth. I did not come to bring peace but a sword.' (Matt. 10:34)

3. The Apostle Peter regarded Jesus as Lord: 'Jesus Christ – He is Lord of all.' (Acts 10:36)

4. The angel Gabriel is said to have announced to Mary that Jesus would be given the throne of King David: 'He will be great, and will be called the Son of the Highest: and the Lord God will give Him the throne of His father David.' (Luke 1:32)

These Biblical verses suggest that both Jesus and the Apostles believed that Jesus was indeed a sovereign Lord/Ruler/King. But the Lordship of Jesus that they recognized was spiritual and was not concerned with material rulership. 'Abdu'l-Bahá explains:

> His Word was indeed a sharp sword! The Throne upon which He sat is the Eternal Throne from which Christ reigns for ever, a heavenly throne, not an earthly one, for the things of earth pass away but heavenly things pass not away . . . Thus, all the spiritual prophecies concerning the coming of Christ were fulfilled, but the Jews shut their eyes that they should not see, and their ears that they should not hear, and the Divine Reality of Christ passed through their midst unheard, unloved and unrecognized. (*Paris Talks* 56)

There is Biblical evidence, therefore, suggesting that Jewish expectations were based on literal interpretations of Old Testament prophecies and that this literalism contributed to their failure to recognize the true Lordship of Jesus Christ. This evidence points both to the importance of understanding and appreciating the spiritual significance of prophecies and to the need to avoid insistence upon literal fulfilment.

BIBLICAL REFERENCES FOR CHAPTER 7

For future reference it is a good idea to make an outline of this section in a notebook or in your Bible. In Chapter 4 ('Common Criteria') and Part 3 ('Proofs') of Volume 1 in this series, a green marker was used to highlight the appropriate Biblical verses. To create a separate category for prophecies, a blue marker is recommended.

The following passages relevant to the spiritual significance of prophecies about Jesus could be highlighted.

1. The Jews expected a Ruler:
    Matt. 2:3–6
    John 12:12–13
    John 19:19–21
2. Old Testament prophecies describing the Messiah as Ruler:
    Mic. 5:2 (Ruler)
    Isa. 66:16 (Sword)
    Isa. 9:6–7 (Throne)
3. Jesus indicates He is a Ruler or King:
    John 18:37
    Matt. 27:11
    Matt. 22:42–5/Psalm 110:1
    Mark 15:2
    Luke 23:1–3
    Acts 10:36 (Peter indicates Jesus is Lord of all)
    Luke 1:32 (Throne)
    Matt. 10:34 (Sword)

It may also be useful to outline the following:
    Eph. 6:17, 2 Cor. 10:3–5 (Symbolism of sword)
    Acts 7:49 (Symbolism of throne)

Concerning the 'Smitten Shepherd argument', note verses:
    Zech. 9:9
    Zech. 13:7
    Matt. 21:2–7

part three

THE RETURN OF CHRIST
AND
THE 'DAY OF GOD'

chapter 8

BASIC THEMES IN NEW TESTAMENT PROPHECY

THE PRESENCE OF GOD

The most important theme in New Testament prophecy, as in the Old Testament, is the presence of God, and this theme is central to those prophecies that concern the return of Christ. Christ's return is often referred to as 'the second coming', a phrase that originates from a question the disciples asked Jesus: 'What will be the sign of Your *coming*?' (Matt. 24:3). The word 'coming' is the translation of the Greek word 'parousia', which means 'presence'.[18] During the time when most educated people read Latin, this word was translated into the Latin using the word 'adventus'. Hence, some Christians also refer to the return of Christ as the 'second coming', the '*parousia*', and/or 'second advent'. The disciples, therefore, did not actually ask about the 'coming' of Christ, but rather about the future 'presence' of Christ. The two words can mean essentially the same thing and

---

18. This fact is well known to Christian scholars. Marvin R. Vincent, for example, writes that the word 'coming' was 'originally, *presence*, from παρειναι, to be present' (*Vincent's Word Studies of the New Testament*, vol. 1, 127). The Christian scholar and specialist in prophetic studies John F. Walvoord writes, 'The word most frequently used in the Scriptures to describe the return of Christ is [parousia] . . . It involves all that the English word *presence* connotes' (see 'New Testament Words for the Lord's Coming', *Bibliotheca Sacra*, 101:284–89, July, 1944). The popular Christian dictionary, *Vine's Expository Dictionary of Biblical Words*, states 'parousia literally means "a presence", *para*, "with", and *ousia*, "being" (from *eimi*, "to be"), denotes both an arrival and a consequent "presence with" . . . Parousia is used to describe the presence of Christ with His disciples on the Mount of Transfiguration, 2 Peter 1:16. When used of the return of Christ, at the rapture of the church, it signifies, not merely His momentary "coming" for His saints, but His presence with them from that moment until His revelation and manifestation to the world' (see entry for 'Coming', 111).

there is no need to stress this point unduly, because the future presence of Christ refers to His coming or future advent, but a better understanding does suggest that the symbolism of Jesus' prophecies was concerned with the presence of God, since these prophecies were in response to questions about His future *presence*. This also suggests that the symbolism used by Jesus in response to this question may be better understood when viewed in the light of other Biblical symbolism about the presence of God, such as that discussed in Chapter 2.

In this section of the book the emphasis now shifts to New Testament texts. In Part One, the *theological message* and *symbolic method* of prophecy was explained in relation to the Old Testament, and these points are equally relevant to the New Testament. The most effective key to understanding the prophecies explained in the next five chapters is Bahá'u'lláh's teaching concerning the 'presence of God' (*Certitude* 138–46) and another teaching that has been called the 'two poles' of predictive prophecy (see page 24 and *Certitude* 118). Once it is understood that the disciples of Christ were asking about the signs that will indicate the future presence (*parousia*) of Christ (Who signifies God's presence), then each of the signs can be understood as it relates to this theme. The appearance of this divine presence is the central theme, and a secondary theme is the condition of those who turn away from it and those who turn towards it (the two poles of predictive prophecy).

In the next five chapters symbolism will be classified as:

1. The Tribulation
2. The Rapture
3. The Return of Christ
4. The Battle of Armageddon
5. The Millennial Kingdom

The symbolism concerning the historic return of Christ is central and relates to the presence of God. The symbolism of the tribulation and the battle of Armageddon describes life (individually and collectively) without this divine presence, and the symbolism of the rapture and the Millennial Kingdom concerns the life of those who attain the presence of God. The return of Christ is the central spiritual event, and the other four topics divide equally according to the two predictive poles of prophecy.

OLD TESTAMENT SYMBOLS IN THE NEW TESTAMENT
In Chapter 2, we examined the following topics in Old Testament symbolism:

1. The first seven days of Genesis
2. The original garden of Eden (or garden of God)
3. The Tabernacle (and the Temple)
4. The promised land
5. The reign of King David

All five forms of symbolism reappear in the New Testament, and each relates in some way to the five forms of New Testament symbolism selected for study in the next five chapters, where the relationships and parallels will become clearer. An introductory overview may be useful before taking a closer look.

The Old Testament symbolism involving the 'Day' of God takes a variety of forms in the New Testament. It is the Day of Christ's future appearance, a New Testament version of prophecies concerning the 'anointed' One, or Messiah; it is also a Day of wrath *and* a Day of blessing. The Old Testament Day of Wrath becomes, in the New Testament, the 'tribulation' and the 'Battle of Armageddon'.

The symbolism of the Davidic Kingdom is also combined with the symbolism of the garden, as found in Genesis, to communicate the ideal nature of the coming new world order (Rev. 21–2). The anthropomorphic[19] symbolism of God's

---

19. The term 'anthropomorphic' means that God is depicted as taking on human form. This simply expresses close communion with God.

actual presence on earth in this ideal new order is also used in New Testament prophecy (Rev. 21:3). The Old Testament symbolism of the reign of King David is transformed in New Testament prophecy into the coming reign of Christ (or God) on earth. In the Old Testament, messianic prophecy often used the symbolism of David and the 'anointed' (Christ) King. In the New Testament, the 'anointed' is simply understood to be Jesus Christ.

Old Testament promises about the restitution of the Jews are comparable to New Testament prophecies concerning the *rapture* (the gathering together of the believers), and the return to the promised land is comparable to New Jerusalem prophecies of the Kingdom of God on earth.[20] The Old Testament symbolism of the Tabernacle, the Temple and the Holy City of Jerusalem is also incorporated into New Testament symbolism involving the establishment of the Millennial Kingdom of God, and the 'New' Jerusalem.

Beliefs and interpretations arising from the doctrine of the second coming are, for Christians, probably among the most controversial doctrinal issues. Their varying beliefs reflect the difficult and often speculative nature of the interpretation of prophecy. Because there are so many conflicting opinions, it is not possible to give an adequate overview of the diversity of thought among Christians. Some understand prophecies from a very literal point of view, others symbolically, and perhaps most combine these two approaches. Moreover, there are those who argue that certain prophecies have a literal fulfilment in events already past, while others hold that such prophecies will be fulfilled literally in the future, and so on.

Discussing these issues with Christians can be difficult because many deny that the Biblical passages involved can be understood as symbolizing great spiritual truths and events.

---

20. This symbolism does not, however, preclude the literal fulfilment of Old Testament prophecies concerning the Jews returning to the land of Palestine in this age.

Nevertheless, emphasizing the many areas of agreement, discussed in Volume 1 of this series and in the previous chapters of this volume, can help create a foundation of fellowship, making it easier to discuss and explain the Bahá'í point of view regarding the interpretation and meaning of prophecy.

Because of the difficulties caused by the many differences of opinion among Christians and the sheer number of prophetic verses, the following chapters examine only some aspects of five main forms of prophetic symbolism involving the second coming of Christ. The topics covered are those most essential for understanding the issues and discussing them with Christians, whatever their personal views may be.

chapter 9

THE TRIBULATION

CHRISTIAN BELIEFS ABOUT THE TRIBULATION
The term 'tribulation' is derived from Jesus' prophecy about 'the tribulation of those days' (Matt. 24:21, 29). To Christians, it generally signifies a time of terrible physical destruction and suffering. The events expected to characterize the tribulation are viewed as signs that will precede the return of Christ. Some Christians believe the tribulation occurred in the early history of the Church, when Christians were persecuted. Others believe we are now living in the tribulation period, and still others believe the tribulation is in the future and will be worse than any suffering that has so far occurred.

When Jesus spoke of a tribulation that would come, He also stated:

> Now learn this parable from the fig tree: When its branch has already become tender and puts forth leaves you know that summer is near. So you also, when you see all these things, know that it is near, at the very doors. (Matt. 24:32)

Because of this teaching, Christians often interpret tragic world events as signs that Christ will return soon. In Matthew 24, Christ describes conditions Christians commonly believe are part of, or a prelude to, the tribulation. Jesus states, 'you will hear of wars and rumours of wars' (Matt. 24:6). There will be 'famines, pestilences, and earthquakes in various places' (Matt. 24:7) and the believers will suffer, 'they will deliver you up to tribulation and kill you, and you will be hated by all nations for My name's sake' (Matt. 24:9). Many Christians interpret all these signs in a literal way.

In addition to these, there is another sign, which Jesus seems to emphasize more than the others, and this deals with the guidance of the soul and heart of the believer, and concerns the threat of false prophets and deceptions.[21] It is with this sign that Christ begins His discourse:

> Take heed that no one deceives you. For many will come in My name, saying 'I am the Christ', and will deceive many. (Matt. 24:4–5)

Only a few verses later Christ again states:

> Then many false prophets will rise up and deceive many. (Matt. 24:11)

And again in the same discourse Christ reiterates the warning:

> Then if anyone say to you, 'Look, here is the Christ!' or 'There!' do not believe it. For false christs and false prophets will arise and show great signs and wonders, so as to deceive, if possible, even the elect. (Matt. 24:23–4)

This theme is also emphasized in the writings of the Apostle Paul, who speaks of a great apostasy when 'in latter times some will depart from the faith, giving heed to deceiving spirits and doctrines of demons, speaking lies in hypocrisy' (1 Tim. 4:1–2). This particular theme of deception, given such emphasis in the New Testament, is also a theme Bahá'u'lláh stresses when He explains the meaning of the tribulation.

---

21. Biblical criteria for separating true from false prophets are explained in Volume 1 of the *Preparing for a Bahá'í/Christian Dialogue* series (Chapter 4: 'Common Criteria').

BAHÁ'Í TEACHINGS CONCERNING THE TRIBULATION

In *The Book of Certitude*, Bahá'u'lláh elaborates on the meaning of Jesus' prophecies in Chapter 24 of the Gospel of Matthew. The term 'tribulation' is rendered 'oppression', according to the literal meaning of the original Greek. Therefore, in *The Book of Certitude*, the verse reads 'Immediately after the oppression of those days' (*Certitude* 24–7, 29–33). Bahá'u'lláh explains that the oppression, or tribulation, is symbolic of a spiritual crisis, that is, a crisis characterized by people's search for spiritual truth and their inability to find sure guidance. This, Bahá'u'lláh explains, is primarily a result of the religious leaders of humankind having become corrupt and self-seeking, as well as simply ignorant of the true meaning of Scripture.

The appearance of false christs, false prophets, and what St Paul terms 'deceiving spirits and doctrines of demons' (1 Tim. 4:1) suggests that the end time, the tribulation, will be a time of great spiritual confusion and destruction. It is this confusion that Bahá'u'lláh indicates is the primary meaning of the tribulation. The false prophets, the corrupt religious leaders, the wars and disputes can all be viewed as aspects of one long and pervasive spiritual crisis. The loss of souls to ignorance and deception is a greater calamity than the loss of bodies to physical destruction. Bahá'u'lláh explains:

> As to the words – 'Immediately after the oppression of those days' – they refer to the time when men shall become oppressed and afflicted, the time when the lingering traces of the Sun of Truth and the fruit of the Tree of knowledge and wisdom will have vanished from the midst of men, when the reins of mankind will have fallen into the grasp of the foolish and ignorant, when the portals of divine unity and understanding – the essential and highest purpose in creation – will have been closed, when certain knowledge will have given way to idle fancy, and corruption will have usurped the station of righteousness. Such a condition

as this is witnessed in this day when the reins of every community have fallen into the grasp of foolish leaders, who lead after their own whims and desire. On their tongue the mention of God hath become an empty name; in their midst His holy Word a dead letter. (*Certitude* 29)

This message is supported by St Paul, who said, 'in the last days perilous times will come' (2 Tim. 3:1). Paul describes how immorality will abound and people will be 'always learning and never able to come to the knowledge of the truth' (that is, they learn information but are unable to discern between right and wrong; 2 Tim. 3:7). These words suggest that the tribulation is a time when humankind does not know where to turn to 'acquire spiritual knowledge and apprehend the Word of God' (*Certitude* 32). Many people think 'faith' means giving up thinking and questioning, but it is faith in the new Manifestation of God that enables the believer to have the most important knowledge of all, the knowledge of what is right and wrong for the age in which he or she lives.

The corrupt religious leaders 'who lead after their own whims and desire' (*Certitude* 29) are largely responsible for the tribulation. Bahá'u'lláh goes on to say, 'such is the sway of their desires, that the lamp of conscience and reason hath been quenched in their hearts' (*Certitude* 29). He describes such leaders as 'voracious beasts' who have 'gathered and preyed upon the carrion of the souls of man' (*Certitude* 31). These words of Bahá'u'lláh suggest that St Paul's prophecy has been fulfilled:

For I know this, that after my departure savage wolves will come in among you, not sparing the flock. (Acts 20:29)

Christ also points out the corruption that will come into the Church:

> Not everyone who says to Me, 'Lord, Lord', shall enter the kingdom of heaven, but he who does the will of My Father in heaven. Many will say to me in that day, 'Lord, Lord, have we not prophesied in Your name, cast out demons in Your name, and done many wonders in Your name?' And then I will declare to them, 'I never knew you; depart from me you who practise lawlessness!' (Matt. 7:21–3)

It is not certain that 'that day' here means the time of the tribulation, but it seems probable, and it is very significant that Christ would reject His own seeming followers, those who call Him 'Lord' and 'cast out demons' in His name. The fact that Christ says they will prophesy in His name suggests that in that day, the false prophets[22] and deceivers will not be only from among those outside the Church, but also those who are inside. These 'savage wolves' that, St Paul warns, will come in among the Church will be one of the causes of the tribulation.

Today the Christian Church has been divided into thousands of competing denominations. Conflicts about the meaning of the Scriptures, disputes over questions of leadership, and divisions over the moral and spiritual issues of our time (even such issues as slavery in the nineteenth century and women's rights in the twentieth), have led many churches to compromise their positions as religious guides and adopt views entirely inconsistent with Jesus' teachings. All of these factors have caused confusion and grief among Christians and a pervasive religious decline. As Shoghi Effendi writes, 'the defenders of the Christian Faith, the preponderating religion of the western world, are realizing, in the first century of the Bahá'í Era, how their influence is being undermined by a flood of conflicting beliefs, practices and tendencies which their own bankruptcy had helped to create' (*World Order* 185).

---

22. In the New Testament, the term 'prophet' is sometimes used to refer to leaders in the Church. See, for example, 1 Cor. 12:28. The different Biblical meanings are explained in Volume 1 of the *Preparing for a Bahá'í/Christian Dialogue* series (96–9).

Bahá'u'lláh rebukes leaders of the Church who have betrayed their offices as severely as Christ criticized the corrupt Pharisees of His day (cf. Matt. 23).

> Though they recognize in their hearts the Law of God to be one and the same, yet from every direction they issue a new command, and in every season proclaim a fresh decree. No two are found to agree on one and the same law, for they seek no God but their own desire, and tread no path but the path of error. In leadership they have recognized the ultimate object of their endeavour, and account pride and haughtiness as the highest attainments of their heart's desire. (*Certitude* 30)

The Church used to be the guiding lamp of society, and laws were often founded upon the ethics of the New Testament. Today the influence of the Church has diminished, and many people have left it to look elsewhere. Bahá'u'lláh writes:

> What 'oppression' is more grievous than that a soul seeking the truth, and wishing to attain unto the knowledge of God, should know not where to go for it and from whom to seek it? For opinions have sorely differed, and the ways unto the attainment of God have multiplied. (*Certitude* 31)

The opposing conditions of tribulation and spiritual well-being relate to the soul's ability to attain to the presence (*parousia*) of God. While some Christians are looking outside the Church for the signs of the tribulation, Bahá'u'lláh's writings suggest they should also look inside the Church.

The other prophecies associated with the tribulation – wars, famines, pestilences and earthquakes – may also be primarily symbolic in significance. However, the possibility of a dual significance, of both a literal and a spiritual meaning, is not improbable. Disputes and the waning of religious influence often bring about wars and famines, and in this sense, the literal and the spiritual are closely related.

A symbolic interpretation of the term 'earthquakes' may be suggested by 'Abdu'l-Bahá's comment that 'the earthquake of doubts' (*Some Answered Questions* 60–1) brings about the shaking down of religious institutions. Another clue may be found in Bahá'u'lláh's statement, 'by the term "earth" is meant the earth of understanding and knowledge' (*Certitude* 48). In this sense, 'earthquakes' occur in our way of thinking, beliefs and ideologies. This passage by Bahá'u'lláh concerns the fulfilment of Jesus' prophecy about earthquakes:

> 'Earthquakes have broken loose, and the tribes have lamented, for fear of God, the Lord of Strength, the All-Compelling'. Say: 'The stunning trumpet-blast hath been loudly raised, and the Day is God's, the One, the Unconstrained.' And they say: 'Hath the Catastrophe come to pass?' Say: 'Yea, by the Lord of Lords!' (*Tablets of Bahá'u'lláh* 117–18, also *Epistle* 132)

This can be interpreted as meaning that all that was secure has been, so to speak, shaken down. The old foundations of society, government and religion are no longer stable.

In the spiritual sense, 'wars' (Matt. 24:6) may refer to the destruction brought about by violent disagreements in the religious and moral life of humankind. Sectarian disputes, doctrinal controversies, religious animosities – all these constitute real wars in human souls.

'Famines' (Matt. 24:7) may indicate being deprived of spiritual food, the bread from heaven, and the loss of true understanding. One verse suggesting such a meaning appears in the Old Testament book of the prophet Amos:

> 'Behold, the days are coming,' says the Lord God,
> 'That I will send a famine on the land,

Not a famine of bread,
Nor a thirst for water,
But of hearing the words of the Lord.' (Amos 8:11)

In this passage famine is given a spiritual meaning, a famine of the hearing of the word of God. Perhaps this is one of the significances of the term 'famine' used by Jesus in Matthew 24. 'Pestilences' (Matt. 24:7), which indicates diseases or plagues, may mean spiritual diseases and illnesses, that is, immorality, and the consequences of error and materialism. Shoghi Effendi spoke, for example, of the 'cancerous growth of racial prejudice' (*Advent of Divine Justice* 23) and also likened materialism to a cancer (*Citadel of Faith* 125). These are, of course, only one interpretation of these terms.

It should also be noted that Bahá'u'lláh's explanation of the tribulation discusses not only this day but also the appearance of Muḥammad. Bahá'u'lláh begins His discourse on Chapter 24 of Matthew by stating that it is the 'literal interpretation of the words of Jesus' that has caused the Christians to deprive themselves 'of the streaming grace of the Muḥammadan Revelation and its showering bounties' (*Certitude* 26).[23] However, this tribulation or oppression is, according to Bahá'u'lláh, 'the essential feature of every Revelation' (*Certitude* 31). Bahá'u'lláh writes:

> Unless it cometh to pass, the Sun of Truth will not be made manifest. For the break of the morn of divine guidance must needs follow the darkness of the night of error. For this reason, in all chronicles and traditions reference hath been made unto these things, namely that iniquity shall cover the surface of the earth and darkness shall envelop mankind. (*Certitude* 31–2)

---

23. This means the tribulation referred to by Jesus was first fulfilled before the appearance of Muḥammad.

Most prophecies are archetypal, that is, they not only refer to specific events, but also describe conditions that recur in the spiritual history of humankind – hence, it is possible and correct to apply them to different eras.

Although Jesus' prophecies concerning the tribulation appear in His last great discourse (Matt. 24), this teaching also appears in the Old Testament (for example, Amos 5:18–20, Zeph. 1:14–16) and in other portions of the New Testament (for example, 2 Pet. 3:12). The Old Testament prophet Joel spoke of the coming 'day of the LORD' with these words,

> Alas for the day!
> For the day of the LORD is at hand;
> It shall come as destruction from the Almighty.
> (Joel 1:15)

And again,

> Let all the inhabitants of the land tremble;
> For the day of the LORD is coming,
> For it is at hand:
> A day of darkness and gloominess,
> A day of clouds and thick darkness. (Joel 2:1–2)

It is likely that Joel spoke with the awareness that the people had turned or would turn away from God, and therefore there was reason for the people to be afraid of the coming day of the Lord. If the people were faithful, nothing could be greater and more blessed than the day when one could attain the presence of the Lord. The prophet Zephaniah also preached a similar message (see Zeph. 1:14–16; cf. *God Passes By* 95).

In these words of Joel there is a message very much like Jesus' prophecy of the tribulation, and it is a theme that dominates the Book of Joel. When St Peter was preaching that Jesus was the one foretold in Scripture, he turned his attention to Joel's message, quoting Joel's words concerning the 'last days'

(Acts 2:16–21). Similarly, St John wrote to the Christians of his day, saying, 'Little children, it *is* the last hour' (1 John 2:18).

This may seem confusing: how could St Peter say, concerning the events of his time, 'this is what was spoken by the prophet Joel' and then go on to quote references which were about the 'last days'? If the day of Christ, the time when St Peter was preaching, was the last day, why did Jesus and the Apostles speak of a future day?[24]

When a Manifestation of God appears, the past age has ended and the new has begun. This is one way of understanding why Christ said, 'I am the . . . Beginning and the End' (Rev. 1:8; *Selections from the Writings of 'Abdu'l-Bahá* 13). In this way, every new age is 'the last days' or, as it is also called, 'the time of the end' (see, Dan. 8:17; 11:35, 40; 12:4, 9; also 'the end of the days', Dan. 12:13). The 'last days' can, therefore, simply be thought of as the last days of one age – and St Peter was, therefore, right in saying that their day was the last day spoken of by Joel, even as Shoghi Effendi also applies the message of Joel to this age (*God Passes By* 95).

In many passages, Shoghi Effendi made a connection between the turmoil of our age and the crisis of the end times, spoken of in prophecy:

> The convulsions of this transitional and most turbulent period in the annals of humanity are the essential prerequisites, and herald the inevitable approach, of that Age of Ages, 'the time of the end', in which the folly and tumult of strife that has, since the dawn of history, blackened the annals of mankind, will have been finally transmuted into the wisdom and the tranquility of an undisturbed, a universal, and lasting peace, in which

---

24. To understand the deeper significance involved in this question see Bahá'u'lláh's explanations of the terms 'last' and 'first' in *The Book of Certitude* (161–3, 179).

the discord and separation of the children of men will have given way to the worldwide reconciliation, and the complete unification of the divers elements that constitute human society. (*Promised Day* 117)

Bahá'u'lláh also spoke of a coming calamity, and Shoghi Effendi indicates that this prophecy can be identified with similar prophecies in past Scriptures concerning the time of the end. Shoghi Effendi writes:

> Pregnant indeed are the years looming ahead of us all. The twin processes of internal disintegration and external chaos are being accelerated every day and are inexorably moving towards a climax. The rumblings that must precede the eruption of those forces that must cause 'the limbs of humanity to quake' [cf. *Gleanings* 119] can already be heard. 'The time of the end', 'the latter years', as foretold in the Scriptures, are at long last upon us. The Pen of Bahá'u'lláh, the voice of 'Abdu'l-Bahá, have time and again, insistently and in terms unmistakable, warned an unheeding humanity of impending disaster. (*Messages to America* 13–14)

From these words of Shoghi Effendi, and Bahá'u'lláh's interpretation of the 'tribulation' prophesied by Jesus (*Certitude* 29–32), it seems likely that there are a number of related prophecies with both an inner and an outer meaning, which have been fulfilled in past ages and are being fulfilled again in this age. The present tribulation will continue as long as the world turns away from the message of Bahá'u'lláh.

For many Christians, the claims of the Bahá'í Faith do not seem to correspond to Biblical teachings about the tribulation, because they believe the tribulation will first end, and then Christ will establish His Kingdom. The idea that these two processes can occur simultaneously – that is, as the old order collapses, a new order is in the process of being built – is unfamiliar to many Christian interpreters. One way of approaching this objection is to explain this twin phase in the context of the battle of Armageddon. This great struggle signifies a time when the forces of good, led by the returned Christ, battle and defeat the forces of darkness. This was foretold, and it can be seen as signifying a time when both processes are at work in the world, before the eventual establishment of the Kingdom of God.

chapter 10

THE RAPTURE

CHRISTIAN BELIEFS ABOUT THE RAPTURE

The 'rapture' is a term commonly used by conservative Christians to signify a physical resurrection of the believers, expected to occur when Christ returns. Another term used with the same meaning is 'translation', from the verse, 'He has delivered us from the power of darkness and *translated* us into the kingdom of the Son of His love' (Col. 1:13, emphasis added). Beliefs about the rapture are derived mainly from the writings of St Paul (especially 1 Cor. 15:50–2; 1 Thess. 4:14–18), but other important and related verses include Matthew 24:36–42; Mark 13:32; Acts 1:7, 11; Philippians 3:20; Titus 2:13; 2 Peter 3:12; Revelation 1:7.

As explained in Volume 2 of *Preparing for a Bahá'í/Christian Dialogue*, many Christians regard the resurrection of Jesus as a literal event, and as such they assert it constitutes proof that Jesus can and will also raise His followers from the dead when He returns. This is believed to be the meaning of St Paul's message in 1 Corinthians, Chapter 15, and 1 Thessalonians 4:16–17. Although St Paul was not a prophet like Moses or even Isaiah,[25] authoritative Bahá'í writings do acknowledge that

---

25. The term 'prophet' used here is synonymous with the phrase 'Manifestation of God'. Both the *dependent* prophets, such as Isaiah, Jeremiah, etc., and the *independent* prophets or supreme Manifestations of God, such as Buddha, Jesus Christ, Muhammad and Bahá'u'lláh, possess all the attributes of God and an equal station in relation to divinity, but their station in this world differs. These points are explained in *The Book of Certitude* (152–4, 176–81); see also Hornby, ed., *Lights of Guidance*, nos. 1683–96,

he spoke of the future hour and advent of the Bahá'í Faith. Shoghi Effendi writes,

> To the hour of His [Bahá'u'lláh's] advent St Paul had alluded as the hour of the 'last trump', the 'trump of God' . . . (*God Passes By* 96)

In the above passage, Shoghi Effendi is referring to the two main passages in the writings of St Paul that Christians emphasize in connection with the rapture (1 Cor. 15: 51–3; and 1 Thess. 4:16–17). The word 'trump' is a translation of a Greek word which means a reverberating sound, like the sound of a trumpet, and so it is sometimes translated as *trumpet*. In Scripture, the term 'trumpet' is said to have accompanied the Revelation of the Law (the Ten Commandments on Sinai; Exod. 20:18) and to symbolize the voice of the Manifestation of God, as, for example, when John says, 'I heard behind me a loud voice, as of a trumpet' (Rev. 1:10). The loud voice is that of Jesus Christ, as is evident in the next verse (Rev. 1:11). The trumpet sound is used to summon John to the presence of God (Rev. 4:1). The sound of the trumpet is also said to accompany the appearance of Christ (Matt. 24:31).

The first of the above references alluded to by Shoghi Effendi is contained in a letter St Paul wrote to the new Christians in the town of Corinth:

> Behold, I tell you a mystery: We shall not all sleep, but we shall all be changed – in a moment, in the twinkling of an eye, at the last trumpet. For the trumpet will

---

pp. 500–3. For more information concerning the distinction between dependent and independent prophets see 'Abdu'l-Bahá, *Some Answered Questions* 164–6. St Paul made statements that can be regarded as prophecies, but these statements do not appear to be independent inspirations. Rather, he made these statements based on his faith in and knowledge of the Scriptures and apostalic teaching.

sound, and the dead will be raised incorruptible, and we shall be changed. For this corruptible must put on incorruption, and this mortal must put on immortality. (1 Cor. 15:51–3)

In this passage, St Paul tells the Corinthians that in the end time (signified by the 'last' trumpet sound) not all will sleep, that is, fail to be aware of the return of Christ. In 'the twinkling of an eye', some will be 'changed'. That is, as suddenly as the act of belief itself, some will attain to immortality, or eternal life.

The second passage appears in St Paul's first letter to the Church at the town of Thessalonica. St Paul writes:

For the Lord Himself will descend from heaven with a shout, with the voice of an archangel, and with the trumpet of God. And the dead in Christ will rise first. Then we who are alive and remain shall be caught up together with them in the clouds to meet the Lord in the air. (1 Thess. 4: 16–17)

When these events occur, some Christians believe the physical bodies of the believers will be transformed into spiritual bodies (1 Cor. 15:44). It is also believed by some that their physical bodies are made spiritual because the effects of Adam's sin are removed from the believers (that is, those effects of Adam's primal sin which, according to the doctrine of original sin, are passed from one generation to the next). The removal of this inherited sin also takes away the effects of sin, most notably physical death itself.

This is also how some Christians understand the prophecy 'there shall be no more death' (Rev. 21:4). According to this literal interpretation, Adam and Eve could have lived in the Garden of Eden forever had they not sinned. When they sinned, death came into the world, and everyone since Adam's time has died a physical death. However, when Christ returns, it is said that He will raise dead Christians from their graves and they with all living true Christians will be 'raptured', taken up into the air to meet Christ as He appears in the clouds. When Christ raises the Christians from the dead He will give them eternal life. All true Christians and Christ will then live together, without ever dying, in the Kingdom that Christ will establish and rule for a thousand years.

St Paul's teachings concerning the rapture, as described in 1 Thessalonians 4, involve what could be regarded as two distinct elements – the resurrection of the dead and the movement of these dead, plus others who were not dead, into the sky or heavens. In the Bible, both types of symbolism already existed before St Paul used them. In the Old Testament Book of Ezekiel, for example, the prophet has a vision of a valley full of dry bones (37:1–14). In this vision, God tells Ezekiel to 'prophesy to these bones' that they will come together and breath will enter into the bodies made of these bones. Ezekiel does as he is commanded, and the bones come to life:

> Then He [God] said to me, 'Son of man, these bones are the whole house [that is, nation] of Israel. They indeed say, "Our bones are dry, our hope is lost, and we ourselves are cut off!" Therefore prophesy and say to them, "Thus says the Lord God: 'Behold, O My people, I will open your graves and cause you to come up from your graves, and bring you into the land of Israel. Then you shall know that I am the Lord, when I have opened your graves, O My people, and brought you up from your graves. I will put My Spirit in you, and you shall live, and I will place you in your own land.'"' (Ezek. 37:11–14)

In this vision the symbolism of the raising of the dead is very graphic. Most Christian commentators recognize that the Book of Ezekiel contains symbolic visions. Nevertheless, some insist that the meaning of this vision is literal.

There are, however, a number of clues suggesting the symbolic and poetic nature of this text. Ezekiel, for example, sees the bones covering the valley, yet God speaks of opening the graves, suggesting that the bones are covered and would not be visible. The symbolism of the text is clear, and trying to force it into a literal framework only obscures the beauty of expression. In the time of Ezekiel (sixth century BC), the people of Israel had been defeated and were captives to a foreign power. They had lost hope and felt cut off from God. God assures Ezekiel that He will once again breathe His Spirit into the nation, and in this way, Israel is given hope.

The description of people being caught up into the air recalls the story of the prophet Elijah, who, according to the Scriptures, was suddenly taken 'up by a whirlwind into heaven' on a 'chariot of fire' with 'horses of fire' (2 Kgs. 2:11). The Book of Ezekiel speaks of the resurrection of the dead, whereas the story of Elijah gives an instance of a person being taken up to heaven. St Paul combines these two forms of symbolism to create a powerful image of the last times. People will rise from their graves and be taken up into the heavens so that they can be in the presence of Christ.

The Book of Revelation also provides a vision of the last days. Here the first earth is said to have passed away and there is both a new heaven and a new earth on which the believers live in the presence of God (Rev. 21:1–3). Christian commentators have tried to explain the sequence of events, devising such complex theories as the 'partial rapture position', the 'post-tribulation rapture theory', the 'mid-tribulation rapture position', and the 'pre-tribulation rapture theory', and so on.[26] If, however, the symbolism of St Paul's teachings is understood in light of other symbolic passages, there is no need to try to work out how such extraordinary sequences of events would take place.

Based on literal interpretation of St Paul's words as described above, some Christians argue that there is no reason

---

26. See, for example, J. Dwight Pentecost's *Things to Come: A Study of Biblical Eschatology* (1958).

to investigate the claims of Bahá'u'lláh. They assert that if Christ had returned, they would have been raised up into the air to meet Him, and since this hasn't happened, He hasn't returned. Interpretation of the Bible is at the heart of all these issues. One can either interpret it literally and reject Bahá'u'lláh, or interpret it spiritually, and recognize the Bible's affirmation of Bahá'u'lláh's appearance.

BAHÁ'Í BELIEFS ABOUT THE RAPTURE

I can find no *direct* interpretation of 1 Thessalonians in authoritative Bahá'í writings. The theme of 1 Thessalonians is, however, a theme related to other verses found in the Bible – the resurrection of the dead in the time of the end, or the 'Day of Resurrection'. This theme is common to both the Bible and the Qur'án, and it is discussed in *The Book of Certitude*, as well as in many other writings of Bahá'u'lláh.

It is, therefore, possible to apply these explanations in the Bahá'í writings to the question of St Paul's prophecy. One way of approaching the issue of the rapture is to consider the possible symbolic meaning behind the terms and phrases used by St Paul, such as 'heaven', 'clouds', 'dead in Christ', 'air' and so forth. Since these terms have already been discussed in the previous volumes of the *Preparing for a Bahá'í/Christian Dialogue*, there is no need to describe them with the same thoroughness here or to reiterate the Biblical evidence supporting the Bahá'í point of view.

Briefly, here is one possible interpretation of 1 Thessalonians 4:16–17: The 'dead in Christ' signifies those 'dead in unbelief' (*Certitude* 114) who became discontented with Christianity and who fell away from the Christian life. The 'dead in Christ will rise first' indicates that many of the first Christians to believe in Bahá'u'lláh will be those who became disenchanted with, and fell away from, Christianity.

Next, St Paul states, 'We who are alive and remain shall be caught up together with them in the clouds to meet the Lord in the air'. This, perhaps, refers to those who are still following Christ and who truly seek to be Christians. These persons are next to recognize the Revelation of Bahá'u'lláh and to be caught up in the clouds. By clouds is meant 'clouds of knowledge' (*Gleanings* 45) or the divine teachings and laws 'that are contrary to the ways and desires of men' (*Certitude* 71). Because these teachings are contrary to the desires of people, they are like clouds, obscuring some people's sight so that because of their own personal desires, they do not see the spiritual truth. The believers are caught up in these clouds (representing the Law of God) while, at the same time, the disbelievers fail to recognize the truth because of their disinclination or opposition to the new laws.

Thus both Christians and non-Christians will eventually be caught up together, or, in other words, come to embrace the Faith of Bahá'u'lláh. This interpretation suggests that the promised rapture has already taken place. The 'dead' and 'living' who have been raised are those following Bahá'u'lláh today – the Bahá'ís. Bahá'u'lláh writes:

> The shout hath been raised and the people have come forth from their graves, and arising, are gazing around them. (*Gleanings* 41)

In another passage, He writes,

> Speed out of your sepulchers. How long will ye sleep? The second blast hath been blown on the trumpet. On whom are ye gazing? This is your Lord, the God of Mercy. (*Gleanings* 44)

The references in the Scriptures to the 'Day of Resurrection' are clearly recognized as symbolic in Bahá'í Scripture. Bahá'u'lláh explains: 'You will readily recognize that the terms sovereignty, wealth, life, death, judgement and resurrection, spoken of by the Scriptures of old, are not what this generation hath conceived and vainly imagined'. (*Certitude* 107)

Explaining the meaning of the resurrection of the dead in relation to the ministry of Muḥammad, Bahá'u'lláh writes:

> By 'trumpet' is meant the trumpet-call of Muḥammad's Revelation, which was sounded in the heart of the universe, and by 'resurrection' is meant His own rise to proclaim the Cause of God. He bade the erring and wayward arise and speed out of the sepulchers of their bodies, arrayed them with the beauteous robe of faith, and quickened them with the breath of a new and wondrous life. (*Certitude* 116–17)

In this verse, the meaning of resurrection is the distinction between the life of belief and the death of disbelief. Those who live only for themselves and the gratification of their bodies are, so to speak, buried in the graves of their bodies. The purpose of religion is to call people forth from such graves, so that they can discover and realize their true potential, a potential transcending the life of the flesh. This message is expressed with great beauty in Jesus' teachings:

> It is the Spirit who gives life; the flesh profits nothing. The words that I speak to you are spirit, and they are life. (John 6:63)

In this verse, Jesus points to the essential correlation between God's words and the life of faith. Those who lived by these words were resurrected from the graves of their own flesh into the life of the spirit. This correlation shows how the *Word of God* and the fulfilment of prophecy are linked intimately. Bahá'u'lláh writes:

> Moreover, thou shouldst not perceive the fulfillment of the Return and the Resurrection save in the Word of thy Lord, the Almighty, the All-knowing. (*Tablets of Bahá'u'lláh* 183–4)

This message can also be found in the writings of the Báb. Referring to the Day of Resurrection in relationship to the Day of Muḥammad, He writes:

> The Day of Resurrection is a day on which the sun riseth and setteth like unto any other day. How oft hath the Day of Resurrection dawned, and the people of the land where it occurred did not learn of the event. Had they heard, they would not have believed, and thus they were not told!
>
> When the Apostle of God [Muḥammad] appeared, He did not announce unto the unbelievers that the Resurrection had come, for they could not bear the news. That Day is indeed an infinitely mighty Day, for in it the Divine Tree [the Manifestation of God] proclaimeth from eternity unto eternity, 'Verily, I am God. No God is there but Me'. Yet those who are veiled believe that He is one like unto them, and they refuse even to call Him a believer, although such a title in the realm of His heavenly Kingdom is conferred everlastingly upon the most insignificant follower of His previous Dispensation. Thus, had the people in the days of the Apostle of God [Muḥammad] regarded Him at least as a believer of their time how would they have debarred Him, for seven years while He was in the mountain, from access to His Holy House [the Ka'bah of Mecca]? Likewise in this Dispensation of the Point of the Bayán [the Báb], if the people had not refused to concede the name believer unto Him, how could they have incarcerated Him on this mountain, without realizing that the quintessence of belief oweth its existence to a word from Him? Their hearts are deprived of the power of true insight, and thus they cannot see, while those endowed with the eyes of the spirit circle like moths round the Light of Truth until they are consumed. It is for this reason that the Day of

> Resurrection is said to be the greatest of all days, yet it is like unto any other day. (*Selections from the Writings of the Báb* 78–9)

In another passage, the Báb again explains the meaning of the Day of Resurrection:

> What is intended by the Day of Resurrection is the Day of the appearance of the Tree of divine Reality [the Manifestation of God], but it is not seen that any one of the followers of Shi'ih Islam hath understood the meaning of the Day of Resurrection; rather have they fancifully imagined a thing which with God hath no reality. In the estimation of God and according to the usage of such as are initiated into divine mysteries, what is meant by the Day of Resurrection is this, that from the time of the appearance of Him Who is the Tree of divine Reality, at whatever period and under whatever name, until the moment of His disappearance, is the Day of Resurrection. (*Selections from the Writings of the Báb* 106–7)

In this passage, the Báb identifies the Day of Resurrection with the exact period of the ministry of each Manifestation of God. During this period, the people of the former religion are rewarded and punished according to their own response to the new Revelation. From this explanation, the primary meaning of 'Day' of Resurrection is evident. This is, no doubt, 'one of the mysteries hidden in the symbolic' term resurrection (*Certitude* 117). However, in a broader sense, the Day of Resurrection, or the resurrection of the dead, extends, like the Day of Judgement, to each individual who responds to the Word of God *throughout the entire age*. In the early stags of the Second World War and 49 years after the ministry of Bahá'u'lláh, Shoghi Effendi wrote, for example, about the crisis, then 'sweeping the face of the earth' and spoke of it as 'this judgement of God' (see *Promised Day* 3–4, also 111). Similarly, 'Abdu'l-Bahá would continue to speak of the resurrection of souls even after the strict limits of Bahá'u'lláh's 40-year ministry.

> The light hath shone forth, and radiance floodeth Mount Sinai, and a gentle wind bloweth from over the gardens of the Ever-Forgiving Lord; the sweet breaths of the spirit are passing by, and *those who lay buried in the grave are rising up* – and still do the heedless slumber on in their tombs. (*Selections from the Writings of 'Abdu'l-Bahá* 14, emphasis added)

It therefore seems that the Day of Resurrection, or the rapture as it is sometimes known, refers primarily to the birth of a new Revelation, the time of the ministry of each Manifestation of God, and beyond that to the awakening of souls to the new Faith of God throughout the age. It is accomplished through the Word of God and is effected most in those who respond directly to that Word.

chapter 11

THE RETURN OF CHRIST IN THE CLOUDS OF HEAVEN

CHRISTIAN BELIEFS ABOUT THE RETURN OF CHRIST IN THE CLOUDS OF HEAVEN

Some Christians believe that the return of Christ involves the actual return of Jesus of Nazareth. Such Christians believe Jesus physically ascended into heaven and will, therefore, return in like manner. In support of this belief the following passage is often cited:

> Now when He [Jesus Christ] had spoken these things, while they [the disciples] watched, He was taken up, and a cloud received Him out of their sight. And while they looked steadfastly toward heaven as He went up, behold, two men stood by them in white apparel who also said, 'Men of Galilee, why do you stand gazing up into heaven? This same Jesus, who was taken up from you into heaven, *will so come in like manner as you saw him go into heaven*'. (Acts 1:9–11, emphasis added)

In addition to Acts 1:9–11, Christians often quote several other verses that they feel should be understood literally. They believe Christ's return, unlike His first ministry, will be universally visible, because the Bible states that:

> All the tribes of the earth . . . will see the Son of Man coming on the clouds of heaven with power and great glory. (Matt. 24:30)

This is, of course, the verse Bahá'u'lláh comments on in *The Book of Certitude* (24-5, 66-74), and to which reference has already been made. In another verse, St John writes that 'every eye will see Him' (Rev. 1:7). From their interpretation of these verses, it is hard for Christians to understand how Bahá'u'lláh can be the expected return of Christ, since these signs have not literally occurred.

In order to demonstrate the connection between Bahá'u'lláh's life and such Biblical prophecies, it is important first to be detached from the assumption that the narratives of the Bible are attempts to convey objective historical events and must be understood literally. Scripture is concerned ultimately with the salvation of souls and with conveying spiritual knowledge (John 6:63, *Promulgation* 245-6), and it is therefore essential to seek to understand the 'inner real meanings of the Holy Scriptures' (*Promulgation* 460), the 'things of the Spirit of God' that are 'spiritually discerned' (1 Cor. 2:14). The writers of the Bible recorded many facts, but they also used symbolism to convey the spiritual significance of those facts, a significance otherwise not apparent to many people. They wrote not merely to record what they knew, saw, or heard, but to inspire faith in those who heard this record. St John spelled this out very clearly, when he wrote:

> These [signs] are written that you may believe that Jesus is the Christ, the Son of God, and believing you may have life in His name. (John 20:31).

BAHÁ'Í BELIEFS ABOUT THE RETURN OF CHRIST IN THE CLOUDS OF HEAVEN

To establish the validity of Bahá'u'lláh's claims and His fulfilment of the prophecies mentioned in the Bible, there are three points that can be explored:

1. The way in which the New Testament indicates that John the Baptist was the return of Elijah.

2. Clues in the New Testament narrative of Acts 1:9–11 that suggest Acts 1:9–11 should not be viewed literally.
3. The plausible symbolic meaning of the Biblical terms used to describe the return of Christ.

Since the Biblical equation between John the Baptist and Elijah is explained in Chapter 17, only the last two of these points will be examined here.

Clues in the Narrative Account of Acts 1:9–11
The passage cited above is from the Book of Acts, which is a 30-year account of the ministry of the Apostles (mainly St Peter and St Paul) after the ascension of Christ. Some scholars believe that the Gospel according to Luke and the Book of Acts are actually two parts of one work, written by the same author, and as such it is in some ways similar to Nabil's narrative the *Dawn-Breakers*.

Acts begins with what may be called a resumptive preface, a reference to 'my former book' (1:1; presumably the Gospel of Luke), and a statement of purpose. Since Acts takes up the ministry of the Apostles where the Gospel ends, it makes a second volume in need of the new introduction provided (1:1–4). The author then refers to the appearance of Christ to the Apostles and their questioning of Him. In His last words, Jesus commands them to testify to the truth of the Gospel 'to the end of the earth' (1:8). After this, Jesus ascends to heaven (1:9–11). The message of this account forms a logical and appropriate introduction to the work of the Apostles described in the rest of the book, and whether it is understood symbolically or literally, its message is evident. It teaches first that when the Apostles had questions they turned to Christ, secondly that Christ did not reveal some things (1:6–7), but they did understand that they were to testify to the truth of Jesus, and thirdly that their ministry was authorized by Jesus Himself.

The experiences of the early Church – symbolized by the reappearances of Christ over a period of 40 days after His crucifixion and ascension – make an effective starting point for the ministry of the Apostles, especially in light of the last question the Apostles asked Jesus, 'Lord, will You at this time restore the kingdom to Israel?' (Acts 1:6). This issue was central to the Jewish rejection of Jesus; Jesus had not overthrown the Romans and restored Israel as a sovereign nation. This is what many Jews seem to have expected the promised Messiah to do, and since Jesus did not, they denied that He was the Messiah.[27]

When the Apostles ask this question, Jesus tells them it is not for them to know the exact time. Jesus instead tells them to testify to the truth, and then He ascends to heaven. The ascension or resurrection of Jesus is, of course, the central symbol of the New Testament, meant to express the fact that Jesus was not defeated at the cross and that He was therefore the Messiah foretold in Scripture. Even after the cross, He was guiding His followers to victory and ruling from heaven. This central truth is therefore stressed at the beginning of the ministry of the Apostles, so as to affirm that what they were doing was not pointless. Although the account should not be interpreted literally, it does express the truth of the fact that after Jesus' crucifixion, the Apostles were guided by Him from beyond the limitations of this life.

A number of symbolic meanings are suggested in the description given in Acts, and one detail particularly worth noting concerns the two men in white apparel. They are said to speak to the Apostles, asking, 'Men of Galilee, why do you stand gazing up into heaven?' (1:11). These individuals may be regarded as angels because of their 'white apparel', which recalls the description of the two angels Mary encountered at the tomb of Christ (John 20:12). If not angels, they are at least

---

27. See 'Abdu'l-Bahá, *Promulgation* 198–200, 246, 291–3.

individuals sent or inspired to speak as guides to the Apostles. Why then do they ask this question about 'gazing up into heaven'?

If they were able to speak confidently about Jesus' return, they knew surely that Jesus had just ascended into heaven, and that the Apostles had witnessed this event. It therefore seems strange that they would ask such a question, and it may be a clue that the account is not a literal description. Christ's reappearance, also, will not be an event viewed by gazing, literally, upward into heaven. Christ's ascension was spiritual, and His return will be in like manner.

Jesus' resurrection into heaven is symbolic of a spiritual reality, as 'Abdu'l-Bahá has explained (*Some Answered Questions*, Chapter 23).[28] That is, His resurrection represents the restoration of spiritual life among the believers, especially the Apostles, after they had forsaken Him when He was arrested and crucified (Matt. 26:56, John 18:15–17). Therefore, when the men in white apparel say, 'This same Jesus, who was taken up from you into heaven, will so come in like manner as you saw Him go into heaven' (Acts 1:11), this means that, the Cause and spiritual teachings of Jesus will be raised up again in the end times just as they were raised up among the first Christians.

The Clouds of Heaven
As mentioned above, another verse that bears on these issues is Jesus' prophecy in Matthew:

> All the tribes of the earth . . . will see the Son of Man coming on the clouds of heaven with power and great glory. (Matt. 24:30)

---

28. For a more detailed examination of the Resurrection, see Volume 2 of the *Preparing for a Bahá'í/Christian Dialogue* series (Part 4).

Bahá'u'lláh Himself comments directly on this prophecy:

> And now, with reference to His words: 'And then shall all the tribes of the earth mourn, and they shall see the Son of Man coming in the clouds of heaven with power and great glory'. These words signify that in those days men will lament the loss of the Sun of the divine beauty, of the Moon of knowledge, and of the Stars of divine wisdom. Thereupon, they will behold the countenance of the promised One, the adored Beauty, descending from the heaven and riding upon the clouds. By this is meant that the divine Beauty will be made manifest from the heaven of the will of God, and will appear in the form of the human temple. The term 'heaven' denoteth loftiness and exaltation, inasmuch as it is the seat of the revelation of those Manifestations of Holiness, the Day-springs of ancient glory. These ancient Beings, though delivered from the womb of their mother, have in reality descended from the heaven of the will of God. Though they be dwelling on this earth, yet their true habitations are the retreats of glory in the realms above. Whilst walking amongst mortals, they soar in the heaven of the divine presence. (Certitude 66–7)

In another passage Bahá'u'lláh continues this theme, giving specific elaboration of the term 'clouds', which He says means 'those things that are contrary to the ways and desires of men' (Certitude 71). He writes:

> These 'clouds' signify in one sense, the annulment of laws, the abrogation of former Dispensations, the repeal of rituals and customs current amongst men, the exalting of the illiterate faithful above the learned opposers of the Faith. In another sense, they mean the appearance of that immortal Beauty in the image of mortal man, with such human limitations as eating and

drinking, poverty and riches, glory and abasement, sleeping and waking, and such other things as cast doubt in the minds of men, and cause them to turn away. All such veils are symbolically referred to as 'clouds'. (*Certitude* 71–2, see also *Selections from the Writing of 'Abdu'l-Bahá* 167–8)

In addition to these explanations it is worth keeping in mind the parallel afforded by Christ's original *descent* from heaven (John 6:38, 41), the spiritual meaning of which was missed entirely by the people to whom Christ was speaking (John 6:42; cf. *Bahá'í World Faith* 387). In addition to Bahá'u'lláh's explanation in *The Book of Certitude* concerning Matthew 24, 'Abdu'l-Bahá offers another point that is helpful for understanding this issue. In His explanation of the resurrection (*Some Answered Questions*, Chapter 23), He cites the Gospel of John (verses 3:13, 6:38 and 6:42) to demonstrate that the term 'heaven' is not a geographical or physical reality but represents a *spiritual existence*. Jesus stated He was in heaven (John 3:13) and also that He had come down from heaven (John 6:38). When the Book of Acts speaks of Jesus ascending up into heaven, it seems likely that the term 'heaven' is meant in the same way as in the teachings of Jesus.

Every Eye Will See Him
As mentioned above, some Christians also stress the prophecy that 'every eye will see Him'. The verse in the Book of Revelation states:

> Behold, He is coming with clouds, and every eye will see Him, and they also who pierced Him. (Rev. 1:7)

Since not every eye has seen the appearance of Bahá'u'lláh, some Christians argue He cannot have fulfilled the prophecy.

The simplest explanation of this is that it is a manner of speaking, not a technical expression meant to refer to the physical eyes of every human being on the planet. This is supported by a prophecy concerning John the Baptist, cited in the Gospel of Luke:

> And he [John the Baptist] went into all the region around the Jordan, preaching a baptism of repentance for the remission of sins, as it is written in the book of the words of Isaiah the prophet, saying:
>
> 'The voice of one crying in the wilderness:
> "Prepare the way of the Lord,
> Make His paths straight.
> Every valley shall be filled
> And every mountain and hill brought low;
> And the crooked places shall be made straight
> And the rough ways made smooth;
> And all flesh shall see the salvation of God".'
> (Luke 3:4–6)

In this passage, it is clear that the prophecy is fulfilled in the preaching of John the Baptist and the coming of Jesus Christ, yet on no account did every eye literally see either of them, much less were the mountains literally brought down.

The prophecy 'every eye will see Him' can be understood as simply a way of speaking meant to express the openness of Jesus' return. It will not be kept to a chosen few, to a particular nation, Christian denomination, or an elite group of individuals. It will be, as the Bahá'í Faith has been, proclaimed openly to all people throughout the world. 'Every eye' may simply suggest the idea that every type of person will be able to see the coming of the new Revelation. In one sense, this means both bad and good people will be able to embrace the teachings and laws of Bahá'u'lláh. This is probably the primary intention of the prophecy.

Nevertheless, as clear as this is, not everyone will be satisfied with the above explanation. In approaching this question, it is therefore also useful to consider the symbolic nature of the word 'eye'. St Paul refers to the 'eyes of your understanding' (Eph. 1:18), a terminology also suggested by Jesus' words (Matt. 13: 15–16). Furthermore, when the verse in the Book of Revelation refers to 'Him', there is no reason to insist that this means His physical person rather than the spiritual reality of His sovereignty and Revelation, nor does it indicate that it means all eyes will see Him at once, rather than that all people will eventually come to see the truth of His Revelation.

Another answer to this question may be suggested in the following passage, specifically revealed by Bahá'u'lláh to the Christians:

> Verily, We behold all created things moved to bear witness unto Us. Some know Us and bear witness, while the majority bear witness, yet know Us not. (*Tablets of Bahá'u'lláh* 15)

When Bahá'u'lláh states that all created things bear witness to Him, this appears to assert the fulfilment of the prophecy that every eye will see Him. 'Some know Us and bear witness' may indicate the believers, those who have embraced Bahá'u'lláh's Revelation. And the 'majority' who 'bear witness, yet know Us not', may mean those who are not believers. This second group may represent the rest of humanity, who are witnessing the effects of Bahá'u'lláh's Revelation and teachings but are unaware of their source.

From this point of view, all have seen Him coming on the clouds of heaven, both those who believe and those who do not. The new spirit affecting this age has left no one untouched. Most people today are, in some way, embracing Bahá'í teachings without having knowledge of the Bahá'í Faith. The recognition of the need for equality between men and women, for racial justice, for an international system of government, for a world language, and for many more such elements of Bahá'í teachings has come to be characteristic of the spirit of this age.

The last part of the Revelation 1:7 – 'and they also who pierced Him' – is believed by some Christians to indicate the particular Roman soldier who pierced Jesus' side and His other persecutors (John 19:34). The return of Jesus' persecutors signifies, from the Bahá'í point of view, the return of their spirits. The malevolent spirits of Christ's oppressors can be compared with those who persecuted Bahá'u'lláh and who persecute His followers even today. Bahá'u'lláh explains this concept of return in *The Book of Certitude* (158–9).

The above points provide plausible alternatives to the literal interpretations often found among conservative Christians. The Bahá'í Faith does not challenge the authenticity or inspiration of the prophesies stating that Christ will return in the clouds of heaven. Rather, Bahá'u'lláh proclaims in very forceful language that these signs have come to pass:

> And among them is he who saith: 'Have I been assembled with others, blind?' Say: 'Yea, by Him that rideth upon the clouds!' (*Epistle* 133)

And in another passage Bahá'u'lláh states:

> He, verily, hath again come down from heaven, even as He came down from it the first time. (*Tablets of Bahá'u'lláh* 11)

In this second quotation, Bahá'u'lláh stresses that Jesus came down from heaven the first time He appeared, as the Gospel itself testifies (John 6:38), and that this is how His return should also be understood. This verse, from Bahá'u'lláh's 'Tablet to the Christians' (*Lawḥ-i-Aqdas*), is well worth committing to memory, as it captures succinctly all that is most essential for understanding the symbolism of the resurrection and return of Jesus Christ.

chapter 12

THE BATTLE OF ARMAGEDDON

CHRISTIAN BELIEFS CONCERNING ARMAGEDDON
The battle of Armageddon is understood by many conservative Christians as an epic, physical battle between the forces of good and evil. It is one of the prominent features of the Day of Judgement or Day of God in the end times. According to many Christian commentators, it is to coincide with the return of Christ and precede the establishment of the Kingdom of God. Armageddon has often been a popular subject of discussion among Christians, particularly those who took an interest in the world's growing arms race during the 'Cold War' years (1950–90), the Israeli-Arab conflicts in the Middle East, and the spread of militant communism to many countries throughout the world.

The so-called cold war between the United States of America and the Soviet Union inspired many evangelical Christians in America to preach that the prophecies concerning Armageddon referred to a nuclear war. Armageddon became the subject of numerous sermons, books, and films. Interpreting these prophecies broadly and literally, some Christians have argued at times that fulfilment could be seen in current world affairs, and this assertion appeared to some people to have a startling accuracy.

The most significant references to the battle of Armageddon are thought to be in the books of Ezekiel and Revelation, also known as the Apocalypse. The word 'apocalypse' is derived from the Greek word meaning 'to reveal', so to speak of the Book of Revelation or the Apocalypse is the same thing. Because

Revelation contains so many descriptions of disasters and destruction, its title has come to be synonymous in modern English with war and/or disasters. Events are often described in the news as being 'apocalyptic' in nature. It is also an accepted academic term used to describe a type of scriptural symbolism. The similarity between the cryptic and often obscure symbolism of the Book of Revelation and other books such as Ezekiel has led some scholars to refer to this type of symbolism as 'apocalyptic'. Most scholars would, for example, also consider Jesus' last sermon (Matt. 24) to be in the apocalyptic style.

The term 'armageddon' appears only once in the Bible, in Revelation 16:16. It is thought to refer to a future battle, so in addition to this one reference, other passages involving battles, such as Revelation 19:17–21 and Ezekiel 39:1–4, are believed by some Christians to be descriptions of Armageddon. Some believe that this battle will occur on the plain of Esdraelon in Israel, others that it will extend throughout the whole country of Israel (or Palestine), with the conflict centred around Jerusalem. The term 'ar-mageddon' mentioned in Revelation 16:16 means literally 'hill of Megiddo', and refers to the ancient Canaanite fortress of Megiddo. This site was on the main commercial route of ancient Israel, and whoever controlled it had power over Israel's economic well-being. The site became the scene of a decisive battle in Israelite history (see Judg. 4 and 5). It therefore seems likely that the term 'armageddon' came to be used in the Book of Revelation to symbolize the battle of the Lord and the intervention of God in history to preserve His people.

According to conservative Christian belief, there are three primary persons (or entities) who will wage war against Christ when He returns and against His hosts (angelic army) in this end-time battle. They are Satan; his human agent, the beast, or antichrist; and the false prophet who acts as the beast's minister of religion. Although the beast described in Scripture is undoubtedly antichrist in nature and spirit, there is no direct connection between the antichrist referred to by John in his Epistles and the beast described in the Book of Revelation. The term *antichrist* is not mentioned in Revelation, nor does the Scripture support the belief that there is to be only one antichrist who will appear at the end of the age – St John describes the antichrist as 'already in the world' (1 John 4:3) and writes that 'even now many antichrists have come' (1 John 2:18).

Satan's human agent, the beast, and 'the kings of the earth' will go into battle against the returned Christ and His hosts. This is described in Revelation 19:

> And I saw the beast, the kings of the earth, and their armies, gathered together to make war against Him who sat on the horse and against His army. Then the beast was captured, and with him the false prophet who worked signs in his presence, by which he deceived those who received the mark of the beast and those who worshipped his image. These two were cast alive into the lake of fire burning with brimstone. And the rest were killed with the sword which proceeded from the mouth of Him who sat on the horse. (Rev. 19:19–21)

According to Scripture, Christ and His hosts are victorious and Satan is bound for 'a thousand years' (Rev. 20:3). It was common from the 1960s to the 1980s for some Christians to assert that this battle signified a conflict involving a Soviet, Chinese and Arab alliance waging war against Israel (with the implication that America was on the side of Christ). Some expressed the belief that Christ would literally be involved in this international battle. The beast was seen as a totalitarian world political ruler, and because of the philosophical assertion of atheism in Marxist philosophy, the Soviet Union was regarded by many as a likely instrument of this apocalyptic beast.

Peace movements, and individuals or organizations working for world unity and world government, have also been accused by some Christians of preparing the way for the antichrist, or beast. For example, the Bahá'í effort for world unity was labelled another preparation for the coming antichrist by Kurt Kosh in his book *Occult ABC*, a charge asserted in varying degrees by other Christian authors.

Such accusations can be countered by using the information outlined in Volume 1 of *Preparing for a Baháʼí/Christian Dialogue, Understanding Biblical Evidence*; here it is pointed out that the Bible gives clear and unmistakable criteria, which exclude any possibility that Baháʼu'lláh is an antichrist, the beast or a false prophet. Moreover, it should be noted that none of the literal and political interpretations of Revelation to date construct a picture that corresponds to the history or administration of the Baháʼí Faith.

BAHÁʼÍ TEACHINGS RELATING TO ARMAGEDDON

If Scripture is primarily concerned with the spiritual life of humankind and the soul of the individual, it is reasonable to assume that the great battle mentioned in the Bible concerns the struggle of the soul against evil. Specifically, the battle is between the forces of disbelief and evil that oppose those who believe in Baháʼu'lláh and His teachings. Baháʼu'lláh is at the head of this battle, in that He has appeared in the world and armed His followers with His teachings (the sword of His words). The battle is the opposition to His teachings throughout the world. Through the power and truth of His teachings, He has prevailed over this opposition, or, as prophesied, He has defeated His enemies with a word from His mouth (Rev. 19:15). The beast who opposes Baháʼu'lláh can refer to the individuals who persecuted Him and/or the sin within all people that opposes the Word of God.

The battle of Armageddon is at the opposite pole from the resurrection of the dead, in the sense that this battle is the result of failure to recognize God's teachings for this age, and the resurrection of the dead is the blessing of having attained to that recognition. Those who have turned away and those who are resurrected must play their respective roles in this great struggle.

Some very relevant insights into the interpretation of Chapters 19–22 of the Book of Revelation can be gained by examining how 'Abdu'l-Bahá interprets earlier portions of the same book. 'Abdu'l-Bahá explains how similar symbols in Revelation pertain to the past spiritual developments and crises of Islam. It is only reasonable that the rise of a major world religion in the Holy Land would be mentioned and figure prominently in John's prophecies and vision of the future.

'Abdu'l-Bahá interprets references to the beast in Revelation 11 as signifying events associated with evil individuals whose actions seriously damaged the Faith of Islam, specifically the usurping of power by those who were not sincere Muslims (see *Some Answered Questions*, Chapters 11 and 13). The beast signifies the 'dynasty of the Umayyads' (*Some Answered Questions* 51, 69–70). The war against the two Witnesses (Rev. 11:7) is correlated to the Umayyads' wrongful opposition to 'the religion of Muḥammad' and 'the reality of 'Alí', the rightful successor of Muḥammad (*Some Answered Questions* 51). The wealthy and corrupt Umayyads used violence to further their imperial ambitions, and even killed the rightful successors to Muḥammad. Because of their aggression and greed, Islamic government was never established according to the spirit of the Qur'án. These actions brought division into Islam and 'the holy city' or 'sanctuary' (indicating true *Islam*, or literally, the *submission to God*) was trampled under foot (Rev. 11:2, Dan. 8:13–4). History seems to suggest that the Umayyads fit John's descriptions very well. 'Abdu'l-Bahá also interprets later portions of this chapter, as well as portions of the last chapters of the Book of Revelation, in relation to the Bahá'í Faith.

As in Chapter 11 of Revelation, where a beast is described as waging war against the two Witnesses (Muḥammad and 'Alí), in later chapters (19–20) another beast and, this time, a false prophet, arise to wage war against God's Messenger (Bahá'u'lláh, the Lord of Hosts).[29] Two individuals fit this

---

29. These chapters contain many references applicable to Bahá'u'lláh, and when understood from this point of view, these chapters cannot refer directly to the Umayyads and it must be assumed that the terms *beast* and *false prophet* refer to individuals in this age who possessed similar malevolent characteristics.

description of the beast and false prophet especially well: Siyyid Muḥammad, regarded as the 'Antichrist' of the Bahá'í Revelation (*God Passes By* 164) and Mírzá Yaḥyá (also known as Ṣubḥ-i-Azal, literally meaning the *Morn of Eternity*). These two exerted every effort to defeat Bahá'u'lláh's Cause and to turn people against Him, including the most powerful rulers of the land, the Sultán of the Ottoman Empire, Sultán 'Abdu'l-'Azíz, and the Sháh of Persia, Násiri'd-Dín-Sháh.

But events described at the end of the Book of Revelation differ from those described in Chapter 11, where the two Witnesses are described as being killed by the beast. This time, instead of the holy sanctuary being made desolate, the text assures us that the forces of darkness are defeated, the Lord of Hosts triumphs, killing the beast with a sword that proceeds from His mouth. This sword symbolizes the Word of God, with which Bahá'u'lláh has defeated His adversaries.

This is one way of understanding the conflict described in the Book of Revelation. In a broader sense, the struggle that the believers of Bahá'u'lláh are waging against the sin within themselves and in the world around them is an ongoing Armageddon. Many passages by Shoghi Effendi suggest this:

> The stage is set. The hour is propitious. The signal is sounded. Bahá'u'lláh's spiritual battalions are moving into position. The initial clash between the forces of darkness and the army of light, as unnoticed as the landing, two milleniums ago, of the apostles of Christ on the southern shores of the European continent, is being registered by the denizens of the Abhá Kingdom. The Author of the Plan that has set so titanic an enterprise in motion is Himself mounted at the head of these battalions, and leads them on to capture the cities of men's hearts. (*Citadel of Faith* 26)

In this passage it is clear that the battle is not over, nor is Bahá'u'lláh absent from the scene. In another passage Shoghi

Effendi refers to the Baháʼís as 'the all-conquering army of the Lord of Hosts, the torchbearers of a future divinely inspired world civilization' (*Citadel of Faith* 109) and again as the 'steadily advancing army of the Lord of Hosts, whose reinforcing strength is so essential to the safeguarding of the victories which the band of heroic Baháʼí conquerors are winning in the course of their several campaigns in all the continents of the globe' (*Citadel of Faith* 117).

These passages show how this conflict can be understood in the broad symbolic sense of the spiritual struggle taking place throughout the world today. However, ʻAbduʼl-Bahá also applies the Armageddon imagery from the Book of Revelation to wars of our age. Just before World War I, ʻAbduʼl-Bahá, stated 'we are on the eve of the Battle of Armageddon' (*Baháʼuʼlláh and the New Era* 223, see also *Tablets of the Divine Plan* 22). This suggests that the Book of Revelation can refer to many events, occurring over a long span of time, in which the forces of darkness appear to be engulfing much of the world. ʻAbduʼl-Bahá does not say that one side, such as America and Britain, represent the hosts of the Lord, or the Spirit of Christ, and the other side, Germany, represents the armies of darkness headed by the beast. It is unlikely, in my opinion, that such an interpretation could be forced upon the Book of Revelation even with regard to World War II. *World-wide* nationalism and racism precipitated these crises, and whichever nation first challenged the others would necessarily have to be opposed. Conflicts such as these are representative of Armageddon in that they are attempts by the forces of darkness in the world to assert principles directly contrary to the teachings of Baháʼuʼlláh. ʻAbduʼl-Bahá apparently foresaw that lack of spirituality and disregard for Baháʼuʼlláh's teachings would inevitably lead to such violence and destruction. These world-encompassing wars proved the spiritual bankruptcy of the ideologies of the time and brought many reluctant people closer to acceptance of the truths of Baháʼuʼlláh's teachings. As World War II was beginning, Shoghi Effendi wrote:

The powerful operations of this titanic upheaval are comprehensible to none except such as have recognized the claims of both Bahá'u'lláh and the Báb. Their followers know full well whence it comes, and what it will ultimately lead to. Though ignorant of how far it will reach, they clearly recognize its genesis, are aware of its direction, acknowledge its necessity, observe confidently its mysterious processes, ardently pray for the mitigation of its severity, intelligently labor to assuage its fury, and anticipate, with undimmed vision, the consummation of the fears and the hopes it must necessarily engender.

This judgment of God, as viewed by those who have recognized Bahá'u'lláh as His Mouthpiece and His greatest Messenger on earth, is both a retributory calamity and an act of holy and supreme discipline. (*Promised Day* 4)

It is clear from *The Book of Certitude* (33, 204) and 'Abdu'l-Bahá's discourses (*Some Answered Questions* 122–7) that Scripture has multiple meanings. It is logical that, if the religion of Muḥammad is valid, as the Bahá'í writings assert, Islam should hold a prominent place in the prophetic message of the New Testament. It should also come as no surprise that a book with as much symbolism as the Book of Revelation is capable of giving guidance applicable to many different circumstances.

'Abdu'l-Bahá regards the symbolism of the Book of Revelation as being applicable to the story of Islam (*Some Answered Questions*, Chapters 11, 13), to the unfolding of the Bahá'í Faith (*Selections from the Writing of 'Abdu'l-Bahá* 12–13), and to some modern world events (*Tablets of the Divine Plan* 22).

Chapter 13

THE MILLENNIAL KINGDOM

CHRISTIAN BELIEFS CONCERNING THE MILLENNIAL KINGDOM

Millennial is a term derived from the Latin 'mille' meaning a *thousand*,[30] used to refer to the time when believers will live and reign 'with Christ for a thousand years' (Rev. 20:4).

Among Christians, including conservative Christians, there is considerable disagreement about the nature and establishment of the Millennial Kingdom. Three basic terms are used to describe the most commonly accepted views about the Millennial Kingdom: Post-millennialism, A-millennialism and Pre-millennialism.

- **Post-millennialism:** This view holds that Jesus will return after the Christians have established the Millennial Kingdom. The phrase 'a thousand years' is viewed symbolically as a long duration of unspecified length. Some Christians believe this kingdom will be, or has been, established directly through the work of the Holy Spirit and the preaching of the Gospel. Others maintain it will come about as a result of general humanitarian efforts and prayers.

---

30. A translation of the Greek *chilioi*, hence the term 'chiliasm', another Christian term for millennialism.

- **A-millennialism:** The A-millennialist interpretation holds that the Kingdom of God signifies either the present reign of Christ in the Church or His present reign in heaven. No literal kingdom will be established on earth.

- **Pre-millennialism:** The Pre-millennial view is that Christ will return, conquer the antichrist, eradicate evil from the world, and then establish a thousand-year rule over the earth. Pre-millennialists tend to maintain that Revelation 20 should be interpreted literally. This view was espoused in varying degrees by early Christian writers until the time of Augustine, and has been revived in modern times. This may be the most popular view among conservative Protestant Christians today.

BAHÁ'Í BELIEFS CONCERNING THE MILLENNIAL KINGDOM

The Bahá'í view is in agreement with some portions of all these views. The Bahá'í teachings agree with Post-millennialists about the active spiritual and human role involved in the establishment of the Kingdom. During this time, individuals will have to act upon the new teachings and plans set forth in the new Revelation given by God.

Similarities between the Bahá'í view and the A-millennialists can be seen in the acknowledgement that Revelation 20 should be interpreted symbolically. Agreement with the Pre-millennialists can be found in the belief that the Kingdom is to be established after the historic return of Christ. This, the Bahá'í Faith believes, has already happened, and for this reason Bahá'ís can confidently work towards the establishment of the Kingdom of God on earth, a Kingdom already present in the hearts of those who believe in, and have come to know, Bahá'u'lláh. Addressing the Christians, Bahá'u'lláh writes:

O people of the Gospel! They who were not in the Kingdom have now entered it, whilst We behold you, in this day, tarrying at the gate. Rend the veils asunder by the power of your Lord, the Almighty, the All-Bounteous, and enter, then, in My name My Kingdom. (*Proclamation* 91)

The nature of this promised Kingdom is described by St John in the Book of Revelation:

And I saw a new heaven and a new earth, for the first heaven and the first earth had passed away. Also there was no more sea. Then I, John, saw the holy city, New Jerusalem, coming down out of heaven from God, prepared as a bride adorned for her husband. And I heard a loud voice from heaven saying, 'Behold, the tabernacle of God is with men, and He will dwell with them, and they shall be His people, and God Himself will be with them and be their God. And God will wipe away every tear from their eyes; there shall be no more death, nor sorrow, nor crying; and there shall be no more pain, for the former things have passed away.' Then He who sat on the throne said, 'Behold I make all things new.' And He said to me, 'Write, for these words are true and faithful'. And He said to me, 'It is done! I am the Alpha and the Omega, the Beginning and the End. I will give of the fountain of the water of life freely to him who thirsts. He who overcomes shall inherit all things, and I will be his God and he shall be my Son. But the cowardly, unbelieving, abominable murderers, sexually immoral, sorcerers, idolaters, and all liars shall have their part in the lake which burns with fire and brimstone, which is the second death'. (Rev. 21: 1–8)

Many conservative Christians expect these prophecies to be fulfilled literally. 'Abdu'l-Bahá, however, indicates that they have been fulfilled through the outpourings of Bahá'u'lláh's Revelation and its effect on the hearts of believers. 'Abdu'l-Bahá writes:

> Oh ye beloved of God! O ye children of His Kingdom! Verily, verily, the new heaven and the new earth are come. The holy City, new Jerusalem, hath come down from on high in the form of a maid of heaven, veiled, beauteous, and unique, and prepared for reunion with her lovers on earth. The angelic company of the Celestial Concourse hath joined in a call that hath run throughout the universe, all loudly and mightily acclaiming: 'This is the City of God and His abode, wherein shall dwell the pure and holy among His servants. He shall live with them, for they are His people and He is their Lord.'
>
> He hath wiped away their tears, kindled their light, rejoiced their hearts and enraptured their souls. Death shall no more overtake them neither shall sorrow, weeping or tribulation afflict them. The Lord God Omnipotent hath been enthroned in His Kingdom and hath made all things new. This is the truth and what truth can be greater than that announced by the Revelation of St John the Divine?
>
> He is Alpha and Omega. He is the One that will give unto him that is athirst of the fountain of the water of life and bestow upon the sick the remedy of true salvation. He whom such grace aideth is verily he that receiveth the most glorious heritage from the Prophets of God and His holy ones. The Lord will be his God, and he His dearly-beloved son.
>
> Rejoice, then, O ye beloved of the Lord and His chosen ones, and ye children of God and His people, raise your voices to laud and magnify the Lord, the Most High; for His light hath beamed forth, His signs have appeared and the billows of His rising ocean have

scattered on every shore many a precious pearl.
(*Selection from the Writings of 'Abdu'l-Bahá* 12–13)

These words of 'Abdu'l-Bahá are phrased to suggest the symbolic nature and spiritual significance of John's writings. Notice the similarity between John's vision of life in the new Kingdom and life in the original garden described in the Book of Genesis. To be in the presence of God (Rev. 21:3) is to ascend to a condition above the suffering of material existence – to return to the shade of the tree of life in paradise. *The Book of Certitude* can further help us understand the particular expressions and terms used by St John. The phrase 'a new heaven and a new earth' (Rev. 21:1) can, for example, be understood in light of this explanation:

> Even as the visible sun that assisteth, as decreed by God, the true One, the Adored, in the development of all earthly things, such as the trees, the fruits, the colors thereof, the minerals of the earth, and all that may be witnessed in the world of creation, so do the divine Luminaries, by their loving care and educative influence, cause the trees of divine unity, the fruits of His oneness, the leaves of detachment, the blossoms of knowledge and certitude, and the myrtles of wisdom and utterance, to exist and be made manifest. Thus it is that through the rise of these Luminaries of God the world is made new, the waters of everlasting life stream forth, the billows of loving-kindness surge, the clouds of grace are gathered, and the breeze of bounty bloweth upon all created things. (*Certitude* 33–4)

In this passage Bahá'u'lláh describes, in the form of an analogy, how the Manifestations transform the spiritual world of humankind. Through the effect of their Revelations 'the world is made new'. By 'world' Bahá'u'lláh means humankind's total spiritual experience; spiritual life is renewed, unity is established, old ways of seeing things are replaced with a new vision and purpose.

John writes, 'I saw a new heaven and a new earth, for the first heaven and first earth had passed away' (Rev. 21:1). In certain instances, Bahá'u'lláh explains, the term 'earth' signifies 'the earth of understanding and knowledge', and 'heavens' means 'the heavens of divine Revelation' (*Certitude* 48, see also 44). And, in another instance, He refers to the changing of 'the earth of their hearts' (*Certitude* 46). If we apply these explanations to John's words the meaning of 'new heaven' and 'new earth' is a new Revelation and a new spiritual life among humankind.

This implies that the words 'Behold, I make all things new' (Rev. 21:5) involves the two spiritual factors of the Revelation of Bahá'u'lláh and its effects on the hearts of humankind. John writes, 'And God will wipe away every tear from their eyes; there shall be no more death, nor sorrow, nor crying; and there shall be no more pain, for the former things have passed away.' Because these occurrences relate not only to the 'new heaven', (that is, the new Revelation) but also to the 'new earth' (humanity's heart and understanding), it is our responsibility to receive and respond to the message of Bahá'u'lláh. These blessings do not simply appear, they are bestowed on those who thirst (Rev. 21:6), overcome (Rev. 21:7), and persevere (Rev. 3:12). These rewards concern the 'life of faith' (*Certitude* 144) and 'the paradise of the love of God' (*Certitude* 118).

This explanation also reflects the Bahá'í view that worldly orientation is non-existence in comparison with spiritual life. 'Abdu'l-Bahá explains:

> For those who believe in God, who have love of God, and faith, life is excellent – that is, it is eternal; but to those souls who are veiled from God, although they have life, it is dark, and in comparison with the life of believers it is nonexistence. (*Some Answered Questions* 243)

The words of St Paul also testify to this point of view:

> Therefore, if anyone is in Christ, he is a new creation; old things have passed away; behold, all things have become new. (2 Cor. 5:17)

From this passage it is clear that even in the time of Christ it could be said that the old creation was replaced with a new one. This passage, plus the prophecies in the Book of Revelation suggest New Testament agreement with Bahá'u'lláh's teaching that in every age the Manifestation of God renews the world.

BIBLICAL REFERENCES FOR PART THREE

There are no verses suitable for an outline of the chapters concerning the Battle of Armageddon and the Millennial Kingdom, although the verses mentioned above could be listed. Since these verses involve prophecies, use a blue highlighter and include them as notes on prophecy, as described in Volume one of *Preparing for a Bahá'í/Christian Dialogue*. Some of the following verses are already listed in previous outlines, so it is necessary to mark them in a way that does not become confused with the other outlines. This can be done by simply making a highlighter mark in the margin and writing the next verse number within that mark.

The Tribulation (*Certitude* 29–32):
    Matt. 24:4–5
    Matt. 24:11
    Matt. 24:23–4
    1 Tim. 4:1–2
    2 Tim. 3:1–7
    Matt. 7:15–16
    Matt. 7:21–3
    Acts 20:29
    Amos 8:11

The Rapture:
   1 Thess. 4:16–17
   1 Cor. 15:44
The Return of Christ:
   Return of Elijah/John the Baptist (outlined in Chapter 17)
Spiritual meaning of descent from heaven (*Some Answered Questions*, Chapter 23, *Certitude* 66–7, 71–2):
   John 3:13
   John 6:38, 41
   John 6:42

part four

BAHÁ'U'LLÁH
IN
BIBLICAL PROPHECY

chapter 14

PROPHECIES REFERRING TO BAHÁ'U'LLÁH

INTRODUCTION
The prophecies examined in the following chapters are quoted directly in the authoritative Bahá'í writings and are taken primarily from Shoghi Effendi's book *God Passes By* (94–6). The list of prophecies is very brief, considering the large number in the Bible referring to the second advent of Christ. Also, the selected prophecies do not cover all those mentioned in the Bahá'í writings; in fact, they are not even all the Biblical prophecies listed in *God Passes By*. Bahá'u'lláh, in one of His Tablets, writes:

> Were We to make mention of all that hath been revealed in these heavenly Books and holy Scriptures concerning this Revelation, this Tablet would assume impossible dimensions. (*Gleanings* 13)

As this passage suggests, many chapters in the Bible concern the second advent of Christ – the appearance of Bahá'u'lláh – and the establishment of the Kingdom of God on earth. The prophecies in this chapter consist of only a verse or two selected from such passages. Each student of Scripture can use the prophecies cited here as a starting point, adding further references later, and reading more of the text to get a better understanding of the Biblical contexts.

In addition to emphasizing only prophecies mentioned in the authoritative Bahá'í writings, an effort has been made to base the commentary on explanations also available there. The aim of this analysis is not to list prophecies that merely refer to Bahá'u'lláh, but to provide sufficient explanations as to how Bahá'u'lláh has fulfilled these prophecies, and thus also provide a general understanding of Biblical prophecy that will enable the student of the Bible to read other prophecies with confidence and decide whether they have been fulfilled by Bahá'u'lláh, and if so, how.

IDENTIFYING BIBLICAL PROPHECIES MENTIONED IN BAHÁ'Í WRITINGS

There are many prophecies in the Bible; some Christian scholars say that roughly 30 per cent of the Bible is in fact prophecy. Of these, it is important to distinguish correctly those that refer to Bahá'u'lláh. In past interpretations, some people concluded that certain prophecies referred to specific events or people, but with the passage of time the importance of those events has diminished, or new information has emerged that necessitated the abandonment of earlier interpretations. To ensure that the prophecies referred to in this book are representative of Bahá'í teachings and actually do refer to Bahá'u'lláh, follow two main rules which are applicable to any study of prophecy:

1. Focus only on those Biblical prophecies quoted in authoritative Bahá'í texts.

2. When the fulfilment of prophecy is indicated, but no direct Biblical quotation is given in Bahá'í Scripture, match the possible key words or concepts with passages found in the Bible. In this way, it may be possible to identify Biblical prophecies alluded to in Bahá'í Scriptures.

It helps to note passages where Bahá'u'lláh, 'Abdu'l-Bahá and Shoghi Effendi mention specific prophecies applicable to Bahá'u'lláh or His Revelation. For example, Bahá'u'lláh mentions a number of Biblical prophecies in *Epistle to the Son of the Wolf* (143–8), and He also quotes two of the same prophecies in another Tablet found in *Gleanings from the Writings of Bahá'u'lláh* (13). 'Abdu'l-Bahá explains in Chapter 12 of *Some Answered Questions* that Bahá'u'lláh fulfils the prophecy of Isaiah 11:1–10. And, as mentioned previously, Shoghi Effendi cites in *God Passes By* (58, 92–6, 110, 139, 151, 172, 183–4, 194, 210, 213, 248, 249, 305, 348) many Biblical prophecies that apply to Bahá'u'lláh and the Bahá'í Faith.

These references provide clear and reliable examples of prophecy pointed out in the authoritative Bahá'í writings. By studying these examples first, it is possible to learn characteristics of Biblical prophecy which are most applicable to the Bahá'í Faith. Through this knowledge, each student of Scripture can find other prophecies that refer to Bahá'u'lláh and this Day, but which are not quoted directly in Bahá'í Scripture.

Prophecies cited by Shoghi Effendi in *God Passes By*, for example, show that some Bible prophecies use certain titles to refer to Bahá'u'lláh. Noting these titles and locating them in other parts of the Bible can occasionally help in the identification of additional verses referring to Bahá'u'lláh. For example, Shoghi Effendi points out that David 'sung in his Psalms, acclaiming Bahá'u'lláh as the "*Lord of Hosts*" and the "*King of Glory*"' (*God Passes By* 95). These two titles appear together in Psalms 24:10. However, the title 'Lord of Hosts' appears seven more times in Psalms and well over 200 times in the Old Testament. Noting Shoghi Effendi's reference to Psalms 24:10, therefore, it is possible to begin a study of many other passages, some of which are prophecies. Crucial to this process is the need to understand what such titles mean, and the context in which they are used, as will be explained later.

In other cases, instead of titles there are certain words that provide clues, such as the word *Day*, which may mean the Day of God (Jer. 30:7, Joel 2:11), that time at the end of one age and the beginning of a new one when God intervenes in history to redeem humankind; or the word *judge* (Isa. 2:4), indicating the day of judgement – that is, the time when it becomes necessary to follow God's *new* teachings or suffer the consequences, the Day in which the prevailing standards of the world are judged in relation to the new Revelation. Such words embrace concepts that appear in many verses and often refer both to our age and the appearance of Bahá'u'lláh.

Bahá'u'lláh does not always directly quote a Biblical prophecy to point out that it has been fulfilled. In some cases He mentions key phrases recognizable by the student of the Bible. For example, Bahá'u'lláh makes this statement:

> Out of Zion hath gone forth the Law of God, and Jerusalem, and the hills and land thereof, are filled with the glory of His Revelation. (*Gleanings* 13)

This passage does not directly quote the Bible, nevertheless, it does refer to key phrases found in the Book of Isaiah, and it can be said with reasonable confidence that Bahá'u'lláh is indicating the fulfilment of several prophetic verses, among which are the following:

> Now it shall come to pass in the latter days
> That the mountain of the LORD's house
> Shall be established on the top of the mountains,
> And shall be exalted above the hills. (Isa. 2:2)

> For out of Zion shall go forth the law,
> And the word of the LORD from Jerusalem. (Isa. 2:3)

Bahá'u'lláh provides many other examples of verses that contain references to the prophecies, but no direct quotations:

> Blessed is the man who hath detached himself from all else but Me, hath soared in the atmosphere of My love, hath gained admittance into My Kingdom, gazed upon My realms of glory, quaffed the living waters of My

bounty, hath drunk his fill from the heavenly river of My loving providence, acquainted himself with My Cause, apprehended that which I concealed within the treasury of My Words, and hath shone forth from the horizon of divine knowledge engaged in My praise and glorification. (*Tablets of Bahá'u'lláh* 17)

Many words and phrases in this passage suggest that Bahá'u'lláh and His Revelation have fulfilled certain Biblical prophecies. For example, the believer who has 'soared in the atmosphere' of Bahá'u'lláh's love may be experiencing in essence the spiritual fulfilment of 1 Thessalonians 4:17, which states that when the Lord returns the believers will be caught up 'to meet the Lord in the air'. The 'Kingdom' could refer to the Millennial Kingdom described in Revelation 20-1. The 'living waters' could refer to Revelation 21:6, 'I will give of the fountain of the water of life freely to him who thirsts' and so on.

This approach is not as reliable as finding a direct quotation. However, as one's scriptural knowledge increases, it is possible to apply this approach with increasing accuracy. Before making outlines of prophecy in the Bible, it is best to compile a list of the Biblical prophecies that refer undoubtedly to Bahá'u'lláh, and to study that list carefully over a long period.

Once references to Bahá'u'lláh or any other Manifestation of God are located, it is important not to assume that such references are only applicable to one Manifestation. For example, in one Tablet, Bahá'u'lláh writes:

The Hour which We had concealed from the knowledge of the peoples of the earth and of the favoured angels hath come to pass. (*Tablets of Bahá'u'lláh* 11)

This verse may allude to, or at least encompass in part, Mark 13:32, a prophecy concerning the second coming, where Jesus states, 'of that day and hour no one knows, neither the angels in heaven, nor the Son, but only the Father'.[31] This reference provides an indication that Bahá'u'lláh is probably associating His Revelation with other prophecies of Jesus recorded in Chapter 13 of Mark. Significantly, these prophecies also have parallels mentioned in other passages of the New Testament, most notably Luke 21 and Matthew 24. As mentioned before, Bahá'u'lláh explains Matthew 24 in connection with Muḥammad (see Certitude, 24–6), but Bahá'u'lláh also indicates that these signs refer to Him. In fact, in The Book of Certitude Bahá'u'lláh says that these particular signs occur with the advent of every Revelation (Certitude 31, 73).

Even though a prophecy may seem to refer especially to one Messenger of God, this does not preclude reference to other Messengers. The implications of Bahá'u'lláh's words in The Book of Certitude are extraordinarily profound in this regard. For example, in the Bahá'í writings Bahá'u'lláh is identified as the 'Son of Man' Who 'shall come in the glory of His Father' (for example, God Passes By 95). This prophecy (Matt. 16:27/Mark 8:38) is so much like Matthew 25:31 in messianic nature, and so much a part of the natural progression of thought in the earlier part of Jesus' sermon (Matt. 24) that it becomes all too apparent that Muḥammad was also the return of the 'Son of Man' Who 'shall come in the glory of His Father'.

In The Book of Certitude, Bahá'u'lláh writes:

> Purge thy sight, therefore, from all earthly limitations, that thou mayest behold them all as the bearers of one Name, the exponents of one Cause, the manifestations of one Self, and the revealers of one Truth, and that thou mayest apprehend the mystic 'return' of the Words of God as unfolded by these utterances. (Certitude 159)

It should, therefore, come as no surprise that both Christ and Bahá'u'lláh can be rightly regarded as the 'Prince of Peace'

---

31. Cf. Epistle to the Son of the Wolf 143.

(*Promised Day* 105, 106); that the Báb could refer to Bahá'u'lláh as the 'Lord of the visible and invisible' (*God Passes By* 97) and that Bahá'u'lláh would apply the same terms to Christ (*Gleanings* 57).

Because of the symbolic nature of prophecy and the oneness of the Manifestations, Biblical prophecy cannot be divided up rigidly into separate categories or put into a simple chronological order. This point is important to keep in mind because there are times when it may seem that a prophecy refers to Bahá'u'lláh, and a Christian may object, saying that Christians have always thought it referred to Christ. It may, in fact, refer to both. In any event, it is important not to argue needlessly about such issues and to keep in mind the ultimate unity of the Manifestations of God. In the deepest *spiritual* sense, what refers to Christ refers to Bahá'u'lláh and what refers to Bahá'u'lláh refers to Christ. The two are one Reality – eternal and unchanging.

In the Gospel, the prophecy of Isaiah 40:3 is applied to John the Baptist. In the *Lawḥ-i-Aqdas*, Bahá'u'lláh refers to the Báb in similar terms. This does not mean the Gospel record is wrong – the verse is manifestly applicable to both. Bahá'u'lláh probably means to indicate that the Báb performed a mission for Him similar to the one John the Baptist accomplished for Christ. In a way, both John the Baptist and the Báb fulfilled Isaiah 40:3, even as both are the return of Elijah (*God Passes By* 58). Moreover, even when a verse seems more applicable to one Prophet than another in the literal sense, it still may be, in a spiritual sense, applicable to other Prophets.

chapter 15

OLD TESTAMENT PROPHECIES THAT REFER TO BAHÁ'U'LLÁH

Shoghi Effendi frequently turned to Biblical prophecy to draw out the divine connection between past events and writings and various aspects of the Bahá'í Faith. This is nowhere more evident than when he writes about the birth of the Bahá'í Revelation (94–6). In one paragraph, he makes reference to nine different Old Testament books, and in another paragraph he touches on prophecies from the New Testament, including references from Jesus Christ, St Peter, St Paul and St John.

In addition to all these and other Biblical prophecies cited in *God Passes By*, Shoghi Effendi quotes passages from Bahá'u'lláh containing references to Biblical prophecies.[32] It is perhaps worth noting that all these are from Books of the Bible recognized as sacred and authoritative by both the Catholic Church and the traditional Protestant denominations. The prophecies mentioned by Shoghi Effendi on pages 94–6 in *God Passes By* form the basis of the following analysis. To help put these prophecies into context, it is perhaps beneficial first to discuss these particular Books of the Bible.

On these pages, Shoghi Effendi cites a total of ten prophets from the Old Testament, beginning with Moses[33] and including David, the greatest of Israelite kings, and Daniel, a major Israelite statesman. In several other later passages, Shoghi

---

32. See, for example, *God Passes By* 207, 210, 213.

33. Moses is not mentioned by name, but rather, the prophecy of verse 33:2 from the Book of Deuteronomy is cited.

Effendi adds references from the prophets Amos and Hosea (*God Passes By* 184). The twelve prophets referred to are:

Moses
David
Amos
Hosea
Isaiah
Zephaniah
Ezekiel
Daniel
Haggai
Zechariah
Malachi
Joel

After Moses and King David, all the remaining prophets appeared after the divided kingdom period explained in Chapter 2. This one period can be viewed as consisting of three stages, all of which centre on the 'exile' of the Jews into the land of Babylon, namely, 'pre-exile', 'exile' and 'post-exile'. It is useful to know the relationship of the prophets to the exile because the contemporary fate of the Israelites influenced how the prophets expressed themselves. Many of their specific prophecies and much of the symbolism they used are concerned with the events of this period. Even when they spoke of the future, contemporary events coloured the way they spoke. It was, for example, just before the exile that Jerusalem was invaded and the holy Temple destroyed. The prophets who spoke after this event, such as Ezekiel and Zechariah, used symbolism about the restoration of the Temple to express their messianic vision of the future.

Prophets appeared before the exile who warned of what was coming, and others came during and at the end of this period explaining why it had happened and prophesying Israel's future restoration. They also spoke of a future Messiah and of the end times. These prophets can be positioned historically as follows:

Pre-exile prophets (in the divided kingdom period):
In Israel: Amos, Hosea
In Judah: Isaiah, Micah, Zephaniah

Exile prophets: Ezekiel and Daniel (Jewish prophets in Persia)

Post-exile prophets: Zechariah, Haggai, Malachi, Joel(?)[34]

Each of these prophets expressed his message in symbols consisting of persons, institutions, places and events that were significant in the history of the Israelite nation, and with a message relevant not just to the future but to the time in which he was living.

The prophecies examined on the following pages were selected because they make direct reference to Bahá'u'lláh, as distinct from prophecies that refer to the hour or advent of Bahá'u'lláh. They are prophecies from Isaiah, Ezekiel and Haggai, one from each of the three periods mentioned above. Each used different titles to refer to Bahá'u'lláh. Many

---

34. The exact dates of these prophets are often disputed. The dating and existence of Daniel is in particular a controversial subject. Many scholars today place the Book of Daniel in the post-exile period, although statements by 'Abdu'l-Bahá do not seem to accord with such views. Though less consequential, the precise dating of Joel is also difficult to ascertain. Otherwise, the arrangement above is generally accepted. Additional information about these prophets can be obtained by consulting Bible dictionaries or other reference books. There is often a partisan division between believing Christian scholars and scholars who tend to discount the supernatural, and this is reflected in available literature. These differences can be seen in the contrast between what is on offer in Christian bookshops and in university bookshops. Some scholars, for example, deny that the prophets had any knowledge of future events, and they therefore date the prophecies after the prophesied events. This method, could of course mean that Bahá'u'lláh's prophecies about Germany were written after

Christians will ask where the name 'Bahá'u'lláh' is mentioned in the Bible. Some Christians may suggest that, since the Arabic title 'Bahá'u'lláh' does not appear in the English translations of the Bible, Bahá'u'lláh cannot be the Promised One. As mentioned on page 36, the name 'Bahá'u'lláh' is actually a title meaning the 'Glory of God'. There are, of course, other titles applicable to Bahá'u'lláh besides the 'Glory of God' and this chapter will examine some of them.

When studying these prophecies, it is important to keep in mind that they are not merely a list of references to Bahá'u'lláh, but rather prophecies expressing the spiritual significance of His Revelation. It is essential to know what the titles in these prophecies mean in order to explain effectively why they are applicable to Bahá'u'lláh. Otherwise, stating the belief that Bahá'u'lláh fulfilled these prophecies has little meaning, if any, to those who do not accept the authority of Bahá'í Scriptures.

THE GLORY OF THE LORD
Shoghi Effendi refers to Isaiah as 'the greatest of the Jewish prophets', and states that he alluded to Bahá'u'lláh as the 'Glory of the Lord' (*God Passes By* 94). The Book of Isaiah gives warnings of the coming judgement of God against the divided kingdom of Israel and Judah, and against other specific nations and even the world. At various points, Isaiah stresses the future glory of Israel and the coming Messiah. Isaiah looks back to the reign of David as a symbol of future blessedness.

World War II. It is easier to defend Bahá'í Scripture from the extremes of this methodology, than it is to defend the Bible. Many believing Christian scholars, however, in their eagerness to defend the Bible and to oppose this type of reasoning, tend to reject the merits of other findings made by such academics. Each side may also use labels, such as 'secularist' or 'fundamentalist', to discount the merits of another person's work. In my opinion and experience, truth often seems to lie in between these two extremes. But the search for truth necessitates avoiding the trap of such partisan tendencies, as they only undermine the work and alienate people from each other.

Shoghi Effendi does not give a verse reference for Isaiah's prophecy, but the phrase 'Glory of the LORD' appears 37 times in the Old Testament, including four times in Isaiah:

The excellence of Carmel and Sharon.
They shall see the glory of the LORD,
The excellency of our God. (Isa. 35:2)[35]

The glory of the LORD shall be revealed,
And all flesh shall see it together;
For the mouth of the Lord has spoken. (Isa. 40:5)

Then your light shall break forth like the morning,
Your healing shall spring forth speedily,
And your righteousness shall go before you;
The glory of the LORD shall be your rear guard.
(Isa. 58:8)

Arise, shine;
For your light has come!
And the glory of the LORD is risen upon you.
(Isa. 60:1)

In each case, the Hebrew word translated as 'LORD' is 'Yahweh', the Hebrew name of God, and some modern translations, such as the *Jerusalem Bible*, translate the phrase as 'the glory of Yahweh'. It can also be rendered 'the glory of Jehovah'.

In the first verse (Isa. 35:2), reference is made to the future glory of Carmel and Sharon. Carmel is a mountain in Israel that Bahá'u'lláh visited and where the Shrine of the Báb is located. Sharon is a coastal plain directly to the south of Mount

---

35. Notice the personification of nature in the preceding verse (Isa. 35:1). Personification is a type of literary expression common to the Book of Isaiah (see Isa. 33:9, 44:23, 55:12) and there are similar parallels in Bahá'u'lláh's writings (for example, *Tablets of Bahá'u'lláh* 14–15). 'Abdu'l-Bahá mentions Isaiah 55:12 in the context of messianic prophecies applicable to Jesus (see *Promulgation* 246).

Carmel. Shoghi Effendi refers to Mount Carmel as ' "the Hill of God and His Vineyard", the home of Elijah, extolled by Isaiah as the "mountain of the Lord" to which "all nations shall flow" ' (God Passes By 194). Here, Shoghi Effendi is referring to passages from Isaiah 2:2 which are repeated in the Book of Micah 4:1–2.

Bahá'u'lláh quotes Amos 1:2, and explains the meaning of Carmel:

> Amos saith: 'The Lord will roar from Zion, and utter His Voice from Jerusalem; and the habitations of the shepherds shall mourn, and the top of Carmel shall wither'. Carmel, in the Book of God, hath been designated as the Hill of God, and His Vineyard. It is here that, by the grace of the Lord of Revelation, the *Tabernacle of Glory* hath been raised. Happy are they that attain there unto; happy they that set their faces towards it. (*Epistle* 145, emphasis added)

Bahá'u'lláh also applies the verses Isaiah 35:1–2 to His Revelation in *Epistle to the Son of the Wolf* 146.

In the above passage Bahá'u'lláh refers to the raising of the 'Tabernacle of Glory'. As explained in Chapter 2, the glory of God always signified God's presence, and this was especially true with regard to the Tabernacle (Exod. 40:34). The Tabernacle was a tent-like structure, carried by the Israelites wherever they went. It was only later that it was superseded by a permanent building, the Temple constructed in Jerusalem. Bahá'u'lláh fulfilled the prophecy both spiritually (simply because of Who He was) and literally, by the fact that He pitched His tent on the slopes of Mount Carmel (*God Passes By* 194).[36]

---

36. See *Epistle* 144–6. Bahá'u'lláh's references to Isaiah's prophecy about the Mountain of God, and in particular, Isaiah's prophecies concerning Carmel and Sharon, which He says 'stand in need of no commentary', appear to be left open to literal interpretation. It is literally true that, as Isaiah prophesied (Isa. 35:1),

Concerning Isaiah 40:5, some Christians believe Isaiah's reference to the 'Glory of the LORD' refers to the first advent of Christ because the preceding verse (3) says 'The voice of one crying in the wilderness'. This is recognized as a reference to John the Baptist because it is quoted as such in the Gospel of Matthew 3:3. However, Bahá'u'lláh also quotes Isaiah 40:9 as a reference to His Revelation (*Epistle* 144–5). This may suggest that *the voice of one crying in the wilderness* (Isa. 40:3) also refers to the Báb, the Herald of Bahá'u'lláh, as suggested by Bahá'u'lláh when He referred to the Báb as 'the Crier, calling aloud in the wilderness of the Bayán' (*Tablets of Bahá'u'lláh* 12). Many Christian commentators, emphasizing the words 'all flesh shall see it together' (Isa. 40:5), also believe the second advent is intended. This phrase from Isaiah is associated with Revelation 1:7, 'Behold, He is coming with clouds, and every eye will see Him', which is commonly understood as a prophecy concerning the second advent, and which has been discussed previously on page 122.

Some Christian scholars also express the view that these passages from Isaiah (40:3–5) refer to both advents of Christ. They point out that it is typical of Old Testament prophecies to blend prophecies of Christ's first and second advents. Isaiah 40:3 refers to John the Baptist and can therefore be related to the first advent of Christ, while they argue that verses 4 and 5 refer to the second advent of Christ. These verses, they say, were not completely fulfilled in the first advent.

In Isaiah 58:8 there is a general assurance of God's protection of Israel if the Israelites live righteously. It can be seen in a

---

Carmel (i.e. Mount Carmel) and Sharon (i.e. the plain south of Carmel) saw the glory of God (Bahá'u'lláh). However, the meaning of the Hebrew words 'Carmel' (lit: *fruitful place, vineyard of God*) and 'Sharon' (lit: *level place*) suggests that actual fulfilment of the prophecies could have taken place through the Revelation of God in every age and continues to take place as the hearts of the believers respond to the Revelation. Although the literal interpretation of Isaiah's prophecy is true, it seems also to have an inner meaning not limited to one geographical location, a meaning eternally present in the relationship between the individual believer and the Revelation of God.

messianic sense, but the message is much broader and more applicable to the time of Isaiah. The assurance, however, does seem to include a promise of the restoration of Jerusalem (58:12). Chapter 58, as a whole, forms a powerful discourse on true fasting.

The final passage, Isaiah 60:1, is clearly about the future glory of Zion and has a messianic message. It speaks of the restoration of Israel (60:21), a time of peace and secure borders (60:18), and the continual light of divine guidance (60:19–20, cf. Rev. 21:23). The full implications of this chapter of Isaiah have not yet been seen, but the signs of the fulfilment of these verses are evident even today.

THE GLORY OF THE GOD OF ISRAEL
Shoghi Effendi explains that the Book of Ezekiel is referring to 'Akká when prophesying about the 'gate' that 'looketh towards the East' (*God Passes By* 184) and further states that it is to Bahá'u'lláh that Ezekiel alludes in the next verse: 'The glory of the God of Israel came from the way of the east' (*God Passes By* 184). Together, these comments indicate that Shoghi Effendi is referring to this passage:

> Afterward he [the angel] brought me [Ezekiel] to the gate, the gate that faces toward the east. And behold, the glory of the God of Israel came from the way of the east. His voice was like the sound of many waters; and the earth shone with His glory. (Ezek. 43:1–2)

The Book of Ezekiel follows a well-structured outline containing a series of overviews of the history of Israel, its response to God and its failures, and the causes of exile in Babylon. Progressively, the text moves towards the restoration of Israel, the return to the promised land, the restoration of a united kingdom, the reign of David and the rebuilding of a new Temple in Jerusalem. The Temple would, of course, be meaningless if God's presence did not return to it as in former times, so much of the messianic content of Ezekiel's vision is concerned with the coming of *the glory of the Lord* to the new Temple. This glory signifies Bahá'u'lláh.

According to the vision, the glory of the Lord (Bahá'u'lláh) enters by way of the 'gate', signifying the fortress city of 'Akká, Israel. A 'gate' is an entrance and can signify both a way for entering a place and, metaphorically, a way for entering into a new understanding or awareness. The suffering of Bahá'u'lláh at 'Akká (a literal place) helped make apparent to the world His true greatness. 'Akká was, in the days of Bahá'u'lláh, a penal colony of the Turkish Empire, and He was sent there in the hope that there He would die and be forgotten. Shoghi Effendi writes: 'The arrival of Bahá'u'lláh in 'Akká marks the opening of the last phase of His forty-year long ministry, the final stage, and indeed the climax, of the banishment in which the whole of that ministry was spent' (*God Passes By* 183). Of 'Akká, Bahá'u'lláh writes:

> Lend an ear unto the song of David. He saith: 'Who will bring me into the Strong City?' The Strong City is 'Akká, which hath been named the Most Great Prison, and which possesseth a fortress and mighty ramparts. (*Epistle* 144)

Here Bahá'u'lláh quotes Psalms 60:9. The Guardian states that 'a door of hope' (Hos. 2:15) also refers to 'Akká (*God Passes By* 184; see also *Selections from the Writings of 'Abdu'l-Bahá* 162).[37]

Christian scholars do not identify the phrase 'the glory of the God of Israel' as a title of Christ, but many see the verse as

---

37. David's reference to the Strong City, can also be understood as the City of God that Bahá'u'lláh refers to in *The Book of Certitude* (196, 199), thus giving it a meaning that goes beyond any limited geographical contexts. Similarly 'Akká can be equated with the Biblical Achor of Hosea's prophecy (*God Passes By* 184) owing to Achor's original meaning – the Valley of Achor literally means *valley of trouble*. Thus, 'Akká can be the 'door of hope' (Hos. 2:15) without any strict geographical parallelism because 'Akká has a parallel *significance* to Achor in that it is the place

messianic. Some associate this passage with Jesus' second advent, while others believe it concerns the first. They believe the passage refers to Jesus for the same reason one can argue that it refers to Bahá'u'lláh – because in the Bible the 'glory' of God represents the presence of God and the Manifestation is the presence of God.

The phrase 'the glory of the God of Israel' is unique to the Book of Ezekiel, where it occurs seven times (8:4, 9:3, 10:19, 10:20, 11:22, 43:2, 44:2). The phrase 'God of Israel', however, appears frequently throughout much of the Old Testament. It is simply a way of stressing that the God Who is meant is not one among the pantheon of gods worshipped by other nations, but the one God Who spoke to the prophets of the past, the God Who made covenants with Israel, and Who liberated Israel from bondage. The phrase 'the glory of the God of Israel', therefore, has essentially the same meaning as 'the glory of God', the two phrases being used in the same way for the same reasons, such as indicating the presence of God in the Tabernacle (for example, Exod. 40:34, Rev. 15:8).

THE LORD OF HOSTS AND THE KING OF GLORY

Shoghi Effendi writes: 'Of Him David had sung in his Psalms, acclaiming Him as the "Lord of Hosts" and the "King of Glory"' (*God Passes By* 95; see also 184). The Book of Psalms is a collection of prayers and songs of praise.[38]

---

where humankind 'troubled' (see Josh. 7) God, and consequently 'Akká can be viewed as the door of hope for the redemption of humankind through Bahá'u'lláh. Equally, 'Akká can be viewed metaphorically as the prison within ourselves, wherein every individual has imprisoned Bahá'u'lláh when he or she turns away from God's glory.

38. The *NIV Study Bible*, which provides an excellent introduction to the Psalms, describes some of the literary characteristics of the text: 'The Psalter is from first to last poetry, even though it contains many prayers and not all Old Testament prayers were poetic . . . The Psalms are impassioned, vivid and concrete; they are rich in images, in simile and metaphor. Assonance, alliteration and wordplays abound in the Hebrew text. Effective use of repetition and the piling up of synonyms and compliments to fill out the picture are characteristic. Key words frequently highlight major

> Lift up your heads, O ye gates!
> And lift them up, you everlasting doors!
> And the King of glory shall come in.
> Who is this King of glory
> The LORD of hosts,
> He is the King of glory.
> (Ps. 24:9–10)

In this passage, the greatest Israelite king indicates that the true King of Glory is the Lord. God's glory – meaning His light (knowledge), presence and sovereignty – are, of course, made most visible in the world through the divine Manifestations of God. Bahá'u'lláh writes that they are all 'honoured with the mantle of glory' (*Certitude* 152). For example, Bahá'u'lláh refers to Muḥammad as 'the King of glory' (*Certitude* 26) and again as 'the King of eternal glory' (*Certitude* 136). As God's supreme Manifestation for this age, Bahá'u'lláh is the true King of Glory.

The title 'Lord of Hosts' appears seven times in the Psalms (24:10; 46:7, 11; 48:8; 84:1, 3, 12) and 235 times in the Old Testament. The title 'King of Glory' appears five times in the Book of Psalms, all in Chapter 24, and is here defined as a title of the Lord of Hosts. Neither title appears in the New Testament, even though they are both equally applicable to Christ.

In a sense, Lord means 'ruler', and refers to spiritual power, divine sovereignty and authority (see *Certitude* 133–4, 106–13, for explanations), and the 'hosts' are His army, meaning His followers – earthly and/or heavenly. The title 'Lord of Hosts' is thought to refer traditionally to God's role as leader of the Israelites when they went into battle, the 'hosts' being the armies of Israel (cf. 1 Sam. 4:4, 17:45; 2 Sam. 6:2). Another passage (Judg. 5:20) suggests that the hosts are the

---

themes in prayer and song. Enclosure (repetition of a significant word or phrase at the end that occurs at the beginning) frequently wraps up a composition or a unit within it.' Like many Bahá'í prayers, several of the prayers in the Book of Psalms contain or begin with the phrases 'O God' and 'O Lord my God'.

stars, symbolizing heavenly beings or angels (cf. *Selections from the Writings of 'Abdu'l-Bahá* 241). This second meaning could be symbolic of saintly people in this world and/or beings in another spiritual realm. Perhaps both these ideas are behind the message of later messianic prophecies concerning the 'Lord of Hosts'. In this way, such prophecies anticipated the day when God would once again lead His people to victory.

These two senses are reflected in the way the title is used in Bahá'í writings. Shoghi Effendi, for example, referred to the believers as the 'stalwart warriors', and 'valiant conquerors' for the 'Lord of Hosts' (*Messages to America* 65, 109). In other passages, he spoke of the believers as the 'all-conquering army of the Lord of Hosts' (*Citadel of Faith* 109), the 'slowly yet steadily advancing army of the Lord of Hosts' (*Citadel of Faith* 117), who hold 'aloft the lance of the Word of the Lord of Hosts' (*Messages to the Bahá'í World* 102). With regard to heavenly powers, he wrote:

> The Lord of Hosts, the King of Kings has pledged unfailing aid to every crusader battling for His Cause. Invisible battalions are mustered, rank upon rank, ready to pour forth reinforcements from on high. (*Messages to the Bahá'í World* 44)

The proofs, therefore, as to whether or not Bahá'u'lláh is the Lord of Hosts are His rule, His victories and His 'hosts'. 'Abdu'l-Bahá writes:

> The blessed Person of the Promised One is interpreted in the Holy Book as the Lord of Hosts, i.e., the heavenly armies. By heavenly armies those souls are intended who are entirely freed from the human world, transformed into celestial spirits and have become divine angels . . . Like unto the apostles of Christ, who were filled with Him, these souls also have become filled with His Holiness Bahá'u'lláh, i.e., the

love of Bahá'u'lláh has so mastered every organ, part and limb of their bodies, as to leave no effect by the promptings of the human world.

These souls are the armies of God and the conquerors of the East and the West . . . This is the meaning of the Hosts of God. (*Bahá'í World Faith* 423–4)

Concerning this age, 'Abdu'l-Bahá also states:

What is meant in the prophecies by the 'Lord of Hosts' . . . is the Blessed Perfection (Bahá'u'lláh) and His holiness the Exalted One (the Báb). (Quoted in *World Order of Bahá'u'lláh* 139; see context.)

All Manifestations of God can be identified correctly as the 'Lord of hosts'. In the above passage, 'Abdu'l-Bahá is simply stressing that these titles are applicable to Bahá'u'lláh and the Báb. Some early Bahá'ís may not have appreciated the messianic significance of Bahá'u'lláh and the Báb until such prophetic connections were pointed out. Concerning Christ, 'Abdu'l-Bahá, for example, stated that His 'standard is still waving; His armies are still fighting' (see *Some Answered Questions* 152–3) and again, Christ's:

'power is eternal; His sovereignty will continue forever, while those who opposed Him are sleeping in the dust, their very names unknown, forgotten. The little army of disciples has become a mighty cohort of millions. The Heavenly Host, the Supreme Concourse are His legions; the Word of God is His sword; the power of God is His victory. (*Promulgation of Universal Peace* 5)

Christians attribute these titles (Lord of Hosts and King of Glory) exclusively to Jesus. Psalms 24:10 was traditionally designated by the Church for reading on the Feast of the Ascension, because it was commonly interpreted as a prophecy referring to the ascension of Jesus into the heavenly Jerusalem. However, some Christian scholars dispute this view, asserting that the Psalm refers to the second advent of Christ.

THE EVERLASTING FATHER AND PRINCE OF PEACE
Shoghi Effendi writes that Isaiah had alluded to Bahá'u'lláh as the 'Everlasting Father', the 'Prince of Peace', the 'Wonderful', and the 'Counsellor' who 'shall be established upon the throne of David' (*God Passes By* 94). These words are from Chapter 9 of the Book of Isaiah:

> For unto us a Child is born, Unto us a Son is given;
> And the government will be upon His shoulder
> And His name will be called
> Wonderful, Counsellor, Mighty God, Everlasting
>   Father, Prince of Peace
> Of the increase of His government and peace
> There will be no end,
> Upon the throne of David and over His Kingdom
> To order it and establish it with judgement and justice
> From that time forward, even forever. (Isa. 9:6–7)

'Abdu'l-Bahá writes:

> Rest thou assured that in this era of the spirit, the Kingdom of Peace will raise up its tabernacle on the summits of the world, and the commandments of the Prince of Peace will so dominate the arteries and nerves of every people as to draw into His sheltering shade all the nations on earth. From springs of love and truth and unity will the true Shepherd give His sheep to drink.
>   ... peace must first be established among individuals, until it leadeth in the end to peace among nations. Wherefore, O ye Bahá'ís, strive ye with all your might to create, through the power of the Word of God, genuine love, spiritual communion and durable bonds among

individuals. This is your task. (*Selections from the Writings of 'Abdu'l-Bahá* 246)

Because of the opening words of Isaiah 9:6–7, 'unto us a Child is born, unto us a Son is given', Christians commonly believe this verse refers to the first advent of Christ. By 'Son', Christians believe Isaiah means Jesus, the Son of God.

However, when this verse is viewed from a more literal point of view, other indications suggest it refers to the second advent of Christ, in phrases such as 'the government will be upon His shoulder' and 'of the increase of His government and peace there will be no end'. The references to the 'judgement' and 'Kingdom' also support the interpretation that this verse can mean the second advent. Christ did not establish a literal government during His first advent, and even many Christians generally associate the 'judgement' and 'Kingdom' with the second advent. Bahá'u'lláh, however, brings a special form of divinely instituted government. Also, the peace that Isaiah speaks of and which the world is awaiting was not established in the past but will be established in this age (*Selections from the Writings of 'Abdu'l-Bahá* 246). Thus, the conditions mentioned in Isaiah 9:6–7 are more applicable to the second advent of Christ.

When interpreted spiritually, Isaiah's prophecy is applicable to both Christ and Bahá'u'lláh. Both revealed teachings by which their followers governed their lives. In this way the government is upon the shoulders of Christ, Muhammad, Bahá'u'lláh and all Manifestations of God. 'Abdu'l-Bahá stated, for example, that 'Jesus Christ, single, solitary and alone, accomplished what all the kings of the earth could not have carried out. If all the kingdoms and nations of the world had combined to effect it, they would have failed', (*Promulgation* 250). In another statement He said that with 'His [Jesus'] word' He 'conquered the East and the West', and that 'He sat' upon 'a heavenly throne', an 'Eternal Throne from which' He 'reigns for ever', and that 'His Kingdom is everlasting' (*Paris Talks* 56). 'Abdu'l-Bahá also stated that Jesus' 'throne and Kingdom were established in human hearts, where He reigns with power and authority without end' (*Promulgation* 292). From these statements about Christ, it is possible to get a better idea of how Bahá'u'lláh fulfils prophecy in this age.

Some Christians agree that these verses allude to the second advent, and that Isaiah is referring to both the first and second advents.[39]

Concerning the title 'Everlasting Father', Shoghi Effendi writes that Bahá'u'lláh 'unequivocally admitted and repeatedly announced' that His mission was to be identified with the 'advent of the coming of the Father Himself' (*Promised Day* 45). Bahá'u'lláh writes:

> Say, Lo! The Father is come, and that which ye were promised in the Kingdom is fulfilled! (*Tablets of Bahá'u'lláh* 11)

And again:

> Blessed be the Lord Who is the Father! He, verily, is come unto the nations in His most great majesty. (*Promised Day* 32; see also 33, 103 and *Tablets of Bahá'u'lláh* 14–15.)

This use of the term 'Father' is a way of signifying the nearness of God. In the Old Testament, God is referred to as Father only a few times, but in the New Testament, Jesus refers to God as 'Father' on numerous occasions. Jesus presents Himself as the Son of God (John 3:16, *World Order* 105) and also identifies Himself as the Father (John 14:7–11). Whereas no prophet in

---

39. See, for example, Alfred and John Martin's *Isaiah: The Glory of the Messiah* 107 (1983).

the Old Testament claimed to be the Father, and Jesus only makes the claim in a somewhat veiled way, Bahá'u'lláh proclaims it openly. In this change, a progressive revelation of God's nearness and immanence can be witnessed.

The title 'Prince of Peace' is applied by Shoghi Effendi to both Jesus Christ and Bahá'u'lláh (*Promised Day* 105, 106). All Manifestations are the Prince of Peace, but Shoghi Effendi seems to wish to stress the greater degree of peace that will be achieved in this age – its literal realization through the collective security taught by Bahá'u'lláh and the provisions of the *Kitáb-i-Aqdas* – by stressing that Bahá'u'lláh is the 'true' Prince of Peace (*Promised Day* 106).

The 'Wonderful', and the 'Counsellor' who 'shall be established upon the throne of David' refer to Bahá'u'lláh as the cause of wonder and approval (wonderful), as the One Who gives counsel by which the world's difficulties are solved, and as the One Who represents the archetypal King and Ruler.

THE DESIRE OF ALL NATIONS
Shoghi Effendi writes that Haggai referred to Bahá'u'lláh as the 'Desire of all Nations' (*God Passes By* 95). This title comes from the Book of Haggai, a short text of only two brief chapters, but with a powerful prophetic message. In it, Haggai calls on the people to rebuild the Jerusalem Temple, and in the course of this message, the text becomes increasingly messianic. The Book of Haggai states:

> 'And I will shake all nations, and they shall come to the Desire of All Nations, and I will fill this temple with glory', says the LORD of hosts. (Hag. 2:7)

This title appears in the writings of Bahá'u'lláh. For example, Bahá'u'lláh writes:

> Say: O men! This is a matchless Day. Matchless must, likewise, be the tongue that celebrateth the praise of

the Desire of all nations, and matchless the deed that aspireth to be acceptable in His sight. (*Gleanings* 39)

And in another passage:

Arise, and serve Him Who is the Desire of all nations, Who hath created you through a word from Him, and ordained you to be, for all time, the emblems of His sovereignty. (*Gleanings* 211–12)

The title raises very significant questions. How can the Messiah of the Judaic-Christian tradition be the 'Desire of all Nations'? Other nations have different religions and await different saviours. Buddhists, for instance, await the appearance of Maitreya. If, as Bahá'ís believe, all these messiahs are Manifestations of the same Divine Reality, then all peoples truly desire the same Messiah. Bahá'ís believe Bahá'u'lláh is not only the fulfilment of the Bible and Qur'án but the fulfilment of 'all the Holy Scriptures' (*Promised Day* 76). Therefore, He truly is the Desire of all Nations. Moreover, this prophecy shows that the plan of God has always been to reach out to all nations.

When referring to Haggai 2:7, one should be aware that some Christians believe that the phrase 'Desire of all Nations' is not an accurate translation of the original Hebrew. Hence, many modern translations present a different rendering of the verse. In the *Jerusalem Bible*, for example, the translation is as follows:

I shall shake all the nations, and the treasures of all the nations will flow in, and I shall fill this Temple with glory, says Yahweh Saboath. (Hag. 2:7)[40]

---

40. 'Yahweh Saboath' is a transliteration of the original Hebrew words usually translated as 'LORD of Hosts'.

The phrase 'they shall come to the Desire of all Nations' is here rendered 'the treasures of all nations will flow in'. The *New International Version* renders the same words 'and the desired of all nations will come'. The conservative Christian scholar Robert L. Alden offers this overview of the translation problem.

> Verse 7 is perhaps the most difficult one in the book. KJV's 'the desire of all nations' is beautifully messianic; most of the modern translations do not, however, support it. The problem centers on the words 'the desired . . . will come'. The noun (ḥemdaṯ, 'desired') is singular, and the verb (ba'u, 'will come') is plural . . . Although this fact troubles many commentators, it is well-known that such irregularities are common in Old Testament Hebrew. Perhaps Haggai was thinking of the plural 'nations' and so chose a verb to match it (cf. A. B. Davidson, *Hebrew Syntax* [Edinburgh: T. & T. Clark, 1894], pp. 159–61; GKC, par. 146).

Alden goes on to point out that the King James version is based on a longstanding traditional interpretation that Jewish teachers passed on to the Christians through the early translator and Christian scholar Jerome. He also points out that the reference to 'glory' in verse 2:7 tends to support the traditional understanding that it is a reference to the Messiah. But, interestingly, Alden also finds himself confronted with the question of other religions. He writes,

> The messianic identification of 'the desired of all nations' raises a difficult question: Were the Gentile nations desiring the Messiah? Certainly the Gentiles who received Christ as Savior view him as desirable. Can that, however, be said of them before their salvation? Despite this and other problems, a messianic

view of v. 7 should not be wholly dismissed. NIV[41] has left the question open by not capitalizing the word 'desired' and by not rendering the word as a plural noun. (See *Expositor's Bible Commentary*, vol. 7, 586)

Alden calls attention to several important points. First, the meaning of the original Hebrew is ambiguous, and for this reason it is necessary to attempt an interpretation of the text in order to translate it. Second, Alden raises the question whether non-Jewish nations (the Gentile nations) would really have a desire for the Messiah. This question has already been answered above, and since the answer is affirmative, the divine intention of the verse would seem to favour the traditional interpretation/translation. This is, however, a controversial issue, and is far from being resolved among Bible scholars.

---

41. NIV signifies the *New International Version*.

chapter 16

NEW TESTAMENT PROPHECIES THAT REFER TO BAHÁ'U'LLÁH

Six titles found in the New Testament are examined in this chapter. These titles are not names of a person, but rather signify a type of person (the Manifestation of God) Who was to come in fulfilment of the next stage of God's redemptive plan. This becomes apparent in the way all six of the titles are applicable to other Manifestations of God. As prophecies, they refer to Muhammad, the Báb and Bahá'u'lláh – but in many ways they are especially applicable to Bahá'u'lláh, as will be explained in the following pages.

Of these prophetic titles, most are to be found in writings traditionally attributed to St John (the Gospel of John and the Book of Revelation). One is found in Matthew and Mark, and all are from prophecies attributed to Jesus, with the exception of the last one (the Glory of God) which is from words attributed to St John.

As has been mentioned, there are other passages in the New Testament referring to the return of Christ and the Day of God. St Peter refers to this day in his second epistle, and St Paul frequently mentions the end times. St Peter's and St Paul's apostolic witness to the future coming of Bahá'u'lláh is affirmed by Shoghi Effendi in *God Passes By* (96). Nevertheless, the focus here will be on Jesus' prophecies found in the Gospel and on several important references containing the phrase 'glory of God' recorded in the Book of Revelation, because these, rather than referring to Bahá'u'lláh's advent, contain specific phrases directly relating to the spiritual reality of Bahá'u'lláh.

Most Old Testament prophecies examined in the previous chapters are from prophetic ministries spanning many hundreds of years (c. 750–450 BC) and from many separate books. The prophecies in this chapter were all revealed in a relatively short period of time. If the Book of Revelation is excluded, most of Jesus' prophecies about the future were revealed towards the end of His short three-year ministry, many in the last few days before He was arrested and crucified. These prophetic passages can be found in Matthew 24 and 25; Mark 13; Luke 21; and John 14–16. Each of these chapters in the first three versions of the Gospel (Matthew, Luke and Mark) appear to contain versions of the same sermon, each author recording the same main points and a few separate details or variations not mentioned by the others. This sermon is commonly called Jesus' Olivet Discourse, because in the Gospel according to Matthew it is clear that He was with His disciples on the Mount of Olives (or Olivet) when He was speaking. The prophecies in John 14–16 are worded differently from those of the other Gospels, but the central theme is the same and the context in Jesus' ministry is also essentially the same.

Although most of the prophetic material in the Gospel occurs at the end of Jesus' ministry and appears in a few specific chapters, there are a few notable exceptions (for example, Matt. 16:27 and Mark 8:38) that will also be examined in the following pages. It is also worth keeping in mind that Bahá'u'lláh specifically mentions all four versions of the Gospel when He refers to the truth of the prophetic testimony of Jesus. When Bahá'u'lláh interprets Matthew 24:29–30 in *The Book of Certitude*, He speaks very highly of Jesus' words, prefacing His nearly fifty pages of explanations by saying that He was only sharing 'a dewdrop out of the fathomless ocean of the truths treasured in these holy words' so that 'discerning hearts may comprehend all the allusions and the implications of the utterances of the Manifestations of Holiness' (*Certitude* 28).

The other great repository of prophetic revelation in the New Testament is the vision of St John, known as the Book of

Revelation (the last book of the New Testament). The identity of this 'John' is unclear, but it is traditionally thought to be the Apostle John. 'Abdu'l-Bahá testified that St John's vision was 'real' and produced 'wonderful effects in the minds and thoughts of men', causing 'their hearts to be attracted' (*Some Answered Questions* 253).

THE COMFORTER

Shoghi Effendi writes that Jesus Christ referred to Bahá'u'lláh as the 'Comforter' (*God Passes By* 95). The following verses are from the *New King James Version* of the Bible, as are almost all the Biblical quotations in this book, and consequently there are slight differences in translation from those found in the *King James Version*. The word 'Comforter' has been translated here as 'Helper'. The original Greek word is *paraclete* (or *paraklétos*) and it can mean *intercessor, consoler, advocate, comforter* and *helper*. It appears four times in the Gospel of John, all within the same general context.

> And I will pray the Father, and He will give you another Helper, that He may abide with you forever. (John 14:16)

> These things I have spoken to you while being present with you. But the Helper, the Holy Spirit, whom the Father will send in My name, He will teach you all things, and bring to your remembrance all things that I said to you. (John 14:25–6)

> But when the Helper comes, whom I shall send to you from the Father, the Spirit of truth who proceeds from the Father, He will testify of Me. (John 15:26)

> Nevertheless I tell you the truth. It is to your advantage that I go away; for if I do not go away, the Helper will not come to you; but if I depart, I will send Him to you. (John 16:7)

Bahá'u'lláh testifies to His fulfilment of these verses in the following passage:

> The Comforter Whose advent all the scriptures have promised is now come that He may reveal unto you all knowledge and wisdom. Seek Him over the entire surface of the earth, haply ye may find Him. (*World Order* 104–5)

Christians generally identify the Comforter with the Holy Spirit that guided the Church after the ascension of Christ (Acts 2:33). Therefore, many Christians will have trouble associating these verses with the second advent of Christ (see *Some Answered Questions* 109 and *Promulgation* 41–2). This difficulty also applies to the title 'Spirit of Truth', considered next.

It should be mentioned that these titles are also applicable to Muḥammad. In answer to an inquiry, Shoghi Effendi stated that 'references in the Bible to . . . "Paraclete" refer to Muḥammad's Revelation' (from a letter written on his behalf, *Letters from the Guardian to Australia and New Zealand* 41).

THE SPIRIT OF TRUTH

Shoghi Effendi writes that Jesus Christ referred to Bahá'u'lláh as 'the "Spirit of Truth" Who "will guide you into all truth", Who "shall not speak of Himself, but whatsoever He shall hear, that shall He speak"' (*God Passes By* 95). These passages appear, broadly speaking, in the same context as the references to the Comforter/Helper mentioned above.

> I still have many things to say to you, but you cannot bear them now. However, when He, the Spirit of truth, has come, He will guide you into all truth; for He will not speak on His own authority, but whatever He hears He will speak; and He will tell you things to come. He will glorify Me, for He will take of what is Mine and declare it to you. (John 16:12–14)

Bahá'u'lláh speaks of His fulfilment of these verses in this following passage:

> This is the Word which the Son concealed, when to those around Him He said: 'Ye cannot bear it now'. . . . The Hour which We had concealed from the knowledge of the peoples of the earth and of the favoured angels hath come to pass. Say, verily, He hath testified of Me, and I do testify of Him. (*Tablets of Bahá'u'lláh* 11)

And in the same Tablet Bahá'u'lláh continues:

> Proclaim then unto all mankind the glad-tidings of this mighty, this glorious Revelation. Verily, He Who is the Spirit of Truth is come to guide you unto all truth. He speaketh not as prompted by His own self, but as bidden by Him Who is the All-Knowing, the All-Wise.
>
> Say, this is the One Who hath glorified the Son and hath exalted His Cause. (*Tablets of Bahá'u'lláh* 12)

In another passage (*Certitude* 20–6), Bahá'u'lláh explains that Muḥammad also fulfilled these prophecies in John 14:28 and 16:12–14.

Christians commonly interpret the 'Spirit of truth' (John 16:13) to be the same as the 'Comforter' (John 14:26, *King James Version*; or 'Helper', *New King James Version*). This is also the Bahá'í point of view. However, as mentioned above, Christians believe these terms are not references to the second advent but refer to the holy Spirit (John 14:26) that guides the Church after the ascension of Christ (Acts 2:33). The Bahá'í view is explained by 'Abdu'l-Bahá in the following manner:

> Consider carefully that from these words, 'for He shall not speak of Himself; but whatsoever He shall hear, that shall He speak', it is clear that the Spirit of truth is

embodied in a Man Who has individuality, Who has ears to hear and a tongue to speak. (*Some Answered Questions* 109)

This need not exclude the possibility that the prophecy refers in a lesser way to the miracle of Pentecost (Acts 2:33). Nevertheless, in addition to 'Abdu'l-Bahá's explanation there are several important points supporting the Bahá'í interpretation.

First, these verses are in the context of Christ's departure and return (compare John 13:36, 14:3, 16:5–16; the earlier message of John in 13:36 and 14:3 is similar to 16:16). Towards the end of each of the other Gospels (Matt. 24, Mark 13 and Luke 21), Jesus delivers a sermon about His return. This sermon was given just before Jesus predicted that St Peter would deny Him and before Jesus was arrested in the garden of Gethsemane. In the Gospel of John, this sermon is missing. The traditional Christian interpretation of the meaning of 'Paraclete' therefore suggests that St John omits this important message altogether in his version of the Gospel. This seems unlikely. All the references to the coming Spirit of Truth and the Paraclete occur in the Gospel of John towards the very end of Jesus' ministry – just after Jesus predicted St Peter's denial and just before He was arrested. This suggests that Jesus continued to discuss this theme after the sermon recorded in the other Gospels, and that St John included it appropriately. In other words, it is apparent from the chronological structure of the Gospels that Jesus was talking about His return at this time, and it is likely that the messages contained in chapters 14–16 of the Gospel of John belong to this theme and were included by John in order to address it.

Second, some Christian interpreters have argued that the Book of Acts is referring to the message in John's Gospel when it speaks of the coming of the Holy Spirit upon the Apostles. It is, however, widely accepted by many scholars, both conservative Christians and non-Christian academics, that the Book of Acts is the second half of the Gospel of

Luke. The reasons for this view are numerous, but a simple comparison of the opening verses of both books and the last chapter of Luke is sufficient to convince most readers. If this view is correct, then it seems likely that the author of Luke would have intended the reference to the Holy Spirit in Acts to be understood in the light of references to the Holy Spirit made in his earlier work, the Gospel according to Luke, rather than the Gospel of John.

THE PRINCE OF THIS WORLD
Shoghi Effendi writes that Jesus Christ referred to Bahá'u'lláh as the 'Prince of this World' (God Passes By 95). The following verse, which is from the New King James Version, uses the word 'Ruler' instead of 'Prince':

> I will no longer talk much with you, for the ruler of this world is coming, and he has nothing in Me. (John 14:30)

'Abdu'l-Bahá explains this verse in the following manner:

> Thou didst ask as to chapter 14, verse 30 of the Gospel of John, where the Lord Christ saith, 'Hereafter I will not talk much with you: for the Prince of this world cometh, and hath nothing in Me'. The Prince of this world is the Blessed Beauty; and 'hath nothing in Me' signifieth: after Me all will draw grace from Me, but He is independent of Me, and will draw no grace from Me. That is, He is rich beyond any grace of Mine. (Selections from the Writings of 'Abdu'l-Bahá 170)

By 'Blessed Beauty' 'Abdu'l-Bahá means Bahá'u'lláh. Bahá'u'lláh applies the title 'Prince of the World' to Himself (Epistle 130) and also to the Báb (Epistle 120).

This title is a particularly controversial one to mention in discussions with Christians. Some Christians believe it is a reference to Satan, whom they assert is the ruler of this world.[42] Christians cite John 12:31 and 16:11 to support this view:

> Now is the Judgement of this world; now the ruler of this world will be cast out. (John 12:31)

> . . . of judgement, because the ruler of this world is judged. (John 16:11)

The Christian view of Satan facilitates the assumption that John intends Satan with the phrase 'ruler of this world', and any discussion about this subject may well lead to a lengthy consideration of such issues as the 'fall of man', the nature of sin, and the substitutionary atonement. It is important to keep in mind that taking up such complex issues might prove a nearly interminable diversion from the discussion of prophecies related to Bahá'u'lláh. Yet, if the issue should come up, and it is not addressed, it may leave the listener with many unresolved doubts.

In general, it is best not to bring up this prophecy until a time when the listener is acquainted with the many other prophecies fulfilled by Bahá'u'lláh and the proofs that establish His station and true nature. This is an example of how prior knowledge of Christian views can help one avoid bringing up a subject in which differences of opinion may hopelessly sidetrack the discussion. But if someone who is aware of the Bahá'í interpretation of John 14:30 brings up the matter, it is important to be ready to explore the question. The following four observations will help support the Bahá'í point of view:

---

42. For a scholarly treatment of how this interpretation may have originated, see A.F. Segal's 'Ruler of this World: Attitudes about Mediator Figures and the Importance of Sociology for Self-Definition' (E. P. Sanders, et al., *Jewish and Christian Self-Definition*, vol. 2, 245–68). Segal offers reasons why this Christian interpretation of 'Ruler of this World' came to be written into the Gospel. Without assuming that it was *written into* the Gospel, it is easy to see these as reasons why it came to be the accepted Christian interpretation of the text.

1. The verse itself does not offer an interpretation of the title 'ruler of the world', therefore the assumption that it refers to Satan is only based upon interpretation.

2. The verse does not use the word Satan, nor is the title 'ruler of this world' associated elsewhere in the Bible with Satan. Therefore what is inferred from the meaning of the verse is not based on a strong or clear Biblical association of the terms.

3. The words 'Prince' and 'Ruler' are both used in reference to Jesus Christ (Isa. 9:6, Mic. 5:2, Acts 3:15) and therefore do not in themselves identify or refer to Satan.

4. It cannot be said that the phrase 'of the world' offers a conclusive reference to Satan since the world is not the exclusive dominion of Satan. As David states, 'For all that is in heaven and earth is Yours; Yours is the Kingdom, O LORD' (1 Chr. 29:11). It is God Who is the ultimate Ruler of the World.

These observations show that there is no conclusive evidence that this passage refers to Satan. According to the three verses in John cited above, the Ruler of this World 'is coming', has 'nothing in' Jesus, 'will be cast out', and is 'judged'. With regard to the first of these, it is evident that Satan is not coming, but is, so to speak, already in the world. And even though it can be said that Jesus' presence is also always in the world, Christ unmistakably prophesied that He would return. It follows that the Ruler is One Who is to go away and to come back, and this of course refers to the going of Jesus and His later return. 'The ruler of this world is coming' can therefore mean that Christ is coming (Rev. 1:7) and will reign for a thousand years (Rev. 20:4).

'Hath nothing in Me', as interpreted above by 'Abdu'l-Bahá, is Christ's indication that His return will be that of an independent Manifestation of God separate from His first ministry in the person of Christ, even as John the Baptist was the return of Elijah yet was also completely independent and preached a message appropriate for heralding Christ.

'Cast out' and 'judged' can be interpreted as allusions to the rejection of Bahá'u'lláh and His consignment to prison. Thus, the words *Ruler*, or *Prince*, and *world*, as well as the context and other prophetic verses, must all be considered carefully in forming an interpretation.

THE SON OF MAN
Shoghi Effendi writes that Jesus Christ refers to Bahá'u'lláh as 'the "Son of Man" Who "shall come in the glory of His Father" . . . "in the clouds of heaven with power and great glory", with "all the holy angels" about Him, and "all nations" gathered before His throne' (*God Passes By* 95). These references to the prophecies of Jesus seem to be a composite of three verses from the Gospel of Matthew, and possibly one from the Gospel of Mark. There are other similar verses, but these are the ones with virtually the same wording:

> For the Son of Man will come in the glory of His Father with His angels, and then He will reward each according to his works. (Matt. 16:27)

> Then the sign of the Son of Man will appear in heaven, and then all the tribes of the earth will mourn, and they will see the Son of Man coming on the clouds of heaven with power and great glory. (Matt. 24:30)

> When the Son of Man comes in His glory, and all the holy angels with Him, then He will sit on the throne of His glory. All the nations will be gathered before Him, and He will separate them one from another, as a shepherd divides his sheep from the goats. (Matt. 25:31–2)

> For whoever is ashamed of Me and My words in this adulterous and sinful generation, of him the Son of Man also will be ashamed when He comes in the glory of His Father with the holy angels. (Mark 8:38)

Although Bahá'u'lláh does not appear to use the title 'Son of Man' directly for Himself, He does indicate that it is applicable to Him by way of alluding to the prophecies containing this title. Bahá'u'lláh indicates the fulfilment of the above verses in many of His Tablets, such as in this very poetic passage:

> He Who is the Father is come, and the Son (Jesus Christ), in the holy vale, crieth out: 'Here am I, here am I, O Lord, my God!', whilst Sinai circleth round the House, and the Burning Bush calleth aloud: 'The All-Bounteous is come mounted upon the clouds! Blessed is he that draweth nigh unto Him, and woe betide them that are far away'. (*Epistle* 57)

It should again be kept in mind that Bahá'u'lláh applies this title in its messianic sense to Muhammad (*Certitude* 24ff.). In other passages He uses it to refer to Jesus Christ (*Gleanings* 85; *Certitude* 133, 134) and, in a non-messianic sense, He frequently uses it to address the peoples of the world individually (most notably in *The Hidden Words*). Some scholars suggest that Jesus used this title frequently to emphasize His humanity, while the title 'Son of God' indicated His divinity. The symbolism of the Messiah appearing in the heavens, the stars falling, and so on, may be intended to emphasize that God is intervening in history (the divine aspect of the new Revelation), whereas the use of the title 'Son of Man' in that same context may be meant to stress that this divine intervention is through a fully human individual (the Manifestation of God). When Bahá'u'lláh uses the expression in *The Hidden Words* to refer to individuals, it seems that it is not intended to be gender specific, but rather to stress each individual's humanity.

The title 'Son of Man' appears 81 times in the Gospel, but it is always used by Jesus to refer to Himself or His future advent rather than by others to refer to Him. In the Old Testament, the phrase is used frequently in the Book of Ezekiel to refer to the prophet Ezekiel, and in the Book of Daniel to refer to Daniel and to the future Messiah. Daniel's messianic use of the phrase (Dan. 7:13) is very similar to Jesus' use of it to refer to His return.

> I was watching in the night visions,
> And behold, One like the Son of Man,
> Coming in the clouds of heaven! (Dan. 7:13)

Two similar messianic references occur in the Book of Revelation (1:13 and 14:14). The visionary connection between the appearance of the Son of Man and the clouds of heaven also occurs in the last words of St Stephen before his martyrdom (Acts 7:56). From these observations, it seems that the title is frequently used to refer to living individuals – Ezekiel, Daniel and Jesus – and when it is used in a messianic context it appears among those Scriptures characterized by a high degree of symbolism (such as the Books of Ezekiel, Daniel and Revelation, and Jesus' Olivet Discourse – Matthew 24).

ALPHA AND OMEGA

Shoghi Effendi writes that in the Book of Revelation, the phrases 'Alpha and Omega', 'the Beginning and the End', and 'the First and the Last' allude to Bahá'u'lláh (*God Passes By* 95). These three phrases appear in part or in whole in four different passages, depending on the manuscript used. The documentary evidence for the New Testament is extremely good and there is an abundance of manuscript evidence supporting editions of the text available today. Nevertheless, some ancient copies of the Book of Revelation from which modern editions are derived, contain slight variations. These variations affect the passages using the phrases cited above by Shoghi Effendi. A comparison between the *New King James Version* and the *New International Version* will show the differences.

The following list of verses is taken from the *New King James Version*, and the parts in square brackets are missing from some ancient manuscripts.

> I am the Alpha and the Omega, [the Beginning and the End.] (Rev. 1:8)

> [I am the Alpha and the Omega, the First and the Last.] (Rev. 1:11)

> I am the Alpha and the Omega, the Beginning and the End. (Rev. 21:6)

> I am the Alpha and the Omega, the Beginning and the End, the First and the Last. (Rev. 22:13)

The fourth passage is the one that contains all the phrases mentioned by Shoghi Effendi. This appears to be the one he is referring to, and all the most reliable ancient manuscripts contain the whole of this passage.[43]

The context suggests that the first two passages represent the words of Jesus (Rev. 1:8, 1:11). The third passage is the words of either Jesus or God (Rev. 21:6) and the fourth passage relates to the returned Christ, which now, of course, signifies Bahá'u'lláh. The spiritual reality of all these speakers is one, and such distinctions are therefore only apparent in terms of this world – otherwise all can refer to both Jesus and Bahá'u'lláh as one reality. Nevertheless, Shoghi Effendi's interpretation means that

---

43. Since the three phrases mean the same thing, it is of no real consequence that an important ancient manuscript omits the words 'the Beginning and the End' in verse 1:8. The omission of the whole passage (verse 1:11) is, likewise, of no real consequence since the context already makes it apparent that the speaker is the same as the one identified in verse 1:8.

the risen Christ Who speaks to St John in the vision should be identified as a prophetic allusion to Bahá'u'lláh.

Alpha is the first letter of the Greek alphabet, and Omega is the last. Alpha and Omega therefore suggest the all-encompassing nature of the Manifestation's divinity (both Christ and Bahá'u'lláh) and reinforce the idea of the beginning and the end, which signifies His eternity. In *The Book of Certitude* Bahá'u'lláh explains that the terms 'first' and 'last' refer to all the Manifestations of God (161–4). 'Abdu'l-Bahá specifically refers to Revelation 1:11 when explaining the nature of the Manifestation of God. He states:

> Their heavenly condition embraces all things, knows all mysteries, discovers all signs, and rules over all things; before as well as after Their mission, it is the same. That is why Christ has said: 'I am Alpha and Omega, the first and the last': that is to say, there has never been and never shall be any change and alteration in Me. (*Some Answered Questions* 218–19)

In another connection 'Abdu'l-Bahá refers to the verse in this manner:

> The Creator of all is One God.
> From this same God all creation sprang into existence, and He is the one goal, towards which everything in nature yearns. This conception was embodied in the words of Christ, when He said, 'I am the Alpha and the Omega, the beginning and the end'. (*Paris Talks* 51)

And in another passage 'Abdu'l-Bahá indicates that the author of Revelation is referring to Bahá'u'lláh:

> What truth can be greater than that announced by the Revelation of St John the Divine?

He is Alpha and Omega. He is the One that will give unto him that is athirst of the fountain of the water of life and bestow upon the sick the remedy of true salvation. (*Selections from the Writings of 'Abdu'l-Bahá* 12–13)

THE GLORY OF GOD
Shoghi Effendi writes that 'the Author of the Apocalypse had alluded to' Bahá'u'lláh 'as the "Glory of God" ' (*God Passes By* 95). The 'Apocalypse' is a term sometimes used to indicate the Book of Revelation, as explained previously on page 123–4. Traditionally, this book is ascribed to St John (Rev. 1:1) and accepted as a revelation or vision that came to John enabling him to foretell things, and in some parts containing words attributed to Jesus. Unlike the references to 'Alpha and Omega' that are attributed to the Manifestation of God in the vision, the references to the Glory of God are attributed to St John himself.

The term or title 'Glory of God' appears three times in the Book of Revelation: 15:8, 21:11 and 23. Shoghi Effendi does not state in *God Passes By* whether one or all three of these references allude to Bahá'u'lláh. The verses are:

> The temple was filled with smoke from the glory of God and from His power, and no one was able to enter the temple till the seven plagues of the seven angels were completed. (Rev. 15:8)

> And he carried me away in the Spirit to a great and high mountain, and showed me the great city, the holy Jerusalem, descending out of heaven from God, having the glory of God. And her light was like a most precious stone, like a jasper stone, clear as crystal. (Rev. 21:10–11)

> And the city had no need of the sun or of the moon to shine in it, for the glory of God illuminated it, and the Lamb is its light. (Rev. 21:23)

Each verse refers to the light, presence and triumph of God, which become manifest through the appearance of Bahá'u'lláh. The 'glory' is mentioned specifically to indicate the presence of God. The context of Revelation 21:23 makes it clear that it is applicable to Bahá'u'lláh.

In verse 15:8, the 'glory of God' signifies the presence of God in the Temple (cf. Exod. 40:34; 1 Kgs. 8:10–11). The context of the verse suggests that with the return of God's presence, there will be judgement. In the most general sense, chapter 15 of Revelation conveys an assurance of the victory of the returned Christ over the forces of evil. Christian commentators associate the 'glory of God' with the returned Christ, not as a name, but as Christ signifying and revealing the presence of God's glory. Although 'Bahá'u'lláh' means 'Glory of God', the meaning of this verse makes it applicable to Bahá'u'lláh even if He were to have a different title.

Chapter 21 is a description of the triumphant Millennial Kingdom established by the returned Christ. Again, these verses use the phrase 'glory of God' to refer to the presence of God, which here signifies the fulfilment of God's promise to redeem humankind and to establish His reign on earth. 'Abdu'l-Bahá provides interpretations to parts of Revelation 21 in *Some Answered Questions*, Chapter 13.[44]

Before discussing verses such as these with Christians, it is important to become acquainted with the Book of Revelation and to gain an understanding of its overall outline, its central themes, and some of the general beliefs held by Christians. This may seem an immensely difficult task given the highly symbolic nature of this ancient book, but much can be grasped by simply consulting a Bible dictionary and other reference works. When a general knowledge has been gained, a deeper understanding will come with time. An awareness of the context of a given passage will make it easier to explain, and

---

44. See also *Selections from the Writings of 'Abdu'l-Bahá* 12–13.

almost all of the symbols in the Book of Revelation can be found in earlier books of the Old Testament, particularly Daniel, Ezekiel and Isaiah.

BIBLICAL REFERENCES FOR CHAPTERS 15 AND 16
The verses in these two chapters can be listed under the following headings:

1. Glory of the Lord: Isa. 35:2, 40:5, 60:1
2. Glory of the God of Israel: Ezek. 43:1–2
3. King of Glory, Lord of Hosts: Ps. 24:10
4. Everlasting Father, Prince of Peace: Isa. 9:6–7
5. Desire of All Nations: Hag. 2:7
6. Comforter (or Helper in NKJV): John 14:16, 26; 15:26; 16:7
7. Spirit of Truth: John 16:12–14
8. Son of Man: Matt. 16:27, 24:30, 26:64, 25:31–2; Mark 8:38
9. Prince of this world (Ruler of this world in NKJV): John 14:30
10. Alpha and Omega: Rev. 1:11, 22:13
11. Glory of God: Rev. 15:8, 21:10–11, 21:23

chapter 17

PROPHECIES CONCERNING THE 'MOST GREAT NAME'

Although prophecy does not constitute a conclusive proof, as pointed out in Chapter 4, it does support certain characteristics of Bahá'u'lláh's Revelation. For example, some Christians find it difficult to accept the Bahá'í administrative order, the fact that Bahá'u'lláh has brought new teachings, and that Bahá'u'lláh has a name that is different from the name 'Christ'. It becomes easier for Christians to accept such aspects of the Bahá'í Faith if it can be demonstrated that these things were prophesied in the Bible.

For example, someone may say, 'I can see the greatness of Bahá'u'lláh, and I am willing to acknowledge that He is a Messenger of God. But how can I accept Him as the One foretold in the Bible if He teaches things that are in addition to the message of the New Testament?' In response to such a question reference can be made to the prophecy in the Book of Revelation (Chapter 21) indicating that all things will be made new. This suggests there will be new teachings that were not revealed in former times. Reference could also be made to the verse in Isaiah that states: 'He will teach us His ways' (Isa. 2:3). This suggests additional Revelation from Christ at the time of the second advent.

These examples suggest how prophecy can be used to show that the characteristics of the Bahá'í Faith are part of God's plan as foretold in Scripture. In this respect prophecy is especially valuable.

In this chapter Biblical prophecies relating to Bahá'u'lláh's new name are examined. Many Christians expect that Christ will return with the same name, and they therefore object to the name 'Bahá'u'lláh'. This is a common Christian objection addressed by Bahá'u'lláh in His 'Tablet to the Christians', the Lawh-i-Aqdas:

> Say, O followers of the Son! Have ye shut out yourselves from Me by reason of My Name? Wherefore ponder ye not in your hearts? Day and night ye have been calling upon your Lord, the Omnipotent, but when He came from the heaven of eternity in His great glory, ye turned aside from Him . . . (see Tablets of Bahá'u'lláh 9)

Whenever a Christian objects to some aspect of the Bahá'í Faith, there is usually a reason originating from some understanding of a particular Biblical verse or Christian tradition. Before examining prophecies referring to Bahá'u'lláh's new name, it is therefore important to consider why Christians often object to the name 'Bahá'u'lláh'. The most common objections can be categorized simply as:

1. the 'No Other Name Under Heaven Argument', and
2. the 'Same Name Argument'.

THE 'NO OTHER NAME UNDER HEAVEN' ARGUMENT

Many Christians believe that when Jesus Christ returns He will still be identified by the same name. To support this belief some Christians will cite the following verse, which they believe excludes the association of salvation with any name other than the specific 'Jesus Christ'.

> Nor is there salvation in any other, for there is no other name under heaven given among men by which we must be saved. (Acts 4:12)

Because of the way this verse is interpreted, the name 'Bahá'u'lláh' is a stumbling block for some Christians.

THE 'SAME NAME' ARGUMENT
Some Christians believe the following verse indicates Jesus' name will never change:

> Jesus Christ is the same yesterday, today, and forever. (Heb. 13:8)

This problem is really not very difficult to resolve. The verse must signify Christ's spiritual nature, because Jesus could not have grown from childhood to adulthood if He never changed in any way. From a Bahá'í point of view, this passage refers to Jesus' eternal Lordship and spiritual nature, and with regard to this, as 'Abdu'l-Bahá writes, 'The reality of Christ is ever-living, everlasting, eternal' (*Promulgation* 395).

There are many things that could be said about the theological significance of the divine name. But for the purposes of this book, there are four primary observations to be considered:

1. The meaning of the word 'name' in the Bible, and specifically, in such verses as Acts 4:12. And the spiritual meanings of the names 'Jesus' and 'Bahá'u'lláh'.
2. Jesus has more than one name.
3. A prophet can return yet have a different name.
4. The Bible specifically states Jesus will have a new name.

THE MEANING OF 'NAME' IN THE BIBLE AND THE MEANING OF THE NAMES 'JESUS CHRIST' AND 'BAHÁ'U'LLÁH'
In the Biblical context, a 'name' was not a mere label as it so often is today – that is, it did not only distinguish one person from another. Names in the Bible signify something about a

person or an event associated with that person, and are descriptive of some event or characteristic.

In many cases, it is not possible to know the significance of a name without studying the original language. For example, Christian scholars accept that the Hebrew name *Ezekiel* means 'May God Strengthen', *Isaiah* means 'May Yah[weh] save', *Elijah* 'Yeh[weh] is [my] God', and *Daniel* means 'God is my judge'. But it is not always easy to learn the meaning of a name because the Bible does not always clearly spell out what each name means. However, there are certain accounts recorded in the Bible of persons receiving their names, and these provide examples that indicate how names functioned in ancient times.

Abraham was called originally 'Abram', but, according to Scripture, God changed this name, saying,

> No longer shall your name be called Abram, but your name shall be Abraham; for I have made you a father of many nations (Gen. 17:5)

The direct Hebrew meaning of the name is uncertain, but from this passage, it is clear that the name is intended to signify that He was 'father of many nations'. Were it not prophesied that Abram would be the father of many nations God would not have given this name; Abram's destiny and the new name were linked together – the name expressed what Abram was to be.

Similarly, the Scriptures record how Moses came to be so called. He was named by the Pharaoh's daughter:

> She called his name Moses, saying, 'Because I drew him out of the water' (Exod. 2:10)

Many editions of the Bible, such as some editions of the *New King James Version*, have a footnote with this passage saying that the name literally means 'drawn out'. In other words, the child was called 'drawn out' because He was drawn out of the water. His name signified what had happened to him.

Another example can be seen in the naming of Samuel.

> Hannah [the mother of Samuel] conceived and bore a son, and called his name Samuel, saying, 'Because I have asked [prayed] for him from the Lord'. (1 Sam. 1:20)

Again, the *New King James Version* includes a footnote for this verse, saying the name Samuel means 'Heard by God'.

With regard to Jesus Christ, the Gospel of Matthew states that an angel appeared to Joseph in a dream, saying that Mary was to have a Son:

> She will bring forth a Son, and you shall call His name Jesus, for He will save His people from their sins. (Matt. 1:21)

This passage indicates that He was called Jesus *because* He will 'save His people from their sins', and that this is the meaning of the name 'Jesus'. The name 'Jesus' is from the Greek version of the Hebrew name *Joshua*,[45] which means 'God is salvation'. The connection can, therefore, be observed between the name *Jesus* and the statement that He was given this name because 'He will save His people from their sins'.

The second portion of His name, 'Christ', simply means 'anointed' and is derived from the Greek equivalent of the Hebrew *Messiah* (see p. 20 above). To say that Jesus of Nazareth was the Christ is the same as saying He is the anointed of God, the Messiah, the divine King, the Lord who saves. When Jesus claimed that God had 'anointed' Him 'to preach the gospel to the poor' (see Luke 4:18), he was saying that God had conferred divine authority on Him, that He was the Messiah (or Christ), the King foretold in the Scriptures (see Isa. 61:1–2). It is from this verse in Isaiah that Jesus took His title the 'Christ'. These

---

45. See *Bible Dictionary* 621.

facts are well-known to many Christians, and they can be demonstrated by reference to respected Christian commentaries, dictionaries and Bible study guides.

In the same way, the name 'Bahá'u'lláh' is a title which, when translated from Arabic into English, is rendered 'Glory of God'. The Arabic name 'Bahá'u'lláh' is not found in English translations of the Bible, but rather the words 'Glory of God' or 'glory of the Lord'. Similarly, if you were looking for the Greek name *Jesus Christ*, you would not find it in the Old Testament. What you would find are prophecies concerning the 'Messiah', for example, in Psalms 2:2.

It is clear that when St Peter speaks of 'no other name', he is talking about the person Jesus Christ; not just the name, but the reality of salvation and divine Lordship that Jesus Christ represents, and this is evident from the fact that St Peter does not specify a particular name. When St Peter says that there is no other name under heaven by which people are saved, it is the same as saying that Jesus is the One Who represents God, and that there is no other God by which people are saved. From this point of view, it does not matter whether Jesus is called by another name or returns with a different name.

JESUS HAD MANY NAMES

It is also worth noting that Jesus had other names signifying Who He was. The Book of Isaiah, for example, states:

> For unto us a Child is born, Unto us a Son is given; And the government will be upon His shoulder. And His name will be called Wonderful, Counsellor, Mighty God, Everlasting Father, Prince of Peace. (Isa. 9:6)

This passage, whether it is understood as referring to the first or second advent of Christ, gives many names that are applicable to Him. If 'there is no other name under heaven given among men by which we must be saved' (Acts 4:12), then the question could be asked: Which name, since Jesus has many names? This question is not meaningful because this simply is not how the term *name* is used in the Biblical context, as this verse from Isaiah makes apparent.

Each name mentioned in this verse expresses some characteristic of Christ. For instance, 'Mighty God' expresses Christ's divinity, and 'Prince of Peace' expresses His unifying effect. In that Jesus represented the presence of God among us, He was the 'Father', as He indicated to Philip (see John 14:8–11). If Jesus is called 'Mighty God' or 'Counsellor', surely there is still salvation through Him as long as the reality of *Jesus Christ* is understood. The same is true if Jesus is referred to as the 'Glory of God'.

In another instance the Bible prophesies that 'His name is called The Word of God' (Rev. 19:13) and later in the same chapter, again referring to the second advent, it states:

> And He has on His robe and on His thigh a name written: KING OF KINGS and LORD OF LORDS. (Rev. 19:16)

These verses are commonly believed to be messianic references to Jesus.[46] Furthermore, Isaiah prophesied that the Messiah's name would be *Immanuel* (see Isa. 7:14), and the Gospel of Matthew indicates that this verse was applicable to Jesus (Matt. 1:23). If Isaiah prophesied that the Messiah would be named *Immanuel*, why then is He called *Jesus*? Since Jesus is obviously the Messiah, Isaiah must have intended the name *Immanuel* to convey the spiritual significance of the person Jesus. To make this clear, the Gospel according to Matthew states that *Immanuel* means 'God with us'.

Once the meaning of the names is appreciated, it is not possible to argue either that 'Jesus' cannot be the name of the

---

46. Some may find it interesting to know that the Greek word *onoma* used in Revelation 19:16 is the same word used by St Peter in Acts 4:12 to indicate what is translated into English as 'name'.

Messiah because Isaiah says the Messiah will be named 'Immanuel', or to say that 'Bahá'u'lláh' cannot be the name of the One foretold in Scripture because St Peter said 'there is no other name under heaven'.

In Acts 4:12, St Peter does not mention a particular name or indicate that salvation depends on only one of the names that are used in Scripture to describe and signify Jesus Christ. Obviously, not just any person with the same name can bring salvation; rather, it is the reality of Christ that brings salvation – regardless of the name.

The reality of Christ signified by Peter's words is manifest in this age in the person of Bahá'u'lláh, and this reality is now known by the name *Bahá'u'lláh*. As we have seen, the name or title *Bahá'u'lláh* is Arabic for 'Glory of God' and this name is applicable to Christ even as the name *Christ* is applicable to Bahá'u'lláh. In Revelation, it is written:

> And the city had no need of the sun or of the moon to shine in it, for the glory of God illuminated it, and the Lamb is its light. (Rev. 21:23)

Here, as in many Bible verses, the 'glory of God' is associated with the second advent of Christ. Is it any more difficult to derive the name Bahá'u'lláh from this verse, than it is to derive the name 'Christ' from the verse in Isaiah mentioned above? If Jesus is referred to as the *Glory of God*, it in no way obscures or is contrary to His spiritual role as Saviour. The name 'Glory of God' is applicable to Bahá'u'lláh because He reveals God's presence and because of His great spiritual triumph and sovereignty.

A BIBLICAL EXAMPLE OF A PROPHET WHO RETURNED WITH A NEW NAME

Biblical prophecies concerning the return of Elijah provide a clear example of a prophet who returned and yet assumed a different name. According to Old Testament prophecies, Elijah would return heralding the way for the Messiah:

> Behold, I will send you Elijah the prophet
> Before the coming of the great and dreadful day of the Lord. (Mal. 4:5, see also 3:1)

This prophecy was, according to Jesus Himself (Matt. 11:12–15), fulfilled by John the Baptist. But if John the Baptist were truly Elijah, why didn't he call himself Elijah? When asked by the priests, John the Baptist denied being Elijah:

> Now this is the testimony of John, when the Jews sent priests and Levites from Jerusalem to ask him, 'Who are you?' He confessed, and did not deny, but confessed, 'I am not the Christ'. And they asked him, 'What then? Are you Elijah?' He said, 'I am not'. 'Are you the Prophet?' And he answered, 'No'. (John 1:19–21)

When asked by the Apostles, Jesus Christ *affirmed* that John the Baptist was Elijah:

> And His disciples asked Him, saying, 'Why then do the scribes say that Elijah must come first?' Then Jesus answered and said to them, 'Elijah truly is coming first and will restore all things. But I say to you that Elijah has come already, and they did not know him but did to him whatever they wished. Likewise the Son of Man is also about to suffer at their hands'. Then the disciples understood that He spoke to them of John the Baptist. (Matt. 17:10–13, see also Matt. 11:14)

On the surface, these statements appear to be contradictory. But on close examination, the apparent contradiction can be resolved. In understanding these different answers it is important to notice who posed the question. The Apostles had the necessary spiritual vision to realize Christ meant that John the Baptist was Elijah in spirit, but not in body. The spiritual relationship between John the Baptist and Elijah is expressed in this passage:

> He [John the Baptist] will also go before Him [Jesus] in the spirit and power of Elijah. (Luke 1:17)

Had John the Baptist answered his questioners affirmatively, the priests would have assumed that he was claiming to be the bodily Elijah. 'Abdu'l-Bahá states:

> The explanation is this: not the personality, but the reality of the perfections, is meant – that is to say, the same perfections that were in Elias [Elijah] existed in John the Baptist and were exactly realized in him. Therefore, John the Baptist was the promised Elias. In this case not the essence, but the qualities, are regarded. (*Some Answered Questions* 133)

The example of John the Baptist is an important demonstration that a prophet can return and be called by another name. Elijah returned but was known as John the Baptist, who was the 'spirit and power of Elijah' (Luke 1:17). In the same way Bahá'u'lláh is the spirit and power of Christ.

The example also demonstrates that Bahá'u'lláh need not appear in the body of Jesus in order to be the returned Christ. Bahá'u'lláh is Christ in spirit but not in body; it is the spirit that returns. It is worth noting that some Christian scholars have given interpretations of these Biblical passages that agree with the Bahá'í point of view. Others believe this apparent contradiction is due to errors made in the text by the authors, but the Bahá'í view clearly aligns with those upholding Scripture's integrity.

There is one other very important point about the Elijah/John the Baptist issue that should not be overlooked. Some Christians may argue that Jesus is not to return in 'spirit and power' alone, but also bodily. Because Jesus ascended bodily, according to the literal interpretations of most Christians, they believe He will return bodily. Again, this argument can be considered in light of Elijah's return. According to Scripture, Elijah was also taken up to heaven, and there is no account of his physical death, so it is believed by some that he never died. The following verse records Elijah's departure:

> Then it happened, as they continued on and talked, that suddenly a chariot of fire appeared with horses of fire, and separated the two of them; and Elijah went up by a whirlwind into heaven. (2 Kgs. 2:11, see also 2 Kgs. 2:1)

If this account were literal, that is Elijah's body ascended and he never died, then the Jews could justify their expectations that Elijah would return bodily. Jesus did not say that John the Baptist was Elijah symbolically, or in spirit and power, He said 'he is Elijah' (Matt. 11:14). Nevertheless, Elijah did not return literally from heaven, and John was born on earth, his parents being Zacharias and Elizabeth (Luke 1:13). But the similarities between Elijah's efforts to call his people back to the religion of Moses and John the Baptist's efforts to prepare the people for the coming Messiah testify to the truth of Jesus' words. John is Elijah, but in spirit and not in body.

The Elijah example provides Biblical evidence that suggests Christ *could* return with a new name. There is, however, Biblical evidence that clearly states Christ *will* return with a new name.

THE BIBLE FORETELLS A NEW NAME

In the Book of Revelation, Jesus (or Bahá'u'lláh) appears to St John and indicates that He will have a new name when He returns. This is stated in the following verse:

> He who overcomes, I will make him a pillar in the temple of My God, and he shall go out no more. And I will write on him the name of My God and the name of the city of My God,[47] the New Jerusalem, which comes down out of heaven from My God. And I will write on him My new name. (Rev. 3:12)

Christian scholars commonly believe this passage refers to the second advent of Christ. The Bahá'í writings affirm this belief by stating that 'Revelation 3:12, refers to the Revelation of Bahá'u'lláh' (see Shoghi Effendi, *Letters from the Guardian to Australia and New Zealand 1923–1957* 41).

In this passage Jesus states that whoever 'overcomes' the trials of the tribulation (Rev. 3:10), He will 'make him a pillar in the temple of God'. This means that that person will become a steadfast support holding up the temple or religion of God. Jesus then says the faithful will be inscribed with the name of God and the name of the city of God, the New Jerusalem. 'Abdu'l-Bahá writes: 'The descent of the New Jerusalem denoteth a heavenly Law, that Law which is the guarantor of human happiness and the effulgence of the world of God' (*Selections from the Writings of 'Abdu'l-Bahá* 59). Therefore, one meaning of the first verse is that Christ 'will write on him', symbolically, the law of God. The believer will be characterized by the new law 'which comes down out of heaven from My God'. As explained in Chapter 2, the Temple and Jerusalem derive their central importance from the time when King David brought the Ark of the Covenant (containing the Law) to the city. However, what concerns us at present is the last verse: 'I will write on him My new name'. This passage indicates that both Christ and His followers will have a 'new name'.

---

47. The new name of the city is given in the Book of Ezekiel as 'THE LORD IS THERE' (Ezek. 48:35), a prophecy that is no doubt intended to emphasize the presence of God in the new order.

There are three principal views among Christian scholars regarding the interpretation and meaning of the 'new name'. Some Christians assert that the new name symbolizes a fuller understanding of Christ's divine nature among the believers in the Millennial Kingdom or an imparting of His divine nature to the believers' own natures. This view is based on the understanding of the term 'name' explained above. In an inner spiritual sense this view is no doubt correct, but an outer literal meaning can also be understood from the texts. Others suggest that the new name refers to names mentioned later in the Book of Revelation – the following two verses:

And His name is called The Word of God. (Rev. 19:13)

And He has on His robe and on His thigh a name written: KING OF KINGS AND LORD OF LORDS. (Rev. 19:16)

Still others argue that the new name does not refer to already known names such as in Revelation 19:13 and 16, because Revelation 2:17 mentions that the 'new name' is a name that 'no one knows except him who receives it'. Therefore, Bahá'ís are not alone in considering that there is a Biblical basis for the belief that Christ will have a new name. And 'no one knows except him who receives it' is fulfilled in the fact that only those who receive it (the believers) acknowledge and know that 'Bahá'u'lláh' is Christ's new name. This is, therefore, another Biblical prophecy that can be taken literally.

Concerning the context of Revelation 3:12, it is helpful to note that some of Chapter 1 and all of Chapters 2 and 3 are commonly considered to be words of Christ (or the future Christ) Himself. This belief is based on the narrative and the description the speaker gives of Himself in the vision, 'I am the Alpha and the Omega, the First and the Last' (1:11, 17–18). There are several verses that suggest the text is referring to the second advent of Christ. In verse 3:3 it is written: 'Therefore if you will not watch, I will come upon you as a thief, and you will not know what hour I will come upon you.' Also, in verse 10 the text refers to 'the hour of trial which shall come upon the whole world' and in verse 11, 'Behold, I come quickly!' This language is very similar to other messianic passages such as Matthew 24:42–4 (see *Selections from the Writings of 'Abdu'l-Bahá* 198–9).

THE 'MOST GREAT NAME'

God is unknowable and unseen, yet in the Scriptures there are references to God's face, voice and name. These references are symbolic. No one can see God's 'face', but in the world of creation the Manifestations symbolize God in so far as God can be known, and therefore symbolically speaking, their face is equated with God's face, their voice with God's voice, their name with God's name, and so on (see, for example, *Certitude* 142, 159, 183). Bahá'u'lláh writes that those who turned away from Christ deprived themselves of 'beholding the face of God' (*Certitude* 19).

Bahá'u'lláh stresses the unknowableness of God's name:

> I beseech Thee by Thy Name which no scroll can bear, which no heart can imagine and no tongue can utter – a Name which will remain concealed so long as Thine own Essence is hidden, and will be glorified so long as Thine own Being is extolled – to unfurl, ere the present year draw to a close, the ensigns of Thine undisputed ascendancy and triumph. (*Prayers and Meditations* 94)

However, in some passages, He appears to identify His own name 'Bahá'u'lláh' with God's name, the Most Great Name. This equation is affirmed by Shoghi Effendi (*Letters from the Guardian to Australia and New Zealand 1923–1957* 41). The special station of the name is also seen in the Gospel. Jesus invokes the name of God: 'Holy Father, protect them by the power of your name – the name you gave me – so that they may be one' (John 17:11).

The 'name' usually signifies the character of the bearer in Biblical usage, and the nature and character of God is also identified with Jesus through reference to God's name: Jesus proclaims, 'I have manifested thy name unto the men which thou gavest me out of the world' (John 17:6, KJV). St Peter's statement to the Sanhedrin that 'Salvation is found in no one else [but Jesus], for there is no other name under heaven given by which we must be saved' (Acts 4:12) can be understood as stressing that Jesus represents the 'name' of God. St Paul writes to the Philippians that through Christ's death God 'exalted him [Jesus] to the highest place and gave him the name that is above every name, that at the name of Jesus every knee should bow' (Philem. 2:9–10, cf. Ps. 95:6, Isa. 45:23). Referring to Jesus, the Báb states that God bestowed 'His favour upon the peoples of the world through the influence of Thy [Jesus'] Most Great Name' (*Selections from the Writings of the Báb* 64). Today, conservative commentators generally agree that in 'the name . . . above every name' the 'reference doubtless is to the office or rank conferred on Jesus—his glorious position, not his proper name (cf. Eph. 1:21; Heb. 1:4–5)' (see fn. *New International Version Study Bible*, 1985 ed.).

In this age, from a Bahá'í point of view, the name above every other name is now associated with the Revelation of Bahá'u'lláh. 'Bahá'u'lláh' is the Most Great Name, and the Bahá'í community is the community of the Most Great Name. In His writings, the special significance of the name is made apparent in hundreds of references, and this is yet another example of Bahá'u'lláh affirming an earlier Biblical and symbolic expression that can be found in the Book of Genesis. Commenting on the verse, 'It was then that people began to call on the name of the LORD' (Gen. 4:26), the scholar Claus Westermann writes: 'Worship is here spoken of as "calling on God's name". This means that by means of God's name a genuine contact between humanity and God is effected. In fact, this is the basis of all forms of worship.' (Westermann, *Genesis* 38)

BIBLICAL REFERENCES FOR CHAPTER 17
The following is an outline of the verses contained in this chapter. When outlining these verses in the Bible, use a blue marker, following the procedure described in Chapter 5.

1. Many names are applicable to Jesus
   Isa. 9:6
   Isa. 7:18/Matt. 1:23
   Rev. 19:13
   Rev. 19:16
   Rev. 21:23
2. Return of prophet with new name
   Concerning John the Baptist:
   John 1:19–21
   Matt. 17:10–13 (see also 11:14)
   Luke 1:17
   Concerning Elijah:
   2 Kgs. 2:11 (ascension)
   Mal. 4:5 (return foretold)
3. A new name is promised
   Rev. 3:12
   Rev. 2:17

part five

BIBLICAL PROPHECY
AND
THE QUR'ÁN

chapter 18

THE BOOK OF DANIEL AND THE QUR'ÁN

THE SEAL OF THE PROPHETS

In the Qur'án, Muḥammad is said to be the 'Seal of the Prophets' (Arabic, <u>Kh</u>átimu'n-Nubúwah), which is often understood to mean that He is the *last* of the prophets and that no other prophet will therefore appear after Him.[48] This particular title has been the subject of longstanding and varied commentary in the Islamic world. It has, for reasons that are all too obvious, been the basis of literature written against Bahá'ís. Sometimes, when a Christian learns that the Bahá'í Faith acknowledges the claims of Muḥammad and the inspiration of the Qur'án, he or she will ask how this acceptance of Muḥammad can be reconciled with Muḥammad's claim to be the 'Seal of the Prophets'. Bahá'u'lláh does not deny or ignore the fact that Muḥammad is the 'Seal of the Prophets'. This station is affirmed repeatedly throughout Bahá'u'lláh's writings.[49] The Bahá'í position differs from traditional Islamic belief not in recognition of the title, but with regard to how such a station should be understood.

---

48. See Qur'án 33:40. The Muslim commentator Yusuf Ali writes, 'When a document is sealed, it is complete, and there can be no further addition. The holy Prophet Muhammad closed the long line of Apostles. God's teaching is and will always be continuous, but there has been and will be no Prophet after Muhammad'. See *The Holy Qur'án*, translation and commentary by Yusuf Ali (1119). It should be admitted that Muslims apply the term 'seal' to Jesus; that is, He is often termed 'Seal of Sanctity' because He is thought to have externalized His inner sanctity to the highest degree. Muslims, however, reserve 'Seal of the Prophets' exclusively for Muḥammad. See, for example, Cyril Glassé, *The Concise Encyclopædia of Islam* 353.

49. See, for example, *Epistle* 42, 43, 92, 114, 163; *Certitude* 40, 162, 166, 179.

The Bible, and in particular the Book of Daniel, offers important evidence for understanding the meaning of the Qur'ánic claim that Muḥammad is the 'Seal of the Prophets'. This chapter examines the Book of Daniel's use of the term 'seal' in relation to the Bahá'í interpretation of the statement.

There are frequent uses of the term 'seal' in Biblical texts, but the Book of Daniel provides the basis for connecting the Hebrew term – which is equivalent to the Arabic – to the fulfilment of prophecy in the ministry of Jesus Christ and, therefore, indicating that the title is also applicable to Jesus. Two sources of Scripture, therefore – the Book of Daniel and the Qur'án – apply the same terminology to two different Manifestations of God, and this suggests that the terminology signifies the archetypal fulfilment of prophecy. That is, it is applicable to any and all Prophets who fulfil prophecy and does not therefore mean that any one Prophet is the last historical Prophet.

The purpose of this chapter is not to retrace the history of this issue, but rather to consider briefly how several passages from the Book of Daniel may shed some light on the use of the phrase as it appears in the Qur'án. This knowledge will provide one means of resolving the question: How can Bahá'u'lláh be a Prophet if Muḥammad is the Seal of the Prophets?

It may be useful first to outline six basic reasons why the Book of Daniel might be relevant to the interpretation of the Qur'án.

1. The Qur'án affirms the Torah, and the Book of Daniel may be regarded as a portion of the Torah, or at least belonging to the prophetic witness of Judaism.

2. The Qur'án affirms the Gospel, and Jesus in the Gospel refers to the Book of Daniel.

3. Jesus' reference to the Book of Daniel is contained in His main sermon on the subject of His second advent (the appearance of Muḥammad).

4. The Arabic word for *seal* in the Qur'án is a loan-word from the Hebrew word for *seal* found in the Book of Daniel.

5. Daniel's use of the term 'seal' is in relation to the fulfilment of prophecy and the future Messiah.

6. Some similarities between the symbolism of the Book of Daniel and the Qur'án suggests that Daniel may have influenced the early Jewish-Arabian context of Qur'ánic Revelation.

In the following pages, each of these points will be examined more closely.

THE QUR'ÁN AND THE BIBLE

The Qur'án stands as a witness to and affirmation of the 'Torah',[50] a term that usually signifies in its narrowest sense the laws of Moses, and in its broadest sense the whole of Hebrew Scripture and sacred tradition. However, since the term 'Torah' is not given any explicit definition in the Qur'án, it is difficult to say that the Qur'án's affirmation embraces the inspiration of the Book of Daniel.[51] Nevertheless, Muslims could have found reasons for considering and studying the Book of Daniel in the Qur'án's affirmation of the Gospel.[52] Even if the Qur'án's affirmation of the Gospel is restricted to the words of Jesus recorded in the four versions of the Gospel, this alone would provide an important reference to the Book of Daniel.

---

50. See Qur'án 2:136; 5:49–50, 68. Cf. *Certitude* 84–5. Concerning the acceptance of Israelite prophets see also Qur'án 4:150–1.

51. In the Hebrew Bible, the Book of Daniel was traditionally included among what was called 'The Writings' (Hagiographa), as Daniel was regarded as an Israelite statesman. Nevertheless, he was also considered a great prophet. For statements of 'Abdu'l-Bahá's respect for Daniel as a prophetic witness to the Manifestations of Christ, Muhammad, the Báb and Bahá'u'lláh, see 'Abdu'l-Bahá, *Some Answered Questions*, Chapter 10. See also, Shoghi Effendi, *God Passes By* 58, 95, 110.

52. See Qur'án 2:136, 5:68. For Bahá'u'lláh's view of the Qur'ánic affirmation of the Gospel, see *Certitude* 20; for comments by 'Abdu'l-Bahá see *Promulgation* 201, and *Paris Talks* 47.

In Jesus' last major sermon, the Olivet Discourse, He urges His followers to understand the words recorded in the Book of Daniel:

> So when you see the appalling abomination, of which the prophet Daniel spoke, set up in the holy place (let the reader understand), then those in Judaea must escape to the mountains. (Matt. 24:15)

At the time of Christ, the phrase translated here as 'appalling abomination' would have been a recognizable reference to prophecies in the Book of Daniel, even if 'the prophet Daniel', had not been mentioned by Jesus.[53]

Were it not for the negative attitudes towards the New Testament that developed in the Islamic world, there are several good reasons why Muslim commentators might have noticed and appreciated the significance of this verse in the Gospel. The verse is admittedly somewhat cryptic, as is the whole sermon, but what is clear from the text is that Jesus thought the Book of Daniel had prophetic significance for events that were to occur after Him, and this would naturally be significant with regard to the claims of Muḥammad.[54]

Bahá'u'lláh devotes most of the first portion of *The Book of Certitude* to demonstrating how prophecies from this New Testament sermon (Matt. 24) relate to the appearance of Muhammad. Concluding His explanation, Bahá'u'lláh severely criticizes Muslims for misunderstanding Qur'ánic references to the Gospel, denying the genuineness of the Gospel, and failing to explain the real significance of the Gospel (especially with regard to proving the truth of Muḥammad) to the Christians

---

53. The phrase appears only in the Book of Daniel 9:27, 11:31, 12:11 and in 1 Maccabees 1:54. The reference in 1 Maccabees, however, is not in a prophetic context. For the prophecies of Jesus as they relate to Islam and the Bahá'í Faith, see Sours, *The Prophecies of Jesus*.

54. For an extensive verse-by-verse commentary on Jesus' Olivet discourse (Matt. 24) see Sours, *Prophecies*.

(*Certitude* 83–92). This suggests that, had Muslim commentators been more interested in studying the prophecies of Jesus in order to vindicate Muḥammad, the study of this passage and, consequently, the Book of Daniel, would have been considered important. The understanding of Biblical terminology might have had a significant effect on interpretation of other passages in the Qur'án.

Another very significant point that emerges from Bahá'u'lláh's interpretation of Jesus' prophecies is the influence of cultural conditions on the language and terminology of Scripture. When Bahá'u'lláh explains the meaning of Jesus' use of the term 'sign' (that is, a sign in the heavens), He calls the reader's attention to various instances of stars in heaven said to have accompanied the appearance of the prophets Abraham, Moses, Christ, Muḥammad and the Báb. In His explanation He draws on traditions referring to such signs in both canonical texts and ancient folklore. The explanation indicates that a Messenger of God speaks to people in a terminology familiar to them, and this suggests the need to study Scripture in its cultural context, including traditions and popular folklore – a point widely accepted by scholars today.

THE TERM 'SEAL' IN THE BOOK OF DANIEL

In the Book of Daniel, there are several instances when the term 'seal'[55] is used. Jesus' reference to the 'appalling abomination' in Matthew 24:15, cited above, directs the reader to the context of all these usages (Gabriel's words as recorded in Dan. 9:24–7, and in 12: 4, 10).

The first two, and perhaps the most significant, occurrences are in the following passage:

> Seventy weeks are decreed
> for your people and your holy city,

---

55. The Arabic *khátam*, according to S. Fränkel, is a loan-word from the Hebrew 'hátam'. See *The New Brown, Driver, Briggs, Gesenius Hebrew and English Lexicon* 367.

for putting an end to transgression,
for placing the seal[56] on sin,
for expiating crime, for introducing everlasting
　　uprightness
for setting the seal on vision and on prophecy,
for anointing the holy of holies. (Dan. 9:24)

The Book of Daniel presents this verse as part of an explanation given to the prophet Daniel by the archangel Gabriel. In the immediate context, Daniel has offered a fervent prayer of repentance on behalf of the nation and is supplicating God for guidance concerning the fate of Israel – and in particular, he wants to know this fate in relation to a prophecy revealed to the prophet Jeremiah. This prophecy concerned the number of years 'that were to pass before the desolation of Jerusalem would come to an end' (Dan. 9:2; cf. Jer. 25:11–12, 29:10). It is in answer to this that the angel Gabriel is said to have revealed the above verse. Gabriel also revealed when the period of 70 weeks was to commence, and this period, according to many Christian commentators, culminates with the advent of Christ.[57]

The classic Christian interpretation of this passage is that 70 weeks (490 days) is equal to the 490 years (according to the formula that a day is equal to a year, Num. 14:34; see also Ezek. 4:6) from the 457 BC edict to rebuild Jerusalem to the crucifixion and ascension of Jesus. 'Abdu'l-Bahá affirms the traditional Christian interpretation – that is, that the 70 weeks terminates with the sacrifice of Jesus on the cross (*Some Answered Questions* 41). Therefore, at least from the point of view of

---

56. According to the conservative Christian commentator Gleason L. Archer, the term *lahton* used here (meaning 'to seal up') is 'probably a scribal error' involving the term *lehatem* (meaning 'to bring to an end'). See *Expositor's Bible Commentary*, vol. 7, 119. The difference is slight and largely inconsequential.

57. Perhaps the most extensive historical survey of Christian interpretations relating to this passage can be found in the four-volume study by the Adventist scholar LeRoy Froom, *The Prophetic Faith of Our Fathers* (1948).

Bahá'í interpretation, as well as that of many Christian commentators, this particular aspect of the prophecy concerns Jesus. Daniel 9:24 is concerned basically with the ministry of Christ and its impact on those who believe in Him.

The earthly ministry of Christ only lasted three years – swiftly culminating with the crucifixion. This period is the terminating point of the 70 weeks prophecy, marking the end of the old order and introducing a new one. As outlined in the Daniel verse, it is the end of 'transgression' and 'sin' (that is, for those who abide by the spirit of His Revelation), the beginning of the expiation of 'crime' and the introduction of 'everlasting righteousness' – meaning the rule of Christ in the hearts of believers (the Kingdom of Christ). Beyond this, the verse points to the fulfilment of – or seal on – the vision and prophecy through the appearance of Jesus, and this is the point most relevant to this study of the Qur'ánic phrase 'Seal of the Prophets'.

CHRIST AS 'SEAL OF THE PROPHETS'

Although some Christians are reluctant to see the full implications of the 'seal' realized through the first appearance of Jesus some two thousand years ago, Bahá'u'lláh points out that Christ did appear with 'manifest dominion' and fulfilled the prophecies concerning His appearance 'in the Book of Isaiah as well as in the Books of the Prophets and the Messengers' (*Tablets of Bahá'u'lláh* 9–10).[58] In this way, it is possible to see that through Christ, a 'seal' was put on the vision and prophecy concerning His ministry and divine presence. Or, to put it another way, Christ was Himself the seal on what was said by the prophets.

The connection between the term *seal* and the fulfilment of prophecy is also made by Bahá'u'lláh in the following passage:

---

58. See, for example, *The Expositor's Bible Commentary*, vol. 7, 113.

> It is evident that every age in which a Manifestation of God hath lived is divinely ordained, and may, in a sense, be characterized as God's appointed Day. This Day, however, is unique, and is to be distinguished from those that have preceded it. The designation 'Seal of the Prophets' fully revealeth its high station. The Prophetic Cycle hath, verily, ended. The Eternal Truth is now come. (*Gleanings* 60)[59]

This passage suggests the archetypal nature of prophecy. Various forms of symbolism – such as the Davidic rule, the Day of God, the primal garden, the restored Temple, the New Jerusalem, the united kingdoms of Israel and Judah, and so on – are used in prophetic speech to indicate one central theme, the presence of God. Each prophet that appears – especially the supreme Manifestations such as Christ, Muḥammad and Bahá'u'lláh – represents the presence of God, the ushering in of the Day of God, the restoration of the primal paradise and, in a symbolic sense the 'end time' fulfilment of all that went before (*Certitude* 142–5, 161–70). That any particular prophet does not fully establish the Kingdom of God on earth is an indication of the inadequate human response to His ministry. They are the 'fulfilment', even though the future appearance of another prophet may be indicated by each succeeding prophet. Each fulfils the prophecies because the prophecies are symbols referring to the same reality represented by them all.

---

59. In connection with this passage of Bahá'u'lláh, Shoghi Effendi points out the significance of world unity in relation to the fulfilment of those Biblical and Qur'ánic prophecies referring to the 'Day of God', writing, 'Only those who are willing to associate the Revelation proclaimed by Bahá'u'lláh with the consummation of so stupendous an evolution in the collective life of the whole human race can grasp the significance of the words He [Bahá'u'lláh], while alluding to the glories of this promised Day and to the duration of the Bahá'í Era, has deemed fit to utter' (*World Order* 166–7; see also *God Passes By* 54–5, 100, and *Promised Day* 117). With reference to Isaiah 11:1–10, for example, see 'Abdu'l-Bahá's commentary in *Some Answered Questions* (63–4, 65).

In the above passage, Bahá'u'lláh is indicating *not* that He is the last prophet,[60] but that in this age, the goal of past prophecy will be realized fully. Whereas past ages were not sufficiently mature to respond adequately to the presence of God, this age marks a new stage in human evolution. The hope that all nations would be united and live in peace under the reign of God on earth (as prophesied in, for example, Dan. 7:13–14; Isa. 9:6–7; Rev. 21) will have its realization in this historic cycle initiated by the Revelation of Bahá'u'lláh.

Since the Book of Daniel indicates that Jesus is the seal of the prophets, there is a longstanding Scriptural tradition that the Qur'ánic reference to Muhammad should not be understood to mean that Muhammad is the last prophet or the only seal of the prophets. The Book of Daniel provides a means by which Muslim interpreters could have understood 'Seal of the Prophets' in a broader sense. Obviously, if Jesus was a Seal on the words of the Prophets, and yet prophesied another to come after Him, then the Qur'ánic phrase need not mean that no other prophet will appear after Muhammad.

THE HEBREW ḤÁTAM AS 'SEAL' AND 'LAST'

In the Hebrew, the above usage of 'seal' (*hátam*) has two primary meanings: (1) *authority* and (2) *ending* or *culmination*.

With regard to *authority*, the seal 'on' the vision and prophecy can be likened to the seal of a king on an official document. This is inherent in Gabriel's words indicating the authority of the one foretold: He is the 'anointed', meaning the Messiah or King. The 70 weeks culminates with the appearance of the 'anointed' Ruler – which in this instance means Jesus Christ. Jesus made known His claim to be the Christ or Messiah by reading in the synagogues (see Luke 4:18) the words 'the spirit of the Lord is on me, for he has

---

60. In *The Book of Certitude* (99, 137) Bahá'u'lláh has denied that revelation will ever cease.

anointed me to bring the good news to the afflicted' (Isa. 61:1, 2, emphasis added).[61]

It is Jesus' divine sovereignty and authority which entitles Him to be recognized as the 'anointed' of God – and authoritatively to 'seal' the vision and prophecy, that is, to state unequivocally that He is the fulfilment of the messianic prophecies. He has the authority to say that the prophecy is fulfilled, culminated and concluded in Him. The recognition that Jesus of Nazareth is the *Christ* is, in itself, equivalent to the recognition that He has sealed or fulfilled the *messianic* prophecies. The word 'seal' in Daniel 9:24 has this footnote in the *New Jerusalem* edition of the Bible: ' "To seal" means sometimes "to put an end to", sometimes "to guarantee"; here it has the comprehensive sense of "fulfilling" ' (*New Jerusalem Bible* 1489).

The next significant use of the term 'seal' in relation to prophecy occurs in Daniel 12:4 and is repeated in verses 8 and 9 (cf. Isa. 29:11). Both these verses reinforce the idea of an authoritative seal. Daniel says:

> I listened but I did not understand. I then said, 'My lord, what is to be the outcome?' 'Go, Daniel', he said. 'These words are to remain secret and sealed until the time of the End'. (Dan. 12:8–9)

No literal seal is placed on the Book of Daniel, the term *seal* (*hatumin*) being simply a metaphor based on the ancient practice of sealing documents. The context of both verses suggests that the document is authoritatively sealed (closed up) and is not to be opened (that is, its meaning will not be disclosed) until the appointed authority (the Messiah) reveals the meaning. This sealed meaning need not be stated verbally by the Messiah, but can be realized, or made evident, through His presence.

---

61. In the Gospel according to John, Jesus also states 'on him [i.e. Jesus] the Father, God himself, has set his seal' (John 6:27).

Concomitant to the above is the idea of an *ending*. In a historical prophetic sense, Christ in His divine 'presence' is the ending to all that went before, the conclusion to a line of prophetic expectation – the 'end' that Isaiah, Ezekiel, Daniel and the other Messengers anticipated. In this deeper theological sense, He represents the Godhead that is both the beginning and end of all, for all time. Explaining the significance of the Qur'ánic expression, 'Seal of the Prophets', as it relates to 'the last', Bahá'u'lláh writes:

> Hath not Muḥammad, Himself, declared: 'I am all the Prophets?' Hath He not said as We have already mentioned: 'I am Adam, Noah, Moses, and Jesus?' Why should Muḥammad, that immortal Beauty, Who hath said: 'I am the first Adam' be incapable of saying also: 'I am the last Adam'? For even as He regarded Himself to be the 'First of the Prophets' – that is Adam – in like manner, the 'Seal of the Prophets' is also applicable unto that Divine Beauty. (*Certitude* 162)

Following this passage, Bahá'u'lláh then expands His argument to include all the Manifestations of God:

> Even as in the 'Beginning that hath no beginnings' the term 'last' is truly applicable unto Him who is the Educator of the visible and of the invisible, in like manner, are the terms 'first' and 'last' applicable unto His Manifestations. They are at the same time the Exponents of both the 'first' and the 'last'. Whilst established upon the seat of the 'first', they occupy the throne of the 'last'. Were a discerning eye to be found, it will readily perceive that the exponents of the 'first' and the 'last', of the 'manifest' and the 'hidden', of the 'beginning' and the 'seal' are none other than these holy Beings, these Essences of Detachment, these divine Souls. (*Certitude* 163)

In these passages, Bahá'u'lláh has used *hadiths* (sayings attributed to Muḥammad) concerning the divine station of Muḥammad in order to explain the title 'Seal of the Prophets'. These hadiths put the discussion of Muḥammad's station in the same theological context as various important verses about Christ in the New Testament. For example, Christ is said to have revealed the following to St John at the island of Patmos:

> I am the Alpha and the Omega, says the Lord God, who is, who was, and who is to come, the Almighty. (Rev. 1:8)

This teaching is taken up several times. John is frightened by the vision,[62] and Jesus comforts him, saying 'Do not be afraid; it is I, the First and the Last; I am the Living One . . .' (Rev. 1:17; cf. Rev. 22:13).[63]

The final section of Daniel's vision concerning the sealing of the books, taken together with the earlier prophecy concerning Christ, provides two related ways of seeing the term 'seal'. In one sense, the 'seal' is brought about through the appearance of the Messiah (Christ) who seals the prophecies in the sense of culminating and ending those prophecies leading up to His reign and presence. The other meaning involves unsealing the books at 'the time of the end' (Dan. 12:9).

Although, this section of Daniel presents some specific chronological prophecies, the idea of the 'time of the end' can be understood symbolically and therefore related generally to the appearance of all Manifestations – the 'Day of God'. It is the time of the end of one age and the beginning of another. The old order ceases and a new creation begins. From this point

---

62. The idea of the 'vision' is a metaphor. The author of the Book of Revelation is conveying the magnitude of what he knows quite consciously. See 'Abdu'l-Bahá, *Some Answered Questions*, Chapter 71.

63. See 'Abdu'l-Bahá, *Some Answered Questions* 219.

of view, all Manifestations seal past prophecies by fulfilling them, and through this means of fulfilment also unseal them in the sense of making the meaning of the prophecies evident.[64]

THE ORIGIN OF THE QUR'ÁNIC USAGE

Much of the language and symbolism of the Qur'án reflects the cultural environment of Arabia during the time of Muhammad. There is no conclusive evidence to indicate that the Qur'ánic usage of 'Seal of the Prophets' is connected directly to the Book of Daniel, but ideas about seals are common to both Judaism and Islam, and the Qur'án is not presenting a new type of usage.[65] As far as scriptural influences are concerned, a few pieces of evidence are also worth considering.[66]

The angel Gabriel is assumed to be the angel who appears to Moses (Exod. 3:2), but, apart from Gabriel's appearance to Mary (Luke 1:19, 26), Daniel is the only text (Dan. 8:16; 9:21) within the traditional Biblical canon that actually uses the name 'Gabriel' for an angel who imparts a revelation from God. The apocalyptic imagery of the Son of Man coming on the clouds of heaven is also in Daniel (Dan. 7:13; cf. Matt. 24:30, Qur'án 2:210, 25:25). There are, therefore, three particularly noticeable correlations between the terminology in the Book of Daniel and in the Qur'án: (1) The naming of Gabriel as a messenger of revelation, (2) the use of the term 'seal' in close proximity to the subject of prophecy, and (3) the use of similar apocalyptic symbolism.

---

64. Cf. 2 Cor. 3:7–18.

65. See *The Encyclopaedia of Islam*, vol. IV, 1102–3 and *The Jewish Encyclopedia*, vol. XI, 134–40.

66. This chapter has focused solely on the terms *seal* and *last* as they appear in the apocalyptic texts of the Books of Daniel and Revelation. For other important references in the Hebrew Scriptures and New Testament, which should not be discounted, see *New Bible Dictionary* (2nd ed.) 1081–3. See also Richardson, *Theological Word Book of the Bible* 221–2.

If these traditions from among Jews and Christians were current in Arabia, as is likely, what purpose would a reference to 'seal' – in the sense used in the Daniel text – have served in the Qur'án?[67] It could have been intended as a way of mitigating the effects of certain Christian arguments. The New Testament assertion that Christ is the first and the last, for example, could have been used by Christians as grounds for rejecting another prophet, other than the identical incarnate reappearance of Christ. As a proclamation of Muḥammad's station, 'Seal of the Prophets' suggests equal divine authority with Christ by challenging the suggestion that Muḥammad's claims and position were inferior to those of Christ. The Qur'án's claim that Muḥammad is the seal or last of the prophets, even when taken literally as it has been traditionally understood, proclaims the fulfilment of prophecy and the potential realization of the Kingdom of God on earth.

---

67. The point of this speculation is not to ignore the immediate context of the Qur'ánic reference to Muhammad as Seal of the Prophets, but to explore what additional objective there may have been. There are a number of ways a statement can be made, but the choice of terminology provides emphasis or added depth of meaning. The full passage states: 'Muhammad is not /The father of any/Of your men, but (he is)/The Apostle of God,/And the Seal of the Prophets:/And God has full-knowledge/Of all things' (Holy Qur'án 33:40, trans. Yusuf Ali). Viewed in context, one way of understanding this passage is that Muhammad is saying He is not merely a father of men, but the fulfilment of all the prophecies. As the presence of God on earth, all the great prophetic themes and archetypal prophecies – the Davidic king, the 'anointed', the presence of God in the restored Garden, the new Temple and new Jerusalem, the Lord of Hosts, and so on – are fulfilled by Him. The passage is perhaps complicated by the fact that Muhammad had no sons, and therefore, was literally not the father of men. It seems, however, doubtful that Muhammad intended a literal and gender-specific meaning relating to His own progeny, as there is no apparent connection between His progeny and 'Seal of the Prophets'.

appendix

THE GLORY OF GOD IN THE BIBLICAL TRADITION

In Exodus it is said that 'When Moses went up on the mountain, the cloud covered it, and the *glory of the Lord* settled on Mount Sinai' (Exod. 24:15, emphasis added, NIV). The text adds, 'to the Israelites the glory of the Lord looked like a consuming fire on top of the mountain' (Exod. 24:16). Later this glory is said to fill the tabernacle (Exod. 40:34–5), and through sacrificial offerings, the 'LORD' (for example, in Lev. 9:1–6) – Who is also equated with the 'glory of the Lord' (Exod. 9:6) – appeared to the Israelites (Lev. 9:1ff.). In the Book of Exodus it is said that the people were unable to gaze upon the face of Moses after his encounter with God for it shone so brightly – presumably with the glory of God (Exod. 34:29–35). When Ezekiel describes the majesty of 'a figure like that of a man' 'high above on a throne' (Ezek. 1:26), he says 'This was the appearance of the likeness of the glory of the Lord' (Ezek. 1:28, NIV).

In the Torah, the veil over the face of Moses symbolizes the people's inability to see the light or glory of God. In the New Testament, St Paul picks up this symbol and argues that this veil is taken away through belief in Jesus (2 Cor. 3:15). Using the analogy of the mirror, he adds, 'But we all, with unveiled face, beholding as in a mirror[68] the glory of the Lord, are being

---

68. The word 'mirror' is a translation of the Greek term *katoptrizomai*, meaning to mirror oneself or see reflected, as in a glass.

transformed into the same image from glory to glory, just as by the Spirit of the Lord' (2 Cor. 3: 18: NKJ).

Commenting on the phrase 'glory of God', the Biblical expositor W. E. Vine writes:

> When applied to God, the word represents a quality corresponding to Him and by which He is recognized. Joshua commanded Achan to give glory to God, to recognize His importance, worth, and significance (Josh. 7:19). In this and similar instances 'giving honor' refers to doing something; what Achan was to do was to tell the truth. In other passages giving honor to God is a ... confession of God as God (Psalm 29:1). Some have suggested that such passages celebrate the sovereignty of God over nature wherein the celebrant sees His 'glory' and confesses it in worship. In other places the word is said to point to God's sovereignty over history and specifically to a future manifestation of that 'glory' (Isa. 40:5). Still other passages relate the manifestation of divine 'glory' to past demonstrations of His sovereignty over history and peoples (Exod. 16:7, 24:16). (*Vine's Expository Dictionary* 115)

The 'glory of God' that appeared on Sinai, and later over the Tabernacle of the Law, is traditionally understood in Christian theology to represent the full manifestation of the attributes of God:

> Glory of God expresses the sum total of the divine perfections. The idea is prominent in redemptive revelation: see Isa. 60:1; Rom. 5:2; 6:4. It expresses the form in which God reveals himself in the economy of salvation: see Rom. 9:23; Eph. 1:12; 1 Tim. 1:11. It is the means by which the redemptive work is carried on: see 2 Pet. 1:3; Rom. 6:4; Eph. 3:16; Col. 1:11. It is the

> goal of Christian hope: see Rom. 5:2; 8:18, 21; Tit. 2:13.
> (Vincent, *Word Studies*, vol. IV, 27)

Brockington writes, 'The "glory of God" is, in effect, the term used to express that which men can apprehend, originally by sight, of the presence of God on earth' (from A. Richardson et al. *Theological Word Book* 175). This is a station that Bahá'u'lláh attributes universally to all the Manifestations of God in *The Book of Certitude* (143; see also 'Abdu'l-Bahá, *Some Answered Questions*, Chapter 50).

The glory of God is an indication of the presence of God in the world. These two conceptions – glory and presence – are, therefore, intimately connected in Scripture. Referring to the manifestation of Christ, Brockington writes, 'On earth the glory of God was made known in him [Christ], and men apprehended through him the presence of God' (*Theological Word Book* 175). This theme takes a dominant position in the New Testament.

> Throughout the New Testament Christ is presented as the glory of God made visible on earth to those whose eyes are open to see it; but it is perhaps in the Fourth Gospel that this conception is most strongly stressed. Behind the Johannine *doxa* (Greek *glory*) we must recollect the full biblical richness of the word, as we have described it above. 'We beheld his *doxa*, glory as of the only-begotten from the Father' (John 1:14). The miracles of Christ manifested his *doxa* (2:11). His doxa is not the glory of men but of God (5:41, 17:5, 17:22).
> (*Theological Word Book* 175–6)

Nowhere, however, is this theme more evident than in passages concerning Christ's return (the *parousia*): 'glory slowly became eschatological, so that in the New Testament we find it as an integral part of the life of the Kingdom of God, both realized now and expected in the future' (ibid. 175). Or as Vincent writes:

> The Gentiles, in receiving the manifestation of Christ, did not realize all its glory. The full glory of the inheritance was a hope, to be realized when Christ should appear 'the second time unto salvation' (Heb. 9:28). (Vincent, *Word Studies*, vol. III, 480)

With this in mind, it is easier to appreciate the extraordinary eschatological significance of Bahá'u'lláh's name from a Biblical perspective, as compared to the Qur'ánic. In the Biblical literature the Day of God is primarily expressed in terms of the revelation of the glory of God (for example, Isa. 2:19, 2:21; Rev. 21:23). In Qur'ánic terminology, it is the 'presence' of God at the Day of Judgement that is most often indicated. These two expressions are, as acknowledged in Christian theology, one and the same.

It can be argued, then, that each age in which a supreme Manifestation – such as Moses, Christ or Bahá'u'lláh – appears is considered the Day of God, and through them there is an appearance of the glory of God. Nevertheless, viewed biblically, the supreme nature and distinction of Bahá'u'lláh's Revelation becomes apparent in that two central Biblical themes are actualized in the world in this age – the unity of the nations and the oneness of God. Humankind, created in the image of God, manifests the oneness of God through unification of the world. In past ages, the human race has only reflected this oneness in an incomplete and fragmentary way. When Bahá'u'lláh states the 'spirit of Glory' has appeared to Him, this can be understood as referring to a spirit representing the mediation of God's presence and the end-time fulfilment realized through the oneness of humankind – the central purpose and aim of His Revelation.

ABBREVIATIONS

THE OLD TESTAMENT

Genesis	Gen.		
Exodus	Exod.		
Leviticus	Lev.		
Numbers	Num.		
Deuteronomy	Deut.		
Joshua	Josh.		
Judges	Judg.		
Ruth	Ruth		
1 Samuel	1 Sam.		
2 Samuel	2 Sam.		
1 Kings	1 Kgs		
2 Kings	2 Kgs		
1 Chronicles	1 Chr.		
2 Chronicles	2 Chr.		
Ezra	Ezra		
Nehemiah	Neh.		
Esther	Esther		
Job	Job		
Psalms	Ps.		
Proverbs	Pro.		
Ecclesiastes	Eccles.		
Song of Solomon	Song of Sol.		
Isaiah	Isa.		
Jeremiah	Jer.		
Lamentations	Lam.		
Ezekiel	Ezek.		
Daniel	Dan.		
Hosea	Hos.		
Joel	Joel		
Amos	Amos		
Obadiah	Obad.		
Jonah	Jonah		
Micah	Micah		
Nahum	Nah.		
Habakkuk	Hab.		
Zephaniah	Zeph.		
Haggai	Hag.		
Zechariah	Zech.		
Malachi	Mal.		

THE NEW TESTAMENT

Matthew	Matt.
Mark	Mark
Luke	Luke
John	John
The Book of Acts	Acts
Romans	Rom.
1 Corinthians	1 Cor.
2 Corinthians	2 Cor.
Galatians	Gal.
Ephesians	Eph.
Philippians	Phil.
Colossians	Col.
1 Thessalonians	1 Thess.
2 Thessalonians	2 Thess.
1 Timothy	1 Tim.
2 Timothy	2 Tim.
Titus	Tit.
Philemon	Philem.
Hebrews	Heb.
James	James
1 Peter	1 Pet.
2 Peter	2 Pet.
1 John	1 John
2 John	2 John
3 John	3 John
Jude	Jude
Revelation	Rev.

BIBLES

American Standard Version	ASV
King James Version	KJV
The Modern Language Bible	ML
New International Version	NIV
New King James Version	NKJV
Revised Standard Version	RSV

BIBLIOGRAPHY

'Abdu'l-Bahá. *Paris Talks.* London: Bahá'í Publishing Trust, 1969.
—— *The Promulgation of Universal Peace.* Wilmette, Ill: Bahá'í Publishing Trust, 2nd edn., 1982.
—— *Secret of Divine Civilization.* Wilmette, Ill: Bahá'í Publishing Trust, 2nd edn., 1970, 1975.
—— *Selections from the Writings of 'Abdu'l-Bahá.* Comp. by the Research Department of the Universal House of Justice. Trans. Habib Taherzadeh and a Committee at the Bahá'í World Centre. Haifa, Israel: Bahá'í World Centre, 1982.
—— *Some Answered Questions.* Trans. L. C. Barney. Wilmette, Ill: Bahá'í Publishing Trust, 4th edn., 1981.
—— *Tablets of the Divine Plan.* Wilmette, Ill: Bahá'í Publishing Trust, rev. edn., 1977.
Abu'l-Faḍl, Mírzá. *Miracles and Metaphors.* Trans. Juan Ricardo Cole. Los Angeles: Kalimát Press, 1981.
Báb, The. *Selections from the Writings of the Báb.* Comp. the Research Department of the Universal House of Justice. Trans. Habib Taherzadeh with the assistance of a Committee at the Bahá'í World Centre. Haifa: Bahá'í World Centre, 1976.
Bahá'í World Faith. Wilmette, Ill: Bahá'í Publishing Committee, 1943.
Bahá'u'lláh. *The Book of Certitude (Kitáb-i-Iqán).* Trans. Shoghi Effendi. Wilmette, Ill: Bahá'í Publishing Trust, 2nd edn., 1950.
—— *Epistle to the Son of the Wolf.* Trans. Shoghi Effendi. Wilmette, Ill: Bahá'í Publishing Trust, 3rd edn., 1988.
—— *Gleanings from the Writings of Bahá'u'lláh.* Trans. Shoghi Effendi. Wilmette, Ill: Bahá'í Publishing Trust, 2nd edn., 1976.

—— *The Hidden Words*. Trans. Shoghi Effendi et al. Oxford: Oneworld Publications, 1986.
—— Prayers and Meditations. Trans. Shoghi Effendi. Wilmette, Ill: Bahá'í Publishing Trust, 1972.
—— *The Proclamation of Bahá'u'lláh*. Haifa, Israel: Bahá'í World Centre, 1972.
—— *Tablets of Bahá'u'lláh Revealed after the Kitáb-i-Aqdas*. Comp. the Research Department of the Universal House of Justice. Trans. Habib Taherzadeh with the assistance of a Committee at the Bahá'í World Centre. Haifa: Bahá'í World Centre, 1978.
Beasley-Murray, G. R. *Jesus and the Future*. London: Macmillan, 1954.
Bible, New Jerusalem. London: Dorton Longman & Todd; New York: Doubleday, 1985.
Encyclopaedia of Islam. Vol. IV. Leiden: E. J. Brill, 1978.
Esslemont, J. E. *Bahá'u'lláh and the New Era*. London: Bahá'í Publishing Trust, 1974.
Expositor's Bible Commentary. Vol. 7. Grand Rapids, MI: Zondervan, 1985.
Froom, LeRoy Edwin. *The Prophetic Faith of Our Fathers*. Vols 1–4, Washington, DC: Review and Herald, 1948.
Glassé, Cyril. *The Concise Encyclopædia of Islam*. London: Stacey International, 1989.
Hornby, Helen, ed. *Lights of Guidance: A Bahá'í Reference File*. New Delhi, India: Bahá'í Publishing Trust, 2nd edn., 1988.
Jewish Encyclopedia. Vol. XI. New York: Funk and Wagnalls, 1905.
La Cocque, André. *Daniel in His Time*. Columbia, SC: University of South Carolina, 1988.
Martin, Alfred and John. *The Glory of the Messiah*. Chicago, MI: Moody Press, 1983.
Nabíl-i-A'zam. (Muḥammad-i-Zarandí). *The Dawn-Breakers: Nabíl's Narrative of the Early Days of the Bahá'í Revelation*. Trans. Shoghi Effendi. Wilmette, Ill: Bahá'í Publishing Trust, 1974.
New Bible Dictionary. Wheaton, Ill: Tyndale House Publishers, 2nd edn., 1982.
New Brown, Driver, Briggs, Gesenius Hebrew and English Lexicon. Peabody, MA: Hendrickson, 1979.
NIV Study Bible. Grand Rapids MI: Zondervan, 1985.
Pentecost, J. Dwight. *Things to Come: A Study in Biblical Eschatology*. Grand Rapids, MI: Zondervan, 1964.

Qur'án, Holy. Trans. and comp. A. Yusuf 'Alí. American Trust Publications for the Muslim Students' Association, 2nd edn., 1977.

Richardson, A., et al. *Theological Word Book of the Bible*. New York: Macmillan, 1978.

Sanders, E.P., et. al. *Jewish and Christian Self-Definition*. Vol. 2. Philadelphia: Fortress Press, 1981.

Shoghi Effendi. *The Advent of Divine Justice*. Wilmette, Ill: Bahá'í Publishing Trust, 1939, 1971, 1990.

—— *Citadel of Faith: Messages to America 1947–1957*. Wilmette, Ill: Bahá'í Publishing Trust, 3rd edn., 1970.

—— *God Passes By*. Wilmette, Ill: Bahá'í Publishing Trust, 1974.

—— *Letters from the Guardian to Australia and New Zealand 1923-1957*. Sydney: National Spiritual Assembly of the Bahá'ís of Australia, 1970.

—— *Messages to America: Selected Letters and Cablegrams Addressed to the Bahá'ís of North America, 1932–1946*. Wilmette, Ill: Bahá'í Publishing Committee, 1980.

—— *Messages to the Bahá'í World 1950–1957*. Wilmette, Ill: Bahá'í Publishing Trust, 1958.

—— *The Promised Day Is Come*. Wilmette, Ill: Bahá'í Publishing Trust, 1980.

—— *World Order of Bahá'u'lláh, The*. Wilmette, Ill: Bahá'í Publishing Trust, 1974.

Sours, Michael. *Preparing for a Bahá'í/Christian Dialogue: Understanding Biblical Evidence*. Oxford: Oneworld Publications, 1990.

—— *Preparing for a Bahá'í/Christian Dialogue: Understanding Christian Beliefs*. Oxford: Oneworld Publications, 1991.

—— *The Prophecies of Jesus*. Oxford: Oneworld Publications, 1990.

Vincent, Marvin R. *Vincent's Word Studies of the New Testament*. Vol. 1; Peabody, MA: Hendrickson (no date).

Vine's Expository Dictionary of Biblical Words. Nashville, TN: Thomas Nelson Publishers, 1985.

Walvoord, John F. 'New Testament Words for the Lord's Coming', *Bibliotheca Sacra*, Vol. 101. July, 1944.

Westermann, C. *Genesis 1–11: A Commentary*. Trans. J. J. Scullion. London: SPCK, 1984.

INDEX
OF BIBLICAL REFERENCES

Gen.
 1:26, p. 25
 2:8–9, p. 15
 3:8, p. 15
 4:26, p. 199
 12:7, p. 19
 15:7–21, p. 19
 17, p. 19
 17:5, p. 188
 17:20, p. 67
 22:18, p. 19
 24:7, p. 19
 25:16, p. 67
 48:7, p. 78
Exod.
 2:10, p. 188
 3:2, p. 215
 3:8, p. 19
 9:6, p. 217
 12:46, p. 71
 16:7, p. 218
 24:15, p. 217
 24:16, p. 217, 218
 33:7–11, p. 49
 34:29–35, p. 217
 20:18, p. 103
 40:34, p. 153, 183,
 40:34–5, p. 217
 40:38, p. 30
Lev.
 9:1–6, p. 217

Lev. (cont.)
 9:6, p. 17
Num.
 9:12, p. 71
 14:34, p. 67, 208
Deut.
 26:9, p. 19
 33:2, p. 148
Josh.
 7, p. 157
 7:19, p. 218
Judg.
 4, p. 124
 5, p. 124
 5:20, p. 158
 9:15, p. 20
1 Sam.
 1:20, p. 189
 4:4, p. 158
 17:45, p. 158
 24:6, p. 20
 24:10, p. 20
2 Sam.
 6:2, p. 158
1 Kgs.
 1:39, p. 20
 8:10–11, p. 183
2 Kgs.
 2:1, p. 195
 2:11, p. 106, 195, 200

2 Kgs. (cont.)
 11:12, p. 20
1 Chr.
 29:11, p. 176
Ezra
 6:8–12, p. 166
 7:12–26, p. 166
Ps.
 2:2, p. 190
 8:2, p. 69
 22:18, p. 71
 24, p. 158
 24:9–10, p. 158
 24:10, p. 143, 160, 184
 29:1, p. 218
 34:20, p. 71
 41:9, p. 71
 46:7, p. 158
 46:11, p. 158
 48:8, p. 158
 60:9, p. 67, 156
 69:4, p. 71
 78:2, p. 70
 84:1, p. 158
 84:3, p. 158
 84:12, p. 158
 95:6, p. 199
 110:1, p. 65, 80, 82
 147:2, p. 63

Isa.
2:1–10, p. 46
2:2, p. 144, 153
2:3, p. 144, 185
2:4, p. 143
2:19, p. 220
6:10, p. 71
7:14, p. 69, 191
7:18, p. 200
9:1, p. 69
9:2, p. 69
9:6–7, p. 79, 82, 161, 162, 176, 184, 190, 200, 211
9:7, p. 65
9:11, p. 20
11:1–10, p. 61, 62, 64, 143
11:11, p. 63, 64
11:12, p. 63
29:11, p. 212
33:9, p. 152
35:1, p. 152, 153
35:2, p. 152, 153, 184
40:3, p. 69, 147, 154
40:5, p. 152, 154, 167, 184, 218
40:9, p. 154
42:1–4, p. 70
44:23, p. 152
45:23, p. 199
53:1, p. 71
53:4, p. 69
53:12, p. 70
55:12, p. 152
58, p. 155
58:8, p. 152
58:12, p. 155
60:1, p. 155, 166, 184, 218

Isa. (cont.)
60:5, p. 167
60:18, p. 155
60:19–20, p. 155
60:21, p. 155
61:1, p. 20, 70, 71, 152, 189, 218
61:2, p. 20, 70, 71, 189
66:16, p. 79, 82
Ezek.
1:26, p. 217
1:28, p. 217
4:6, p. 67, 208
8:4, p. 157
9:3, p. 157
10:19, p. 157
10:20, p. 157
11:22, p. 157
34:13–15, p. 63
36:35, p. 16
37:1–14, p. 105
37:22, p. 63
37:24, p. 20, 65
37:25, p. 65
39:1–4, p. 124
40:34, p. 157
43:1–2, p. 155, 157, 184
44:2, p. 157
48:35, p. 196
Dan.
7:13, p. 179, 211, 215
7:14, p. 211
8:13–4, p. 127
8:16, p. 215
8:17, p. 99
8:24, p. 20
9:2, p. 208
9:21, p. 215
9:24–7, p. 207,

Dan. (cont.)
9:24–7, p. 208, 209
9:27, p. 206
11:31, p. 206
11:35, p. 99
11:40, p. 99
12:3, p. 35
12:4, p. 9, 99, 207, 212
12:8, p. 212
12:9, p. 9, 99, 212
12:10, p. 207
12:11, p. 206
12:13, p. 99
Hos.
2:15, p. 156
3:5, p. 65
11:1, p. 69
Joel
2:1–2, p. 98
2:11, p. 143
2:28–32, p. 51
Amos
1:2, p. 153
5:18–20, p. 98
8:11, p. 97, 137
9:11, p. 65
Mic.
5:2, p. 69, 77, 78, 82, 176
Zeph.
1:15, p. 15
1:14–16, p. 98
Jer.
7:11, p. 69
22:15–16, p. 32
25:11–12, p. 208
29:10, p. 208
30:7, p. 143
31:15, p. 69
32:6–9, p. 70

Index of Biblical References

Hag.
  2:7, p. 164, 165–7, 184

Zech.
  1:14–16, p. 98
  9:9, p. 66, 70, 71, 75, 82
  11:12–13, p. 70
  12:8, p. 65
  12:10, p. 71
  13:7, p. 69, 74, 82

Mal.
  3:1, p. 193
  4:1–2, p. 153
  4:2, p. 50, 153
  4:5, p. 31, 69, 193, 200

1 Macc.
  1:54, p. 206

2 Macc.
  3:3, p. 166

Matt.
  1:21, p. 189
  1:22–3, p. 69, 191, 200
  2:1–11, p. 166
  2:3–6, p. 77, 78, 82
  2:6, p. 69
  2:15, p. 69
  2:18, p. 69
  3:3, p. 69
  4:15–16, p. 69
  7:15–16, p. 137
  7:21–3, p. 94, 137
  8:17, p. 69
  10:34, p. 81, 82
  11:12–15, p. 193
  11:14, p. 193, 195, 200
  12:18–21, p. 70
  13:15–16, p. 121

Matt. (cont.)
  13:35, p. 70
  16:27, p. 146, 169, 177, 184
  17:10–13, p. 193, 200
  17:11–13, p. 31, 69
  21:1–6, p. 66, 70, 71, 75, 82
  21:13, p. 69
  21:16, p. 69
  22:41–6, p. 65, 80
  22:42–5, p. 80, 82
  23, p. 95
  24, p. 90, 119, 124, 146, 169, 173, 179, 206
  24:3, p. 85
  24:4–5, p. 91, 137
  24:6, p. 90, 96
  24:7, p. 90, 91, 96
  24:11, p. 91, 137
  24:15, p. 35, 54, 206, 207
  24:21, p. 90
  24:23–4, p. 91, 137
  24:29, p. 34, 35, 46, 51, 90, 169
  24:30, p. 47, 49, 50, 51, 113, 117, 169, 177, 184, 215
  24:31, p. 46, 103
  24:32, p. 90
  24:36–42, p. 102
  24:42–4, p. 198
  25, p. 169
  25:31, p. 146, 177, 184
  25:32, p. 177
  26, p. 77
  26:31, p. 69, 74

Matt. (cont.)
  26:56, p. 70, 117
  26:64, p. 184
  27:9–10, p. 70
  27:11, p. 80, 82
  27:25, p. 77

Mark
  8:38, p. 146, 169, 178, 184
  13, p. 146, 169, 173
  13:32, p. 102, 145
  14, p. 77
  15, p. 77
  15:2, p. 80, 82
  15:11–14, p. 77
  15:28, p. 70

Luke
  1:13, p. 195
  1:17, p. 194, 200
  1:19, p. 215
  1:26, p. 215
  1:32, p. 81, 82
  3:4–6, p. 120
  4:17–19, 70, 71
  4:18, p. 189
  21, p. 146, 169, 173
  22, p. 77
  23, p. 77
  23:1–3, p. 80, 82
  23:18–23, p. 77
  24:44, p. 70

John
  1:14, p. 219
  1:19–21, p. 193, 200
  2:11, p. 219
  2:19–21, p. 18, 32
  3:13, p. 119, 138
  5:41, p. 219
  6:27, p. 212

John (cont.)
  6:38, p. 119, 138
  6:41, p. 119, 138
  6:42, p. 119, 138
  6:63, p. 114
  7:17, p. 32
  10, p. 74
  12, p. 77
  12:12–13, p. 77, 78, 82
  12:14, p. 71
  12:31, p. 175
  12:38, p. 71
  12:39–40, p. 71
  13:18, p. 71
  13:36, p. p. 173
  14:3, p. 173
  14:8–11, p. 191
  14:16, p. 170, 184
  14:25–6, p. 170
  14:26, p. 172, 184
  14:28, p. 172
  14:30, p. 174, 175, 184
  14–16, p. 169, 173
  14:7–11, p. 163
  14:26, p. 172
  15:25, p. 71
  15:26, p. 170, 184
  16:5–16, p. 173,
  16:7, p. 170, 184
  16:11, p. 175
  16:12–14, p. 171, 172, 184
  16:13, p. 172
  16:16, p. 173
  17:5, p. 219
  17:6, p. 199
  17:11, p. 199
  17:12, p. 71
  17:22, p. 219
  18:15–17, p. 117

John (cont.)
  18:37, p. 80, 82
  19, p. 77, 78
  19:15, p. 77
  19:19–21, p. 78, 82
  19:24, p. 71
  19:28, p. 71
  19:34, p. 122
  19:36, p. 71
  19:37, p. 71
  20:12, p. 116
  20:31, p. 114
Acts
  1:1–4, p. 115
  1:6, p. 116
  1:8, p. 115
  1:9–11, p. 113, 115, 116, 117
  2:14–21, p. 51
  2:16–21, p. 99
  2:33, p. 171, 172, 173
  3:15, p. 176
  4:12, p. 186, 187, 191, 192, 199
  7:49, p. 82
  7:56, p. 179
  10:36, p. 81, 82
  20:29, p. 93, 137
Rom.
  5:2, p. 218, 219
  6:4, p. 218
  8:18, p. 219
  8:21, p. 219
  9:23, p. 218
1 Cor.
  2:14, p. 114
  12:28, p. 94
  15, p. 102
  15:44, p. 104, 138
  15:51–3, p. 103, 104

2 Cor.
  3:7–18, p. 215
  3:15, p. 217
  3:18, p. 218
  5:17, p. 137
  15:50–2, p. 102
  10:3–5, p. 47, 82
Eph.
  1:12, p. 218
  1:18, p. 121
  1:21, p. 199
  3:16, p. 218
  6:17, p. 82
Phil.
  3:20, p. 102
Col.
  1:11, p. 218
  1:13, p. 102
1 Thess.
  4:14–18, p. 102, 103, 104, 107, 138
  4:17, p. 145
1 Tim.
  1:11, p. 218
  4:1, p. 92
  4:1–4, p. 91, 137
2 Tim.
  3:1, p. 93, 137
  3:7, p. 93, 137
Tit.
  2:13, p. 102, 219
Philem.
  2:9–10, p. 199
Heb.
  1:4–5, p. 199
  9, p. 18
  9:28, p. 220
  13:8, p. 187
1 Pet.
  3:15, p. xii
2 Pet.
  1:3, p. 218

2 Pet. (cont.)
  1:16, p. 85
  3:10, p. 68
  3:12, p. 98, 102
1 John
  2:18, p. 99, 125
  4:3, p. 125
  4:7–16, p. 32
Rev.
  1:1, p. 182
  1:7, p. 102, 114, 119, 122, 154, 176
  1:8, p. 99, 180, 214
  1:10, p. 103
  1:11, p. 103, 180, 181, 184, 197
  1:13, p. 179
  1:17–18, p. 197, 214
  2:17, p. 197, 200
  2:21, p. 220
  2:23, p. 220
  3:3, p. 198
  3:10, p. 196
  3:11, p. 198

Rev. (cont.)
  3:12, p. 136, 196, 200
  4:1, p. 103
  11, p. 127
  11:2, p. 127
  11:3, p. 67
  11:7, p. 127
  13, p. 127
  14:14, p. 179
  15, p. 183
  15:8, p. 157, 182, 184
  16:16, p. 124
  19, p. 125
  19:13, p. 191, 197, 200
  19:15, p. 126
  19:16, p. 191, 197, 200
  19:17–21, p. 124
  19:19, p. 47
  19:19–21, p. 125
  19–20, p. 127
  19–22, p. 126
  20, p. 132, 145

Rev. (cont.)
  20:3, p. 125
  20:4, p. 131, 176
  21, p. 54, 87, 145, 183, 185, 211
  21:1, p. 135, 136
  21:1–3, p. 106
  21:1–8, p. 133
  21:3. p. 29, 88, 135
  21:4, p. 104
  21:5, p. 136
  21:6, p. 136, 145, 180
  21:7, p. 136
  21:10–11, p. 182, 184
  21:11, p. 182
  21:23, p. 182, 183, 184, 192, 200
  21–22, p. 87
  22, p. 16
  22:12–13, p. 29
  22:13, p. 180, 184, 214
  22:20, p. 29
  23, p. 182

INDEX

'Abdu'l-Bahá,
  explanation of
    Armageddon, 127, 129
    prophecies, 76–81
    resurrection, 117–19
    '70 weeks', 47, 208
    Two Witnesses, 67
    universal peace, 61–4
  missionary journeys, 5
Abraham, 16, 19, 20, 67, 207
  God's promise to 19–20
  heralded by star, 47
  name, meaning of, 188
Abu'l-Fadl, Mírzá, 40
Acts, Book of, 115, 119, 173
Adam, 8, 9, 15, 17, 46, 104, 213
Adamic cycle, 58, 59
'Akká, 4, 67, 72, 155, 156, 157
  'door of hope', 156–7
  prophetic 'gate', 156
  prophetic 'strong city', 67
Alden, Robert L., 166–7
Alpha and Omega, 133, 134, 178–82, 197, 214
angels, 81, 104, 116, 124, 134, 145, 155, 159, 172, 177, 178, 182, 187, 208, 215
animal sacrifices, 32
Anointed One, 20, 21, 70, 87, 88, 189, 211–12, 216
Antichrist, 124, 145, 126, 132
  of Bahá'í Revelation, 128
Apostles of Jesus, 66, 67, 80, 81, 91, 99, 115–17, 128, 159, 170, 173, 194
apocalypse, 123–4, 182
Ark of the Covenant, 16, 17, 18, 196
Armageddon, 54, 86, 87, 101
  Bahá'í beliefs about, 126–30
  Christian beliefs about, 123–6
Augustine, 132

Báb, the, 4, 11, 12, 17, 21, 26, 27, 30, 55, 57–8, 110–11, 130, 153, 168, 205
  Herald of Bahá'u'lláh, 154
  heralded by star, 207
  Prince of this World, 174
  prophecies concerning, 38–40
  refers to Jesus as God's 'Most Great Name', 199
  return of Elijah, 147
  Shrine of, 152–3
Bahá'í Era, 27, 55, 60, 65, 94, 210
Bahá'u'lláh,
  Alpha and Omega, 134, 179–82
  Blessed Beauty, 174
  Branch, 62
  Christ in Spirit, 8, 194
  Christ, return of, 194
  Church, rebukes leaders of, 95
  Comforter, 170–1
  cycle of, 62
  Davidic King, 67
  Desire of all Nations, 164–7
  Everlasting Father, 3, 5, 163–4
  first and last, 180–1
  forty-year ministry, 112, 146
  Glory of God, 182–3

Bahá'u'lláh (cont.)
  Glory of the God of Israel, 155
  Glory of the Lord, 151
  Gospel, affirmation of, 6–7
  hour of, 103
  imprisoned, 67
  Jesus, affirmation of, 209
    extols words of, 169
  King of Glory, 157
  Kingdom of, 65
  Law of, 11, 17
  Lord of hosts, see Lord of Hosts
  Lord, refers to Jesus as, 147
  Most Great Name, see name
  name of, 151, 190, 192
  one with Christ, 57
  opposed by Mírzá Yahyá, 128
  Prince of Peace, 5, 147, 161
  Prince of this World, 174–7
  prophecy, and, 4–5, 7, 13, 16, 18–19, 21, 26, 30, 36, 72, 142–7, 150, 168
    calls attention to fulfilment of, 3
    de-emphasized reliance on, 37
    gives key for unlocking the mysteries of, 28, 29, 65
  Revelation, purpose of, 60
  Son of Man, 177–9
  Spirit of Truth, 171
  suffering of, 156
  Supreme Manifestations, one of the, 21, 102, 158, 220
  sword of, 128
  Tablets to Rulers, 5
  Temple, 19, 32
  throne of, 21
  throne of David, sits on, 65
  world's response to, 11
  see also Book of Certitude
Bayán, 110, 154
Bethlehem, 47, 69, 77, 78
Bible, 9, 10, 18, 25, 34
  one of the two most widely diffused holy Books, 4
  contains symbolic stories, 9
  messianic hope in, 23
  prophetic language of, 21
  records historical events, 9
  as 'sacred' history, 10
  source of many Bahá'í symbols, 4–5
  terminology, 5
Book of Certitude,
  broke 'seals' of 'Book' referred to by Daniel, 9
  de-emphasises reliance on prophecy, 37
  demonstrates how Muhammad fulfilled prophecies, 206
  evidence, explains, 37–39
  doctrinal work, pre-eminent, xii, 29
  path of true seeker, explains, 55–7
  'presence of God', explains, 11–12, 28–9, 55, 86
  prophecy, fulfils, 2
    explains main characteristics of, 7, 9, 55
    of Jesus, explains, 46, 47, 49, 51, 92, 146, 206
  redemptive history, 4, 22
  reliance upon, 135
  Resurrection, explains Day of, 107
  symbolic terms, explains, 24, 181
  twofold language, 33–5
  methods of interpretation, 46
Briggs, Charles, 24
Buddha, 102
Buddhists, 4

Carmel, Mount, 4, 72, 152–4
Christ, see Jesus
Christian Church,
  bishops of, 3, 35
  clergy, 35, 95
  decline of, 94
  divided, 35, 94
  Holy Spirit, guided by, 172
Christianity,
  born out of Judaism, 5

established great Kingdom, 65
golden age, 54
most widespread religion, 4
Christians,
   Bahá'ís and Christians, often in agreement, 45, 52
   commentaries of, 52
   diversity of views among, 52, 88, 94, 131–2, 150
   literal interpretations and expectations, 34, 88, 106–7, 113, 123
   Muhammad, failed to recognize, 97
   persecution of, 90
   'wolves' among, 93
City,
   David, of, 17
   God, of, 29, 55, 56, 57, 63, 64, 134, 156, 196
   Jerusalem, of, see Jerusalem
   Strong, the 66, 67, 156
Cold War, see War

Daniel, 9, 10, 148, 149, 150, 179, 208
   Book of, 9, 34, 35, 46, 48, 54, 179, 184, 184, 204–16
   indicates that Jesus is Seal of the Prophets, 211–14
   may shed light on Qur'án, 204
   dating disputed, 150
   Jesus refers to, 206
   name, meaning of, 188
   seventy weeks, and, 47
   'Son of Man', called, 179
Dark Age, 65
David, King, 13, 14, 17, 18, 20–1, 65, 67, 71, 78, 79, 80, 81, 87–8, 143, 148, 149, 151, 155, 156, 157, 161, 164, 176, 196, 210, 216
   City of, 17
Day, 94, 96, 143
   Ancient of Days, 64
   of Bahá'u'lláh, 5, 7, 31, 60–1, 63, 133, 143, 163, 210
   of Blessing, 87

equal to one year, 47, 208
Ezekiel, of, 32
first seven, 14, 87
God, of, 12, 14, 21, 23, 29, 60, 87, 123, 143, 168, 210, 214, 220
Judgement, of, 53, 111, 144, 123, 220
King of, 60
last, 12, 34, 38, 93, 98–9, 106, 144, 145–6
Lord, of the, 68, 98, 193
Muhammad, of, 110
promised, 60
Resurrection, of, 107, 108, 110–11, 112, 114
seventh, 15
Wrath, of, 15, 87
1260 days, 67
Dawn-Breakers, The, 27, 115
demons, 91, 92, 94
dialogue, spirit of, xii

Eden, see garden
Egypt, 10, 16, 19, 20, 68
Elijah, 31, 106, 114–15, 147, 153, 177
   ascension of, 106, 195
   Elias in KJV, same as, 31
   name, meaning of, 188
   return of, 192–5
   see also John the Baptist
End, time of the, 9, 59, 92, 99, 100, 104, 107, 117, 123, 124, 144, 150, 168, 212, 214, 220
Era of Fulfilment, 58
Eve, 9, 15, 46, 104
everlasting life, 104, 135
Evil, 24, 53, 123, 126, 127, 132, 183
Exodus,
   most important Biblical event in Israelite history, 10
Ezekiel, 18, 105–6, 149, 150, 175, 196, 213
   'Akká, reference to, 155
   divided kingdom period, lived during, 145, 150
   name, meaning of, 188

Ezekiel (cont.)
  'Son of Man', called, 179
  vision of, 30, 32, 105–6, 156, 217
  writings of, 16, 34, 123, 124, 157, 175, 179, 184, 196n, 213

faith, 93
false christs and false prophets, 91, 93, 94, 124–8

Gabriel, 81, 208, 215
garden,
  of Eden, 14, 15–16, 23, 31, 87, 104, 135, 210, 216
  of Gethsemane, 173
  of God, 15, 87, 112
  of paradise, 15
  renewal, symbol of, 16
Genesis, 135, 199
  seven days of, 12, 14–15
Gethsemane, *see* garden,
Glory of God, 5, 17, 18, 36, 151, 154, 157, 168, 182–3, 190, 191, 192, 213, 217–20
  divine perfections, expresses sum total of the, 218
  redemptive history, prominent in, 218
  signifies presence of God, 183, 219
God,
  activity of, 10
  anthropomorphic symbolism, 88
  belief in, 10, 11
  Bible, central aim of, 9
  blessings of, 11
  City of, *see* City of God
  just and compassionate, 10
  knowledge of, 32
  laws of, 10, 11, 16
  liberates Israelites, 10
  name of, 198
  non-physical or limited being, 12
  personal, 6
  presence of, *see* Presence
  promises of, 3, 5, 6, 16, 25, 27, 28, 30, 58, 62, 63, 163, 183
  walked in garden of paradise, 15
  Word, *see* Word of God
  wrath of, 10, 11, 16
government, 79, 161
  Bahá'u'lláh, of, 162
  Christ, of, 161–2, 190
  Islamic, 127
  Manifestations, of, 162
  world, 125
grace, 6, 26, 28, 56, 97, 134, 135, 153, 174

Herod, 76
history,
  interpreted by Prophets, 10
  interpreted by Shoghi Effendi, 11
  'sacred', 15
Hidden Words, The, 178
Hindus, 4
Holy of Holies, 17, 63, 208
Holy Spirit, 131, 170, 172, 173–4
  Comforter, 171
hour, last, 56, 99, 103, 128, 145, 150, 172, 198

Interpretation, 48, 53–72
  see also history
Isaiah, 7, 10, 102
  name, meaning of, 188
Ishmael, 67
Islam, 127
  Muslim attitudes towards the New Testament, 206
  New Testament prophecy, prominent in, 130
  renaissance, contribution to European, 65
Israelites, 20, 63, 153, 154, 158, 216
  Babylon, captivity in, 18
  Canaan, conquered, 19
  Egypt, captivity in, 10, 16, 19
  disunity among, 18
  'divided kingdom' period, 13

exodus of, 10
history of, 13, 18
'pre-divided kingdom' period, 13
promised land, entered, 17
return to Palestine, 61–4
united, 17

Jehovah (Yahweh, YHVH), 15–16, 152
Jeremiah, 10, 70, 102, 208
Jerusalem, 17, 18, 23, 48, 63, 64, 66, 74, 75, 76, 77, 124, 144, 149, 153, 155, 161, 164, 166, 193, 208, 210
New, 56, 196
Jesus, 3, 13, 20, 21, 24, 31, 50, 66, 67, 68
Alpha and Omega, 180, 181
anointed of God, 189
appeared with 'manifest dominion', 209
ascension of, 172
crucifixion of, 116, 208
death of, 199
disciples of, 85, 113, 115, 169
eternal throne of, 81, 162–3
had many names, 190–1
revealed few specific laws, 11
first and last, 216
founded sacred law on basis of complete spirituality, 11
fulfilled prophecies, 21, 30, 32, 69–72, 73–82
Kingdom, raised up without army, 21, 65
Lordship of, 80–1, 147
Messiah, 21, 36, 76
ministry of, 209
name, significance of, 189
called Mighty God, King of Kings, Immanual, Lord of Lords, 191–2
to have new, 195–6
see also name
Olivet Discourse, 179, 206
Prince of Peace, 147
prophecies of, fulfilled, 3

return of, 86, 113–22
Seal of the Prophets, 209–10
second coming, 74, 85, 89, 145
Smitten Shepherd, 74–5
Spirit of God, 3, 79
Son of God, 114, 178
Son of the Highest, 81
Son of Man, 113, 178
Sun of Righteousness, 35
Sun of Truth, 79
Supreme Manifestation, 21
Temple of God, 32
Torah, promised in, 79
Word of God, 79
Jews,
expectations of, 76–8, 116
literal interpretations of, 78–81
see also Israelites
John the Baptist, 31, 147, 154, 177
return of Elijah, 193–5
John, St, vision of, 214

Kingdom of God, 8, 16, 23, 33, 58, 64, 65, 94, 100, 101, 110, 123, 128, 141, 144, 161, 162–3, 176, 197, 209, 210, 216
Davidic, 87
Millennial Kingdom, 86, 87, 88, 131–7, 145
Kitáb-i-Íqán, see Book of Certitude
Kosh, Kurt, 126

Law (of God), 10, 11, 15, 16, 17, 18, 19, 27, 30, 32, 70, 72, 95, 103, 108, 144, 196, 218
symbolized by New Jerusalem, 196
Lawh-i-Aqdas, see Tablet to the Christians
Lord of Hosts, 19, 143, 157–61

Manifestations of God,
'dependent', 102
Face of God, all signify, 28, 198
fulfil prophecy, 29, 146–7, 162, 168, 181

Manifestations of God (cont.)
  oneness of, 15, 146–7, 162, 168, 180, 181, 213
  presence of God, all signify, 21
  Seal of the Prophets, all signify, 209–10
  'Supreme', 21, 102, 220
Mary, 81, 116, 189, 215
Megiddo, hill of, 124
Messiah, 38, 70, 71, 74, 75, 76, 78, 79, 80, 82, 87, 116, 149, 151, 165, 166, 167, 178, 179, 190, 191, 192, 193, 195, 205, 211, 212, 214
  significance of term, 20, 36, 189
Millennium, 87, 131–7
  A-millennialism, 132
  Post-millennialism, 131
  Pre-millennialism, 132
  Bahá'í beliefs concerning, 132–7
  see also Kingdom
Mírzá Yaḥyá, 4
Mount Carmel, see Carmel
Moses,
  significance of name, 188
  Supreme Manifestation, 220
Muḥammad, 31, 38, 39, 48, 65, 67, 97, 127, 207
  affirmed Gospel, 27
  affirmed Jesus, 27
  affirmed Torah, 27
  government of, 162 (Isa. 9:6–7)
  fulfilled prophecy, 18, 21, 30, 97, 105, 146, 168, 172, 205, 216
  heralded by star, 207
  King of Glory, 158
  laws of, 17
  Lord of hosts, 216
  Messiah, 21
  oneness with other Manifestations of God, 213
  'Paraclete' (Comforter), 171
  possessed all the attributes of God, 102
  represents 'Presence of God', 30
  revealed specific laws, 11
  'Seal of the Prophets', 48, 205, 211, 216
  Son of Man, prophesied by Jesus, 146, 178
  Supreme Manifestation of God, 21, 102, 210
  Temple, re-established, 18
  Throne of David, re-established, 21
  'Trumpet call' of, 105
  Two Witnesses, one of, 67, 126
Muḥammad, Siyyid, 127–8

name,
  Biblical significance of, 187–8
  Most Great, 185, 198–9
  new name, 195–6
  'Jesus Christ' and salvation, 186
  significance of 'Bahá'u'lláh', 190
  name above every name, 199
Noah, 17, 213

Old Testament, 12, 14, 15, 22, 31, 34, 40
  as source of important symbolism, 13, 87–9
Olives, Mount of, 169
original sin, 104
Ottoman Empire, 128

Parousia, 85, 86, 95, 219
Paraclete, 173
  meaning of, 170
  Muḥammad, refers to, 171
Paradise, restoration of, 15, 21, 24, 54, 135, 136, 210
  see also garden

Paul, St, predictions of, 93, 103
Peace, 6, 15, 59, 61–2, 79, 81, 100, 125, 155, 161, 162, 164, 190, 191
Peter, St, 81
  denial of Christ, 173
Pius IX, Pope, 3
Presence of God, 10, 55, 86

Index

highest grace, attainment of, 28
made known by Prophets 10
most emphatically asserted
    theme in holy Scriptures, 11
not physical, 12
signified by presence of the
    Manifestations, 12
prophecies,
    central theological message of,
        11–12
    Christian beliefs about, 73
    circumstantial nature of, 36
    help us understand God, 5
    importance of, 3
    individual experience, and, 53
    fulfilment of, 3
    calls attention to God's presence,
        6
    literal fulfilment of, 48, 57, 65
    messianic, 22, 27–9
    multiple meanings, have, 29, 48,
        65, 130
    numerous, 141–2
    Old Testament, 68
    progressive fulfilment of, 57
    prophetic cycle, end of, 58, 61,
        210
    punishment, of, 22, 23–7
    rewards, of, 23–7
    sealing of, 211
    symbolic nature of, 9, 12, 147
    studying, 45–52
    testing of, 40
    theological message, 9
    three major themes of, 22
    two poles of predictive prophecy,
        24, 86
    studying, benefits of, 5, 41, 185
    veiled language of, 33, 37
Prophets, 94
    Old Testament, 148–9
    dates concerning, 150–1
    see also Manifestations of God
Promised Land, the, 14, 17, 19–20,
    21, 54, 64, 72, 87, 88, 155
'proof-text', 69
Psalms, Book of, 157–8

Queen Victoria, 3
Quddús, 4
Qur'án,
    recounts Biblical stories, 27
    prophecies of, 4, 5
    references: 2:10, p. 215; 2:46,
        p. 29; 2:136, p. 205; 2:249,
        p. 29; 4:150–1, p. 205;
        5:49–50, p. 205; 5:68, p. 205;
        18:111, p. 29; 25:25, p. 215;
        33:40, p. 203, 216

rapture, 88
    Bahá'í beliefs about, 107–12
    Christian beliefs about, 102–7
redemptive history, 6, 22, 26
resurrection,
    of the dead, 105, 106, 107, 109,
        111, 126
    of Christ, 102, 116, 117, 119,
        122
    of Elijah, 106
Revelation, Book of, 182

salvation, 6, 11, 23, 66, 75, 114,
    120, 134, 167, 182, 189, 190,
    191, 192, 199, 218, 220
Sanhedrin, 199
Scripture, 126
    multiple meanings, has, 46, 48,
        65, 130
    purpose of narrative form, 114
    spiritually discerned, 114
seal, meaning of, 211–12
second coming, 85
Sháh, Násiri'd-Dín, 128
Shoghi Effendi, 11, 53
    use of prophecy, 4–5, 99, 100,
        102, 141, 143, 148, 150,
        152–82
Sinai, Mount, 16, 103, 112, 178,
    217, 218
Solomon, 13, 17, 20
stars, heralding Messengers of God,
    47, 48
Stephen, St, 179
Sultán 'Abdu'l-'Azíz, 128

symbolism, 9–10, 12, 30–32
  anthropomorphic, 88
  clouds, of, 107, 108, 113, 117–19
  dead in Christ, of, 107
  earthquakes, of, 95, 96
  end, of, 213
  eyes, of, 119–122
  famines, of, 95, 96–7
  'first' and 'last', of, 99
  Joel, used by, 98–9
  moon, of, 118
  new earth, of, 136
  new heaven, of, 136
  New Jerusalem, of, see Jerusalem
  pestilences, of, 95
  resurrection, of, 109–12
  seal, of, 212
  stars, of, 118
  sun, of, 118
  sword, of, 128
  trumpet, of, 103, 104, 109
  wars, of, 95
  see also prophecy, symbolic nature

Tabernacle, 14, 16–19, 49, 72, 87, 88, 133, 153, 157, 161, 217, 218
'Tablet to the Christians', 122, 147, 186
Temple, 12, 16–19, 21, 23, 30, 32, 57, 63, 87, 88, 118, 150, 153, 155–6, 164, 165, 182, 183, 196, 210, 216
theology, 9, 11–12

thief in the night, 68, 198
Torah, 7, 79, 204, 205, 206, 217
Tree of Life, 16, 135
Transfiguration, Mount of, 85
tribulation, 51
  Bahá'í beliefs about, 92–101
  Christian beliefs about, 90–1
trump, of Godt, 103
trumpet-blast, heralding new Revelation, 55, 96, 103–4, 108, 109
Turkish Empire, 156
twelve princes, 67
two Witnesses, 67

Umayyids, 127

war, 66, 124–5, 127

  cease, will, 23, 58, 61
  Cold War, 123
  nuclear, 123
  World War I, 129
  World War II, 11, 111, 129, 150–1
Westermann, Claus, 199
wolf and lamb, 61
Word of God, 15, 79, 93, 97, 109, 110, 112, 126, 128, 160, 161, 191, 197

Zephaniah, 98
Zion, 17, 18, 68, 144
Zoroastrians, 4

www.ingramcontent.com/pod-product-compliance
Lightning Source LLC
Chambersburg PA
CBHW071338080526
44587CB00017B/2882